GROUP CREATIVITY

Music, Theater, Collaboration

R. Keith Sawyer
Washington University

Psychology Press
Taylor & Francis Group
New York London

Editor:	Bill Webber
Editorial Assistant:	Kristin Duch
Cover Photograph:	Lee Tanner ©/The Jazz Image
Cover Design:	SeanTrane Sciarrone
Textbook Production Manager:	Paul Smolenski
Composition:	The Type House
Text and Cover Printer:	Sheridan Books, Inc.

Library of Congress Cataloging-in-Publication Data

Sawyer, R. Keith (Robert Keith)
  Group creativity : music, theater, collaboration / R. Keith Sawyer.
    p. cm.
Includes bibliographical references and index.
ISBN 0-8058-4435-X (cloth : alk. paper)
ISBN 0-8058-4436-8 (pbk. : alk. paper)
1. Creative thinking—Social aspects. 2. Creation (Literary, artistic, etc.)—Social aspects. 3. Group problem solving. I. Title.
BF408.S285   2003
302.3'4—dc21
                                                2003040830
                                                CIP

GROUP CREATIVITY

Music, Theater, Collaboration

Contents

For Michael Silverstein

Acknowledgments

This book was written during 2002 while I was an assistant professor of education at Washington University in St. Louis. I would like to thank the department and its chair during that time, Jim Wertsch, for providing a collegial and supportive environment for serious scholarship. I am grateful for the institutional support I received during this time, including a Faculty Research Grant that provided partial support. I would like to thank my editor at Lawrence Erlbaum Associates, Bill Webber, for his enthusiasm for the project and for his professionalism in shepherding the book through the usual process.

Some of the chapters in this book draw heavily from articles that have appeared elsewhere, and this material appears with permission. However, all material has been substantially rewritten in some case as to be unrecognizable as being from any of the articles cited here. Consequently, this book should be considered to supersede the following four articles: "Improvisational creativity: An analysis of jazz performance," 1992, *Creativity Research Journal*, 5(3) 253-263; "Creativity as mediated action: A comparison of improvisational performance and product creativity," 1995, *Mind, Culture, and Activity*, 2, 172-191; "The semiotics of improvisation: The pragmatics of musical and verbal performance," 1996, *Semiotica*, 108(3/4). 269-306; "Improvisation and the creative process: Dewey, Collingwood, and the aesthetics of spontaneity," 2000, *Journal of Aesthetics and Art Criticism*, 58(2), 149-161.

1

Introduction

It is Saturday night, April 24, 1993, and I have arrived at this Chicago theater to watch a performance of a cutting-edge improvisational theater group called Jazz Freddy. The actors chose this name to emphasize the similarities between their free-form style of improvisation and the musical interactions of a jazz ensemble. Tonight, Jazz Freddy will perform a fully improvised 1-hour play, in two acts separated by an intermission. The lights come up and the audience applauds as we see the 10 cast members standing in a group facing the audience. Two cast members step to the front of the stage and quiet the audience. The first asks the audience to suggest "an event," and someone shouts, "The Olympics." The second actor asks the audience to provide "a location," and someone shouts, "A convent."

The lights go down; we can see the 10 cast members walking to the sides of the stage to sit in chairs that have been placed there. One of the actors pulls a chair to the center of the stage and sits in it, facing the audience, as the stage lights come up.

Example 1.1. Lights up. We see John carrying a chair to front stage right, and he sits down facing the audience. He mimes working at a desk—takes a cap off of a pen, opens a book, starts to make underlining motions as he studies the page. He stops to rub his eyes. He then turns the page, and underlines some more. The other actors watch intently from the sides of the stage; the audience is completely quiet. After about 20 seconds, Mary stands up from her position at the opposite side of the stage, and walks over to John, miming the act of carrying something in both hands, held in front of her:

1	Mary	Here are those papers.	Puts down the "papers."
2		(2 second pause)	She remains standing.
3	John	Thanks.	Looks up to face Mary.
		(2 second pause)	
4		I really appreciate your doing those copies for me.	
5			Bill approaches from stage left, also carrying "papers," and stops next to Mary.
6	Bill	Here are those papers.	Puts down the papers.
7	John	Thanks a lot,	Still facing the two
8		You guys have really been great.	
		(2 second pause)	
9		I'm gonna stop booking for now	Closes book on desk.
10	Mary	[OK]	
11	Bill	[Sure]	
		(1 second pause)	
12		I'm gonna go get some more papers.	
13	John	Alright	He stands up
		(1 second pause)	
14		Thanks a lot, I appreciate it.	
15	Bill	You're welcome.	
		(1 second pause)	
16		We mean it.	As he says this, Bill touches Mary's arm; Mary reaches up her other hand to grasp his hand; they stand holding hands.
18	John	Thanks for being in my corner.	
19	Bill	We always will be.	

In a few minutes, the actors gradually decide that this scene begins a plot associated with the "Olympics" suggestion. After about 5 minutes and three distinct scenes, the ensemble collectively transitions to a new plot line, this one taking place in a convent.

This Jazz Freddy dialogue demonstrates the key characteristics of group creativity. It is unpredictable, particularly in the timing and pacing of the interaction; the actors do not know who is going to speak next, nor when they will begin speaking. As a result, anyone can take the next conversational turn; it is impossible to know ahead of time who it will be. Even an offstage actor can walk on and take the next turn, as Bill does in turns 5 and 6. In the beginning of this performance, the actors leave unusually long pauses between their turns of dialogue, because they are just getting into the flow of the evening's performance. As the basic elements of the plot begin to emerge, the actors develop a rhythm and the pace accelerates; as the performance progresses, they leave shorter pauses and the dialogue begins to sound more like a normal conversation. The dramatic frame gradually gathers steam; in the first 30-minute act, the group creates two distinct plots, one associated with the Olympics and one taking place in a convent. In the second act, the plots begin to weave together, as several of the female athletes decide to become nuns.

Creative group performance is often referred to as "jamming." The term *jamming* was first used by jazz musicians; a "jam session" is an impromptu gathering of musicians with the purpose of improvising together. The term has a positive connotation; when a performance goes particularly well, the musicians might say "we were really jamming tonight." In the last several decades, the term has been widely used outside of jazz to describe any free-flowing creative group interaction (e.g., Coates, 1997). For example, actress Valerie Harper, who began her career at the Second City, Chicago's legendary improvisational theater, said "I've always found improvisation ... to be close to jazz musicians jamming—you're really listening to each other, really hearing" (Sweet, 1978, p. 319). The *American Heritage Dictionary* (1982) defined the jam session as both a type of jazz performance and also as "an impromptu or highly informal discussion." The Harvard Business School professor John Kao referred to work teams as jamming when they are effective and innovative (Kao, 1996; see chap. 7).

The common thread in all of these uses of the term is that they refer to the collective activity of a group creating together, and they suggest a high degree of improvisation and informality. It might seem a little odd, for example, to refer to the formal conversation at a black tie party at the Ambassador's mansion as "jamming"; and it might likewise seem odd to refer to a performance of the Chicago Symphony as a jam session. Yet in chapters 6 and 7, I argue that even these formal and rehearsed performances involve group creativity. Group creativity is found in all group performances, whether on stage or in the privacy of rehearsal. Group creativity is not only a trivial pastime or an entertainment goal; it is essential in many problem-solving groups, such as a brainstorming session at a small high-technology company, a group of teachers collaborating to develop a new curriculum, or a family working to resolve a financial crisis.

THE CHARACTERISTICS OF GROUP CREATIVITY

Performing groups are often called *ensembles*. The *American Heritage Dictionary* (1982) defined an ensemble as "a unit or group of complementary parts that contribute to a single effect" and also as "a group of supporting musicians, singers, dancers, or actors who perform together." The term derives from the Latin roots *in* and *simul*, "in (or at) the same time." The defining features of group creativity are that it involves two or more people, creating together at the same time.

In group performance genres, the creativity of the performance depends on an intangible chemistry between the members of the group. We are perhaps most likely to associate this type of group creativity with improvised musical performance, because an improvising group of musicians is one of the best examples of group creativity. In jazz, for example, no single musician can determine the flow of the performance: It emerges out of the musical conversation, a give-and-take as performers propose new ideas, respond to other's ideas, and elaborate or modify those ideas as the performance moves forward (Berliner, 1994). As bassist Chuck Israels said, "Playing with musicians is like a conversation. If when I speak, you say 'Yes,' or you look at me and blink your eyes or interject some comment of your own, that keeps me going" (Berliner, 1994, pp. 354–355).

Group creativity is also a significant feature of 20th century theater. The Screen Actor's Guild Awards gives prizes for "best actor" and "best supporting actor," but their most prestigious prizes are those for best cast and best ensemble—because "they recognize what all actors know—that acting is a collaborative art" (http:// www.sagawards. org/about_unique.html; April 20, 2002). Theater historians note that the ensemble style of performance was first advocated by the French director Jacques Copeau in the early decades of the 20th century (Frost & Yarrow, 1990). Copeau was the first director to emphasize that the actors in a production should spend some time together in rehearsal to develop an ensemble feel, rather than simply diving right into the performance of the scripted play under the director's guidance. Copeau's emphasis on the ensemble was derived from his belief that the theater was a form of communion, that it was a shared creative act rather than the manifestation of the director's vision. To teach his group this ensemble feel, Copeau developed a rehearsal technique that made heavy use of improvisational exercises. The ensemble style is now a mainstream element of all modern theater, from serious drama to the comedy of Second City and Saturday Night Live.

Group creativity is particularly important in the more improvisational genres of performance: jazz and improvisational theater. Although group creativity is found in all groups, improvisation is particularly interesting because it exaggerates the key characteristics of all group creativity: process, unpredictability, intersubjectivity, complex communication, and emergence.

Process

The purpose of a jazz improvisation is not to generate a created product that will then be displayed or sold in another context; there is no goal external to the improvisation. Instead, the performance is its own goal. In improvisational creativity, the process is the product, and the researcher is forced to focus on the creative processes of group creativity.

This poses a new problem for psychologists who study creativity, because they have focused on *product creativity*, creative domains in which products are created over time, with unlimited opportunities for revision by the creator before the product is displayed. Product creativity is found in artistic domains such as sculpture and painting, as well as scientific domains, where the products generated are theories, formulas, or published articles. In many creative domains, this private revision process is a solitary one.

My studies of group creativity are part of a recent shift in creativity research from a focus on creative products to a focus on the creative processes that generate them. Yet this recent shift emphasizes those creative processes that eventually result in creative products (Sawyer, 1997a). In contrast, in group creativity, the process is the essence of the genre, and it must be the central focus of any scientific study.

This shift is paralleled by the recent growth of *sociocultural theory* in developmental psychology (Rogoff, 1990, 1998; Sawyer et al., in press; Wertsch, 1998). Sociocultural psychologists emphasize the social and cultural contexts of child development, rather than focusing only on the mental changes within the developing child. Socioculturalists have also noted that "the process is the product," and they focus on developmental processes rather than on developmental outcomes such as the stages or stage transitions of the Piagetian approach. They use a *microgenetic* methodology, closely analyzing small changes over the course of a single encounter with a more experienced partner. My studies of group creativity are sociocultural, because I focus on the interactional processes of group creativity, rather than examining the products that are created by a group.

Unpredictability

In the Jazz Freddy transcript presented in Example 1.1, no actor knows what is going to happen next. At each point in the improvisation, an actor can choose from a wide range of moves to propel the drama forward. Actors cannot know how their turns will be interpreted by the others; each turn gains its final meaning only from the ensuing flow of discourse. Bill has begun by miming various activities at a desk, but he must wait to see how Mary reacts to him before he knows exactly what he is doing at the desk. Bill's action does not fully determine the eventual dramatic meaning of that action; each turn of dialogue, although spoken by a single actor, eventually takes on a dramatic meaning that is determined by a collaborative, emergent process (Sawyer, 2003).

Group creativity ranges across a spectrum from relatively unpredictable to relatively predictable. Predictable performances are those in which the performers' actions are highly constrained by the conventions of a genre or a situation. The highly ritualized initial turns of a courtroom proceeding are almost completely scripted (although see Philips, 1992). Slightly less predictable, although still heavily ritualized, are the opening sequences at the beginning of a phone conversation (Hopper, 1992; Schegloff, 1986). Improvisational theater dialogues represent the extreme of unpredictable, relatively unscripted conversation. In chapter 6, I show how group creativity changes in relatively improvised and relatively ritualized ensemble performances.

This unpredictability and contingency results in performances that, at each moment, have a combinatorial complexity: A large number of next actions is possible, and each one of those actions could result in the subsequent flow of the performance going in a radically different direction. At each moment the performer can choose from a wide range of actions that are consistent with the performance up to that point; a performer's action cannot be predicted by the other performers because there are so many potential creative acts, and the range of potential performances that might emerge multiplies from moment to moment.

Strategy games like chess are characterized by expanding combinatorics. In chess, the combinatorics make it impossible to look ahead and mentally play out all possible ways that the game could go. Suppose that a player has 50 possible moves, and the opponent has 50 possible moves following each of the player's possible moves. This results in 2,500 possible two-move sequences; and looking ahead a third turn would require the player to consider 125,000 three-move sequences. Improv theater has even more extreme combinatorics, because the actor's possible actions come from the full range of human experience.

Several of the early and most influential Chicago improvisers drew explicit analogies with sporting events. The actor and director Del Close noted that in both improvisation and in competitive team sports, the outcome is truly unpredictable. The analogy is apt because many team sports also have expanding combinatorics, and it's why it is so difficult to predict which team will win a game simply based on their record competing with other teams. During the 2002 soccer World Cup, the United States team was not expected to do very well; coach Bruce Arena said, "On paper, it looks to be no match. However, we don't play this game on paper," and the team made it to the quarterfinals for the first time since 1930 (Longman, 2002). In advance of major sports events, bookies place a *point spread* on the game. The point spread predicts which team will win, and by how much.[1] But this represents only a statistical probability; no bookie would bet everything on his prediction of the winner, as fans do. Rather, they are successful because they play the odds in such a way that they come out ahead regardless of the outcome.

The first people to connect improv and sports were Keith Johnstone and David Shepherd, two of the earliest improv directors. Keith Johnstone began to direct "Theatresports" tournaments in Canada in 1977. In 1980, David Shepherd (the producer of the first improv theater in Chicago, the Compass Players, in 1955) inspired by Johnstone's metaphor, returned to Chicago to create what he called the "Improvisation Olympiad" or "ImprovOlympiad" (now known as "ImprovOlympic"). These names demonstrate that actors are well aware of the parallels shared with competitive team sports—their unpredictability, their moment-to-moment contingency, and the importance of the group.

Intersubjectivity

A third defining feature of group creativity is that it is often impossible to determine the meaning of an action until other performers have responded to it. In Example 1.1, Line 1—Mary presenting Bill with papers—has several potential meanings, and these ambiguities are not resolved until the subsequent turns of dialogue. She might be a boss bringing her subordinate additional work. It is not until Bill's response in Line 4 ("I really appreciate your doing those copies for me") that we learn she is helping him. If he had responded "I can't believe you're giving me more work when it's already 7 PM!" then her action would take on a different meaning, and their relationship would be completely different. The response "It's about time, where were you?" would establish yet a third relationship.

This sort of retrospective interpretation is quite common in group creativity. Gioia (1988) noted that the jazz musician cannot "look ahead at what he is going to play, but he can look behind at what he has just played ... he creates his form *retrospectively*" (p. 61). The performance that emerges cannot be explained in terms of actor's creative intentions in individual turns, because in many cases an actor

---

[1]Technically speaking, this is not exactly true: the point spread does not reflect the expected amount of a win, but is designed to encourage the maximum dollar amount of bets to be placed, and thus reflects the bookie's opinions about the collective perceptions of the fans rather than his or her own opinions about the teams.

cannot know the meaning of her own turn until the other actors have responded. As a result, intersubjectivity is fundamentally social and collective, and must be negotiated.

The issue of intersubjectivity or "mutual understanding" was always understood to be a central problem in ethnomethodology (see Garfinkel, 1967, p. 114; Schegloff, 1992; Schutz, 1964). In group creativity, the dependence of each action on the subsequent flow of the performance results in a situation in which it is impossible for the performers to have identical mental representations of what is going on. However, although each performer may have a rather different interpretation of what is going on and where the performance might be going, they are nonetheless able to collectively create a coherent performance. To properly understand group creativity, we need to think of intersubjectivity as "a process of coordination of individual contributions to joint activity rather than as a state of agreement" (Matusov, 1996, p. 34). The key question about intersubjectivity in group creativity is not how performers come to share identical representations, but rather, how a coherent interaction can proceed even when they do not.

Because of the problem of intersubjectivity, skillful group performers try not to propose detailed and specific actions, because it makes it harder for the other performers to come up with an appropriate response. Instead, their individual creative acts are designed to be open ended, extendable, and multiply interpretable. In classes for improvisational actors, the actors are taught several rules that encourage this sort of dialogue, and actors have several pejorative terms for dialogue turns which are too specific and explicit. For example, actors use the term *driving* to refer to an actor who is taking over the scene and not letting other performers influence its direction. A variant of driving is what actors refer to as *writing the script in your head* or *playwriting*—thinking more than one turn of dialogue ahead, such that you have already developed an expectation of what the other actor will say. These terms are always used negatively, and actors are taught not to "drive" or "playwright" (Sawyer, 2003).

When group performers avoid these sorts of moves, the meaning of an individual act emerges from the collective creativity of the group, and the performance that results is a collaborative product. The creativity does not originate in one performer's head, then becoming externalized and imposed on the other performers; rather, the creativity is found in the group process. Group creativity occurs on a collaborative, social plane, rather than in performer's heads.

Complex Communication

Whenever [Severn Darden] does something, he's always halfway acting because he's commenting on what he's doing while he's doing it.
—Actor Bill Alton, referring to a legendary Chicago improviser
(in Sweet, 1978, p. 274)

In group creativity, the performance must be constantly negotiated and constructed from moment to moment. Because of unpredictability, each performer may have a different understanding of what is happening and what might happen next, and to maintain intersubjectivity, the performers have to be able to negotiate among their distinct representations. However, actors do not step out of character to talk about how their scene will develop; this would break the dramatic illusion and lose the continuity of the scene. And of course, musicians cannot do this because the language of music does not allow a reflexive commentary on how the performance is proceeding. Instead, performers have to negotiate their intersubjectivity while enacting the performance. Like Severn Darden, each performer is both performing, and at the same time negotiating this intersubjectivity indirectly or implicitly. This latter communicative function is *metapragmatic* in that its indirect pragmatic effect is to further define the nature of the ongoing interaction itself. Both musical and verbal communications thus have effects on two levels: an enacted, or denotational level, and a metapragmatic, or negotiatory pragmatic level (Monson, 1996; Silverstein, 1993).

The theory of group creativity that I introduce in Chapter 3 builds on theories of metapragmatics to explain group creativity in music and verbal art. By focusing on the pragmatics of performance, my approach differs from past attempts to compare music and language that focused on syntax or semantics.

Emergence

When the consciousness of individuals, instead of remaining isolated, becomes grouped and combined, something in the world has been altered.
—Durkheim (1951, p. 310)

Group creators often say that when the group dynamic is flowing, the performance that results is greater than any one individual; the whole

is greater than the sum of the parts. In group creativity, the group leads each individual to perform at a higher level than he or she would have been capable of alone. It is easy to find examples in popular culture. Think of the many cast members of Saturday Night Live who were inspired comedians on the show, but whose solo movie careers bombed. Or think of musicians who left creative, groundbreaking bands for a solo career that never took flight. Of course, a few solo careers are successful—Sting's career after the Police, and David Byrne's career after the Talking Heads—yet despite their success, they never achieved the level of innovation they each did with their seminal ensembles.

Most successful sitcoms are hits because of the ensemble dynamic of the cast; when the individual members of the cast attempt to create their own star vehicle spin-offs, they are flops more often than not. One of the most popular shows of the 1990s, "Seinfeld," told stories of the everyday events of a group of four close friends living in Manhattan. As of Summer 2002, three of these actors had created new series, and each was terminated after only one season; they failed to successfully connect with an audience or with critics. Most observers then concluded that it had been the ensemble dynamic of the show that made the individual actors look good. One might attribute the success of "Seinfeld" to its star, Jerry Seinfeld, rather than to the ensemble dynamic; yet, stars in other successful sitcoms have attempted to star in later sitcoms and have also failed. Of the cast of "Cheers," the star Ted Danson failed with "Ink"; five other actors attempted new shows, and the only one to be successful was Kelsey Grammar, in "Frasier" (Weinraub, 2002). These examples all demonstrate the importance of emergence in performing groups; the group is greater than the sum of its parts, and its success cannot be attributed to a skilled leader or star, nor to any single member of the group.

In competitive team sports, a player might flourish with one team but languish with another. The NFL salary cap reveals this phenomenon: when a football team starts winning, all of the individual players look better and thus become more valuable on the open market. As a result, the total value of the team—as reflected in the sum of the individual salaries—increases, and climbs above the salary cap limit. The team must then trade individual members in exchange for relative unknowns who are cheaper. Yet after they are traded away, those newly expensive players often don't look as good as they did when they were on the championship team. The fact that they looked good wasn't due completely to their own ability; it was their membership in the team that made them look good, and away from that winning team their performance level is not the same. In group creativity, value or ability is not a property of individuals; it is a property of individuals in groups.

Many scholars now use the term *emergence* to refer to complex systems which have this property that the whole is greater than the sum of the parts. In the terminology of these scholars, a creative group is a *complex dynamical system*, with a high degree of sensitivity to initial conditions and rapidly expanding combinatoric possibilities from moment to moment (Sawyer, 1999). As in many complex systems, the global behavior of the entire system is said to emerge from the interactions among the individual parts of the system, and is thus at a higher *level of analysis* than the parts—the performers. In group creativity we see what Mead (1932, 1934) called the *emergent*: "The emergent when it appears is always found to follow from the past, but before it appears, it does not, by definition, follow from the past" (1932, p. 2). Mead was commenting on the contingency of improvisational interaction: Although a retrospective examination reveals a coherent interaction, at each moment a performer has a range of creative options, any one of which could result in a radically different performance. The "emergent" was the fundamental analytic category for Mead's philosophy, and the paramount issue for social science: He claimed "It is the task of the philosophy of today to bring into congruence with each other this universality of determination which is the text of modern science, and the emergence of the novel" (1932, p. 14).

Group creativity results in the collective creation of a shared creative product, Mead's "emergent." I use the term *collaborative emergence* to refer to emergence in small groups (Sawyer, 1999, 2003). Because group creativity is emergent, the direction the group will travel is difficult to predict in advance. The flow of the performance cannot be predicted even if the analyst has unlimited advance knowledge about the skills, motivations, and mental states of the individual performers. Even with this knowledge, there is simply too much potential variability in what might emerge during the performance; the multiplying moment-by-moment combinatorics make advance prediction practically impossible. For these reasons, group creativity cannot be understood through explanations in terms of individuals and their interactions, an approach known as *methodological individualism* (Sawyer,

2001a, 2002b). Psychology cannot provide a complete explanation of group creativity; we need a group level of analysis, and we need to incorporate methods and concepts from sociology, communication, and organizational behavior.

IMPROVISED VERSUS STRUCTURED PERFORMANCE

Although improvisation is the extreme case of group creativity, it is found in all performing groups, even in those genres of music and theater which are composed in advance, memorized, and rehearsed. All performance requires a group dynamic to work effectively.

Performances of a symphony differ from one night to the next, and in part that's because emergence is unpredictable and is not under the control of anyone. A successful performance depends on the *interactional synchrony* of the performers (see chap. 2). This is less of an issue with genres of music that have a conductor, because the conductor sets the tempo with his baton and indicates the proper starting moment for each new passage and theme. But many scored classical performances have no conductor; these include chamber works, duets, and soloists accompanied by a pianist. In these conductor-less scored performances, the performance has to emerge from the musicians themselves; they have to create their own interactional synchrony. Perhaps this is why many classical musicians prefer chamber performance; they are much more likely to speak of jamming and of being in flow during such performances.

Performances of a scripted play also vary from night to night. Even with weeks of rehearsal, the actors subtly vary many elements of their performance. The intonation of a line may change slightly; one actor may wait an extra second before speaking his or her next line; a new actor might enter the stage a split-second earlier than he or she did the night before. All of these tiny, split-second decisions accumulate to result in the emergence of each specific performance.

Even these structured performances have the defining characteristics of group creativity; they are collective, group efforts, in which no single individual can determine the performance of the group. The performance emerges from the individual and successive contributions of all performers. The outcome of any given performance is unpredictable, and this unpredictability results from the problems of negotiating intersubjectivity and the complex dynamics of interactional synchrony. The group's creativity is negotiated at the metapragmatic level of symbolic communication.

I've chosen to focus on improvisational genres of performance in this book because improvisation is the purest form of group creativity, a Weberian ideal type. In chapter 2 I identify the characteristics of group creativity by reference to empirical studies of jazz and improv theater. Yet even scripted theater and scored musical performance involve group creativity; the participants in these ensembles must engage in sophisticated symbolic interaction to coordinate their performance, and the interactional mechanics of communication in these groups are often quite similar to those in improvisational ensembles. In chapter 6, I explore how group creativity changes when it becomes less improvisational, and in chapter 7 I show how these theories can be applied to scripted verbal performance and scored musical performance.

STUDIES OF GROUP PERFORMANCE

Many distinct social science traditions have addressed creativity in groups. I briefly review these relevant traditions, because they provide many insights into group creativity. After this review, I identify what is missing from these traditions. The purpose of this book is to fill in these missing pieces of the puzzle of group creativity.

Anthropology

Anthropologists have always been interested in language, in verbal art, and in folklore. In traditional folklore studies, a verbal performance was considered to be a realization of a *performance text*, a relatively fixed and ritualized sequence of words that remained the same through history and was repeated essentially verbatim in each performance event. Folklore researchers focused on audiotaping and transcribing the text of a performance, in many cases with the goal of preserving the tradition for posterity. During the 1960s and 1970s, however, as audiotaping became more common and more frequent, researchers began to notice that performances of "the same" text were often radically different. Lord's (1960) study of South Slavic epic poetry was seminal in this shift; Lord discovered that Serbo-Croation epic poetry was performed in a more flexible and variable manner than had previously been suspected. The "same" epic, sung by the same singer on multiple occasions, could vary in length by as much as several thousand lines. Even when the storytellers swore they were repeating verbatim the same epic they had told a week ago, a close analysis of the audiotape showed that although much about the performance remained the same, at many points the words used were very different.

These studies eventually led to a rejection of the traditional folklore approach in favor of a new paradigm called the *ethnography of speaking*. Ethnographers of speaking rejected the idea that a verbal performance was a simple execution of a fixed, pre-existing performance text. Instead, "artistic discourse is viewed as emergent in the event. . . . No longer defined by a canonical written text, it is a kind of practice" (Hanks, 1996, p. 190). In a seminal review article, Bauman and Briggs (1997) contrasted this approach and traditional folkloristics: The ethnography of speaking rejected a view of performance texts as fixed products, and a view of contexts as situations that a text is performed in, instead shifting the focus to *processes of contextualization*.

For example, Duranti's (1992) study of respect words rejected an earlier view that a speakers' choice of a respect word is determined by the social context, in favor of a view that language use can help to create the context (e.g., pp. 87–89). In the earlier view, a respect word is chosen to refer to an individual on the basis of that individual's status and on the nature of the situation. Yet Duranti documented several cases in which the choice of a respect word is not fully determined by the situation, due to occasional ambiguity about what kind of situation is occurring and to the fact that each individual has several different social roles that can be invoked on any given occasion, each warranting a distinct respect word. Thus, speakers might use a respect word creatively, to collaboratively create "a context in which certain particular social personae (those of certain titles, with their associated rights and duties) must count and must be invoked" (p. 87). Therefore, he concluded that we must think of words "not only as labels for an already existing reality but also as ideologically loaded tools for defining the situations in which speakers *qua* social actors co-construct their context" (p. 89).

Ethnographers of speaking consider language use to be inherently creative, and their empirical studies have documented a high degree of group creativity in a wide range of cultures and contexts (Bauman & Briggs, 1997; Bauman & Sherzer, 1974; Hymes, 1962). As Bauman noted in the introduction to a 1974 volume, "Performance here is seen as a creative and emergent accomplishment . . . the deepest problem in the social disciplines [is to understand] the dynamic interplay between the social, conventional, ready-made in social life and the individual, creative, and emergent qualities of human existence" (Bauman & Sherzer, 1974, p. xviii).

Musicology

Musicology has traditionally been the study of musical scores—pieces of paper with musical notation on them. Musicology is a European academic tradition, and European musical genres are primarily scored and then performed; yet this focus on Western traditions has resulted in a neglect of live musical performance (Sawyer, 1997a). Although all of the world's cultures have some sort of musical tradition, only a very small minority have developed a notational system to represent their songs or performances. Musicologists justified their neglect of "performance practice" by assuming that it was a relatively trivial task, primarily a technical one without intellectual interest—the performer reads the score and translates it into the finger movements, breathing, or bowing necessary to generate the sounds. They didn't think performance was important because they were members of a culture whose musical tradition didn't value performance.

There has always been a small minority of musicologists who study music in cultures that have no notational system, and these musicologists always had difficulty applying analytic methods originally developed to study notated European music. The paper-oriented focus of musicology largely forced these *ethnomusicologists* to transcribe the performances into (European) musical notation before they could examine them. Thus many studies of improvisational musics have retained a "compositional" approach, often using techniques developed for the analysis of notated scores. This has the unintended effect of removing many of the uniquely performative elements of world music traditions—emergence and improvisation, the contingency from moment to moment, the interactional synchrony among performers—elements that cannot be fully understood without a consideration of group creativity.

In the 1970s, a new movement rejected this traditional paper focus, instead emphasizing the performative nature of music. These *ethnographers of musical performance* explored music as a form of social in-

teraction, and used anthropological techniques to analyze the surrounding cultural context of each musical performance (Blacking,
1981; McLeod & Herndon, 1980). In this shift to a performance focus,
these musicologists drew explicitly on theories first proposed by
ethnographers of speaking. Using this new focus, ethnomusicologists
began to explore interaction among musicians in an ensemble, and
also interaction between the performers and the audience—all factors
that were ignored in the paper-oriented focus on transcription.

The English musicologist John Blacking was one of the key figures
in the shift to performance. As part of his fieldwork on Venda music in
the 1950s, he studied girls' preparations for a Bepha musical expedition by rehearsing the dance *tshigombela* for several weeks. He observed that the dance varied greatly from one occasion to the next:

> In an oral tradition, rules of musical performance often include a whole
> series of options that can be invoked according to the context of per-
> formance: thus a section may be repeated until every member of the en-
> semble has had a chance to dance, so that the length of the section and
> its rhythmic variations in any performance will depend on who is pres-
> ent and how many dancers there are; a piece may be extended until the
> soloists have run out of different words, or because there are more peo-
> ple present than usual; it may be brought to a speedy conclusion be-
> cause the song leader sees a friend coming into the performance area
> and it is nearly time to close the session; or an earlier appearance of the
> same friend might have stimulated the performance and the prolifera-
> tion of variations, if there was an audience, or brought it to a sudden halt,
> if there were only performers present (Blacking, 1977, p. 7).

Regula Qureshi's (1986) study of the *qawwali*—Sufi devotional music—revealed the ways that performers are influenced by the audience. The *qawwali* is performed in a shrine, with the explicit purpose
of helping those present to attain a state of spiritual ecstasy, and the
performers' payment depends on how effectively they achieve this
goal. Listeners usually enter an ecstatic state upon hearing a particular line of poetry; when this happens, the musicians notice it and then
repeat this line of poetry several times. They may also increase the
tempo with each repetition, a technique to heighten the ecstasy of the
listener. Qureshi videotaped performances and interviewed the singers about what was going on during each performance, and she found
that the musicians are consciously evaluating the social group. They
know who is present, which shrines they are connected with, and how
they are related to each other; they then use this knowledge to

choose songs and verses likely to elicit ecstatic responses from them (cf. Feld, 1982; see chap. 6).

These studies show that group creativity involves many complex social, contextual, and interactional factors. An analysis of group creativity cannot be limited to the performers on stage; in many cases, a complete understanding of the performance requires an understanding of audience–performer relationships. Each *tshigomela* dance performance depends on how many performers are present, on who is in the audience, and on the specific history of the relationships between performers and audience members. Likewise, the *qawwali* performance is modified to suit the audience, and its flow and emergence changes depending on the reactions of the listeners.

Conversation Analysis

Conversation analysts (CA) have engaged in some of the most rigorously empirical studies of group interaction. These studies demonstrate that everyday conversation is a form of group creativity (Sawyer, 2001a). Many of these researchers prepare transcripts that encode pauses down to the tenth of a second, and that encode eye gaze and body posture along with the verbal utterances. These transcripts included information that is often filtered out of transcripts: pauses, false starts, stutters, intonation contours, and representations of speaker overlap.

Sawyer and Berson (2002) demonstrated that participants in interaction attend to this level of detail, albeit subconsciously, in determining how to interact with each other: What sorts of overlap and back channeling are appropriate, how authoritative a speaker's utterance is and thus what sorts of response are appropriate, and when a speaker's turn is complete. For example, they found that students in a study group were rarely interrupted when they were looking down at their notebooks, but that they were often interrupted when they were looking up at other speakers. In Example 1.2, Beth begins turn 11 by reading from her notebook, and is not interrupted until she looks up at the other speakers. Even though Susan and Mary are also looking down, they are still able to detect Beth's gaze shift, and subconsciously realize that there is now an opportunity for interruption.

Example 1.2. Study group conversation among four college students. Words in italic font indicates that students are looking at their lecture notes; words in roman font indicate that students are looking up at each other (from Sawyer & Berson, 2002).

(11) B: *So like the younger you are, the (1) more you're gonna recog-*
         nize—you're gonna pay more attention to each,
         [each step.]
(12) S: [So like the] [earlier . . . yeah.]
(13) M: [You're not automa]tized- *automatized.*

Everyday conversation also involves complex interaction, resulting in collaborative emergence in everyday social encounters. A few years ago, a dog bite on my left hand required me to visit the emergency room. The bite was not life-threatening, and consequently I had a small wait while sitting in a chair in the emergency room next to the bed. I carried my coffee in with me, and like any good academic, I had a few journal articles in my briefcase and I began to read and highlight passages while I waited for the nurse. The coffee was sitting at my left, balanced precariously on the thin rail at the side of the hospital bed.

When the nurse entered she walked to a small desk at the far side of the room and did not look at me or speak to me, so I continued reading. After a minute or so, she turned to address me, and a complex dance of interaction unfolded. An audio transcript would indicate that the nurse spoke the following utterance, which took under 5 seconds to speak: "Lemme take a look at that hand (1) and share in your coffee!" Yet the transcript of the spoken words doesn't make sense, because it leaves out all of the nonverbal interaction. The one-second pause, and the comment about the coffee, can only be understood by providing the nonverbal account of the interaction (see Fig. 1.1). During the utterance, the two of us communicated a great deal of information nonverbally; and this nonverbal interaction was closely woven together with the nurse's utterance. In fact, the moment-to-moment creation of her utterance was influenced, from second to second, by the parallel nonverbal interaction of both of us. Although she was the only speaker, we both collaboratively created her utterance (Goodwin, 1981).

This sort of interactional dance occurs with most of us every day: in maneuvering shopping carts past each other down a narrow aisle, in paying for purchases at the cash register. It occurs so quickly, below the level of consciousness, that we rarely take note of it. Yet these examples show that a form of group creativity is found in everyday

0:00	1:00	2:00	3:00	4:00	5:00	6:00
Lemme take a	look at that	hand				
nurse turning and	*walking toward*	*me*				
I put my	*highlighter on the*	*bed*				
	nurse leans	*down to look, but*	*pauses*			
			@I pick up the	coffee cup to	move it behind me,	
					safely out of the way	
				And share in	your coffee!	
						I extend my hand
						Simultaneously,
						nurse leans in

FIG. 1.1. Second-by-second transcription of an emergency room encounter. Each column represents one second of time. Roman typeface represents the utterance of the nurse, and italic typeface represents the nonverbal actions which occurred during the duration of the columns that the words occupy. Simultaneous action occurs in the same column. At second 3:00, as indicated by the @ sign, I realized that she paused because she had seen my coffee and is concerned she'll knock it over.

social life (Sawyer, 2001a). Conversation is not an exchange of mono-
logues; it is often a polyphonic duet (Chafe, 1997; Coates, 1997; Falk,
1980). Studies like these show that everyday conversation is collaborative and interactional, even when only one person is speaking. By
using these detailed transcription conventions, and attending to nonverbal details, conversation analysts have demonstrated that all conversation requires subtle, moment-to-moment group creativity.

STUDIES OF CREATIVITY IN GROUPS

In this book, I focus closely on the genres of interaction that most
strongly demonstrate the essential features of group creativity: musical and verbal creative performance. But because all conversation involves group creativity, the findings I discuss and the theoretical
framework I propose can be used to better understand any conversational small-group encounter. Several research traditions have studied creativity in groups, including work groups and classrooms, and
these traditions are relevant to the study of group creativity, because
the phenomena they study involve creative group interaction, mediated by signs and language; they are improvisational, in that they are
not scripted in advance; and they are collaborative, in that all participants play an important role in the emergent flow of the interaction.

Sociocultural Psychology

Beginning in the 1980s, a group of psychologists known as *socioculturalists* began to study individuals in different social and cultural contexts. They began by studying topics traditionally studied by cognitive psychologists—thinking, planning, remembering, and learning.
They studied how individuals behave intelligently and effectively in
specific cultural contexts, while engaged in well-defined tasks with
culturally valued goals. While observing these psychological processes as they occur in rich social settings, the socioculturalists gradually began to believe that these processes were not, strictly speaking, "psychological"—rather, individual cognitive processes were so
deeply embedded in group practices that it was difficult to identify
what was "individual psychology" and what was "group process."
This position was a shift in focus from the approach of cognitive psychologists, who believed that cognition could be studied as a prop-

erty of the individual, in isolation from any particular surrounding context of performance.

Many socioculturalists study the informal learning of young children, and speak primarily to developmental psychologists or to educational theorists. Rogoff, one of the most prominent advocates of this approach, conducted a study of how girls learn informally by engaging in the practice of selling Girl Scout cookies (Rogoff, Baker-Sennett, Lacasa, & Goldsmith, 1995). She found that a full understanding required not only a study of the cognitive mental processes of the girls, but also required an understanding of the entire social system of activity—the institutionalized practice—that had historically developed to sell cookies. Her research team analyzed the order forms and tracking sheets provided by the Girl Scout organization, and analyzed the informal interactions that take place between mother and daughter as they plan how to organize their orders and how to deliver the cookies when they arrive from the distribution center. One of their main findings was that plans are often modified opportunistically in their collaborative implementation (also see Gardner & Rogoff, 1990).

Another branch of socioculturalism focuses on adult work groups in organizations (Engeström & Middleton, 1996; Nardi, 1996). Hutchins (1995) used anthropological methods to study the navigation teams that direct large navy vessels into the port of San Diego. These are incredibly large ships, and navigation requires a complex array of instruments. Many of the instruments require the dedicated attention of a single navigator, so that the navigation task involves a work team of 5 to 10 trained individuals. By closely studying navigation teams as they piloted ships into and out of the harbor, Hutchins discovered that the team functioned as a unit to solve a collective cognitive task. They engaged in a form of group creativity to solve unexpected problems that arose during the journey; Hutchins documented the communications and the interactional synchrony among team members that allowed them to accomplish this collaborative task. He used the language of cognitive science, but applied it to the group as his unit of analysis, rather than to the single individual. This led Hutchins to argue that, in a sense, the navigation team "decides" and "has knowledge" that could not be found in any one of the members of the team.

Following on seminal studies like these, many other socioculturalists have begun to examine groups as collaborating creative entities, and many of these studies take place in classrooms or other educational settings. For example, in inquiry-based science instruction, children are grouped into teams and assigned research tasks that must be solved collaboratively (e.g., van Boxtel, van der Linden, & Kanselaar, 2000). In informal learning settings like science museums or after-school computer clubs, children typically work together and engage in a great deal of talk with each other while interacting with an exhibit or a computer (Nicolopoulou & Cole, 1993). These studies have shown that children learn unique skills by engaging in these forms of group creativity. I further explore group creativity and learning in chapter 7.

Organizational Behavior and Work Teams

The sociocultural study of work groups in organizations is closely related to a recent trend in studies of organizational behavior: a focus on *work teams*. In particular, there has been a burst of interest in *self-directed* or *self-managed teams* (Belasen, 2000; Evans & Sims, 1997; Lanzara, 1983, p. 86; Weick, 2001). Such teams represent a paradigm shift from the more traditional hierarchical organization, with management exerting control from the top down. Many organization theorists have argued that these empowered teams lead to a flat organizational structure that is more agile, flexible, efficient, productive, and adaptive (Belasen, 2000, p. 252).

Many theorists have emphasized the improvisationality of such teams (Crossan & Sorrenti, 1997; Eisenberg, 1990; Kao, 1996; Miner, Bassoff, & Moorman, 2001; Weick, 2001). In organizations as in improvisational theater, "people are able to accomplish collectively what they could not do individually.... The design that produces this complex mixture tends to be emergent and visible only after the fact" (Weick, 2001, p. 58). Improvisational organizations are emergent and self-organizing, and lead to solutions that have an emergent orderliness, in that small initial structures and decisions can eventually generate a more complex, larger design (p. 67). This recent paradigm shift in organization theory shows that much organizational behavior involves group creativity. Teamwork connects explicitly to the sociocultural focus on group cognition and group problem solving; and organization theorists have explicitly noted the parallels to both jazz and to improv theater. I further explore group creativity and organizations in chapter 7.

Creativity Research

Since the 1980s there has been a burst of scholarly activity surrounding creativity (e.g., Runco & Albert, 1990; Sawyer et al., in press; Sternberg, 1988; Sternberg & Davidson, 1995). The psychology of creativity, a subfield of psychological study, has gone through a parallel shift to that of the socioculturalists in developmental psychology. Prior to the development of the sociocultural paradigm, cognitive psychologists largely believed that the best way to study human behavior was to analyze what was in people's heads. Likewise, creativity researchers thought that creativity could be best understood by analyzing the individual person—his or her motivations, goals, and internal cognitive representations. In the late 1980s, at about the same time as the socioculturalists, creativity researchers began to shift their focus to the social and contextual environments within which creative work occurred (Gardner, 1993; Csikszentmihalyi, 1988, 1996; John-Steiner, 1993, 2000; Sawyer et al., in press). This shift is usually dated to the 1988 publication of an article by Mihaly Csikszentmihalyi which proposed the *systems view* of creativity (see chap. 5). Csikszentmihalyi argued that an individual cannot be defined to be creative universally and in all contexts and domains of activity; rather, individuals could only be said to be creative by reference to some conception of what counted as creative work. Csikszentmihalyi claimed that "what counted" as creative work was always defined by some social group of individuals, which he referred to as the *field*. The field consists of gatekeepers, the senior individuals who evaluate innovative new work and decide which of it is valuable and important; which of it is just derivative, old wine in new bottles; which of it is new, but not really that important; and which of it is new but ridiculous, the work of an eccentric crackpot. Csikszentmihalyi argued that without the field's judgment, no one could state with certainty which category a novel creative product falls into.

This new emphasis on the role of social groups in creativity contributed to an increasing interest in exploring the working processes of creative individuals. By examining their day-to-day activities, researchers were able to document the points at which they interacted with the field, and in some cases, how they received creative inspiration during conversations with colleagues (Csikszentmihalyi & Sawyer, 1995; John-Steiner, 2000). For example, one of the subjects quoted in Csikszentmihalyi and Sawyer (1995) said:

I develop lots of my ideas in dialogue. It's very exciting to have another mind that is considering the same set of phenomena with as much interest as one is. It's very exciting, the sparks, and dynamic interaction, and very much newer things, new ways of looking at things, that come out of those conversations. (p. 348)

Even if the moment of inspiration comes when the creator is in the bathtub or gardening, it may have come only as a result of a prior encounter with a colleague, or exposure to some new ideas at a recent conference. Thus, creativity research has shifted to a concern with group creativity, and an interest in the role that group creativity plays in individual creativity. This book continues in this recent tradition because I focus on the group rather than the individual, and on the social, interactive processes of group creativity. In chapters 4 and 5, I explore the connections between group creativity and creativity in the arts and sciences.

MOVING FORWARD: THE STUDY
OF GROUP CREATIVITY

The above traditions, all emerging in the latter decades of the 20th century, have provided us with many insights about collaboration and creativity in groups.

First, creativity researchers now believe that creativity cannot always be defined as a property of individuals; creativity can also be a property of groups. For example, the performance that is generated by an improvisational theater ensemble is the creative product of the entire ensemble; there is no way to attribute the performance to any single member of the group. In the same way, organization theorists and socioculturalists argue that problem solving in work groups, and learning in classrooms and informal settings, often occurs in social interactions characterized by group creativity. These researchers are still exploring the complex relationship between group creativity and the creativity of individual members of the group. These are different types of creativity; the interactional processes of group creativity that we can observe among improvising actors is not likely to look anything like the cognitive processes going on within any single actor's head.

Second, creativity researchers now believe that even individual creativity is influenced by the immediate social and cultural context, the "domain" and "field" of Csikszentmihalyi's model. John-Steiner (2000) documented that many of the most creative individuals in the 20th century depended heavily on collaboration for their inspirations, relying on close colleagues on an intimate, day-to-day basis while they engaged in their own work.

Third, conversation analysts, organization researchers, and socio-culturalists have demonstrated that creativity is not limited to artists and musicians. Group creativity is also found in everyday life—in children playing together (Sawyer, 1997b) or in a business team trying to design a new product (Moorman & Miner, 1998). Group creativity is found even in the most mundane everyday conversations, because speakers must collaborate to coordinate the mechanics of turn-taking, or even to construct a single utterance.

Yet these traditions have left several questions unanswered, and this book is a contribution to the exploration of these unanswered questions. I begin in chapter 2 by identifying some important properties of group creativity, by drawing on empirical studies of jazz and improvisational theater. These studies reveal the importance of process, mechanism, and communication in group creativity. Yet these are exactly those aspects of group creativity that these several research traditions have had the most difficulty explaining. What are the specific processes of group interaction that lead to the emergence of a form of creativity that is distinct from (and perhaps more than) the creativity of the individuals in the group? What are the social mechanisms that lead to the emergence of group creative products? In this book, I argue that group creativity is a result of certain special properties of creative communication between members. I analyze the kinds of communications that occur between members of creating groups, and how these communications contribute to effective group creativity. In chapters 3 through 6 I develop a theory of symbolic interaction in group creativity; I draw heavily on semiotics, on theories of creative verbal interaction, and on pragmatics.

Music and spoken language are very different symbolic media, and many theories that have attempted to compare music to language have failed. However, my theory of group creativity is unique in its focus on interactional semiotics; because this theory of group creativity is based in the semiotic and pragmatic aspects of symbolic communication, I am able to use it to identify parallels between group creativity in music and in verbal art.

The main implications of the book are for researchers interested in group creativity in music and verbal art. Yet in addition, the book has implications for the widely diverse group of psychologists, sociologists, and organization and communication theorists who study small-group interaction and interpersonal communication. As I described earlier, each of these research traditions has explored creative interaction in collaborating groups. For example, the sociocultural psychologists have examined creative and collaborative emergence in apprenticeship settings such as caregivers interacting with children, and they have found improvisational elements of discourse even in scaffolded activity formats in classrooms (Griffin & Mehan, 1981). Thus this study of group creativity, although it focuses on creative performance genres, provides insights that may generalize to all collaborating groups.

2

Jamming in Jazz
and Improv Theater

True improvisation is a dialogue between people.
—Paul Sills, founder of the Second City Theater, in Sweet (1978, p. 19)

The legendary 1990s Chicago improv group, Jazz Freddy, chose their name because of the similarities between jazz and improv theater. Actor and director Pete Gardner (a.k.a. Pete Zahradnick) said:

Jazz was what it was, that's why I liked it, the improvisation was musical, and it was like riffing. The idea of the jazz thing was it was like knowing a melody that we all knew how to play, and then having all these different sounds come in, and play in there, just like jazz. (Sawyer interview, February 25, 1994)

In interviews with Chicago jazz musicians that I conducted just a few years before my interview with Gardner, many musicians compared their ensemble art to a conversation:

[The ensemble] influences it the same way as if—we're having a conversation now. . . . When I start talking about it, I start thinking about it, putting bits and pieces together, coming up with ideas on how I feel about things, and that way it helps me . . . I can start to know myself better through my conversation and interactions with the world around me, and it's the same thing up on stage, the same exact thing. By talking to people up on stage through your music, you can start working on

28

stuff you've never heard and never done ... you need people to play
with ... when I do it, I'd find that there are these things coming out of
myself, which I didn't even know were there, I'd never heard them, I
didn't know where they came from. ... but playing with the others trig-
gers it, so maybe consciously or subconsciously you'll hear that thing,
that you're trying to find ... by listening to what other people have to
say, and by talking to them about it, it's like talking about—really great
music, it's guys getting together and talking about how sad or lonely
they feel, or how happy or angry. (Sawyer interview, Dec. 2, 1990)

In this chapter, I explore many parallels in the ways that performers in both jazz and improv describe their experiences creating in
groups. In my book *Creating Conversations* (Sawyer, 2001a), I explored
the improvisationality of everyday conversation, and these quotations begin to show us what specific form the parallels might take, because improv theater *is* conversation—a highly improvised, staged
conversation.[2]

These quotations provide several suggestive observations—jazz is
like conversation, conversation is improvised dialogue, and improv is
like jazz. But these general observations don't provide much detail for
a social scientist to work with—they are woefully short on specifics.
Getting a more specific understanding of these common characteristics will help to flesh out the understanding of group creativity in general, because jazz and improv are the two purest genres of group creativity. In chapter 1 I identified the key features of group creativity: It
is unpredictable and emergent, and involves processes of intersubjectivity and complex communication. In this chapter, I extend this
analysis of group creativity by delving more deeply into the phenomenon itself. I do this by focusing on what performers say about the subjective experience of creating in a group; the raw data for this chapter
are interviews with jazz musicians and improvisational theater actors.
I combine my own interviews of both jazz musicians (Sawyer, 1992)
and improv actors (Sawyer, 2003) with a wide range of published interviews of both types of performers, drawn primarily from Berliner's
(1994) book *Thinking in Jazz* and Sweet's (1978) oral history of Chicago
improv, *Something Wonderful Right Away*. I use quotations from the in-

---

[2]There are some differences between spontaneous speech and dramatic dialogue,
particularly in turn-taking technique and the amount of overlap among speakers, as
noted by several conversation analysts (Hafez, 1991; Hopper, 1993; Stucky, 1988, 1993).
These differences do not affect my argument.

terviews to demonstrate key properties of group creativity. For each property I group the comments of both musicians and actors.

Compared to everyday groups like work teams and classroom collaborating groups, jazz musicians and improv actors are remarkably self-reflective about group creativity. There seems to be something about these genres that facilitates and perhaps even requires some critical understanding of what is going on. For example, aspiring improvisers must first take classes in which they are taught a fairly elaborated theory about how improvised dialogue works (Sawyer, 2003). Perhaps it's because unlike in many everyday groups, the process is the product and there is no other external goal.

There are weaknesses associated with the interview method; after all, performers may not fully understand the mental and group processes that are involved in group creativity. In fact, in *Improvised Dialogues* (Sawyer, 2003), I reveal many dimensions of improv that are essential to a coherent performance but that actors are unaware of. As Durkheim (1964) perhaps first observed, "Even when we have collaborated in [a performance], we can only with difficulty obtain even a confused and inexact insight into the true nature of our action and the causes which determined it" (p. xlv). Yet when a phenomenon like group creativity is just beginning to be studied, an interview approach can provide an initial map of the territory, and social scientists have displayed a remarkable lack of interest in group creativity; our understanding of it is embarrassingly minimal (cf. Sawyer, 1997a). Psychologists have not studied group creativity in jazz or theater—perhaps because the ensemble nature of these forms makes them resistant to the individualistic methods dominant in contemporary psychology.[3] Sociologists and anthropologists have generally been equally uninterested in these small group settings (with the exception of the research I described in chapter 1). And in particular, there has been very little study of the social and interactional processes of creative groups.

I begin the chapter by providing two extended examples of group creativity, one of a jazz group, and one of an improv group. Following

---

[3]A few cognitive psychologists studied the mental processes of solitary musical improvisation in jazz and classical musicians. These studies examined cognitive processing models of mental states during improvisation (e.g., Cambor, Lisow, & Miller, 1962; Hermelin, O'Connor, Lee, & Treffert, 1989; chapters in Sloboda, 1988 including Clarke, 1988; Pressing, 1988). But because the focus in cognitive psychology is on internal mental processes, these studies did not examine the interactional and social aspects of group improvisation.

these two examples, the chapter focuses on three general features that are shared by both jazz and improv theater. First, I discuss properties of group interaction, using the concepts of interactional synchrony and group flow. Second, I discuss the tension between structure and innovation in group performance. Third, I discuss the role of the audience. Because these properties are common to improvisations in both musical and verbal language, I suggest they are likely to be found in all improvised group interaction.

SMALL-GROUP JAZZ

Group jazz performance is perhaps the most well-known improvisational performance form in American culture. "Jazz" is a broad term, encompassing 20-piece orchestras with elaborate scoring, to "free jazz," an unstructured small group improvisation. The canonical small jazz group, usually a quartet or quintet, rests between these extremes of structure and nonstructure. This performance format represents a highly developed context within which creative group interaction generates an ephemeral creative product. The real-time nature of the performance leaves little opportunity for conscious reflection; the revision and elaboration required for composition cannot take place.

Each performance begins with a song, more or less arranged in advance, and quickly progresses to group improvisation, usually based on the initial song form. The most commonly performed jazz songs, known as *standards*, are based on the chorus form of the mid-century American popular song. The chorus is a 32-bar structure, grouped into four sections of eight bars each. The group begins by playing the *head*, playing the song's melody "straight" so that the audience can recognize the song. Then the group moves into the main portion of the song's performance, a series of solo improvisations over the 32-bar chorus form. During his or her solo, the soloist is the primary improviser; the remainder of the group is expected to direct their improvisations so that they support the soloist, by reinforcing creative ideas of the soloist or suggesting new ideas to stimulate the soloist.

Monson's 1996 book *Saying Something* analyzed many such examples, along with transcribed musical notation that demonstrated in wonderful detail how musicians converse in a jazz improvisation. Monson described an interview with drummer Ralph Peterson in which she played a tape of a live performance of Peterson's composition "Princess" with pianist Geri Allen and bassist Essiet Okon Essiet. During Allen's solo, Peterson's drum accompaniment was very dense, and there were several instances in which Allen and Peterson traded ideas with each other. Monson and Peterson sat together and listened closely to the tape. Monson (1996) recognized that one of the conversational exchanges seemed to be based on the distinctive, catchy pattern from Dizzy Gillespie's famous performance of "Salt Peanuts," and noted this to Peterson. He replied:

> Yeah! "Salt Peanuts" and "Looney Tunes"—kind of a combination of the two. [Drummer] Art Blakey has a thing he plays. It's like: [he sings a rhythmic phrase from the song]. And [pianist] Geri played: [he sings Allen's standard response]. So I played the second half of the Art Blakey phrase: [he sings the second part of Blakey's drum pattern]. (p. 77)

Geri Allen immediately recognized the musical quotation from her performances with Blakey, and then responded with her usual response, indicating that she recognized and appreciated Peterson's communication (musical transcripts can be found in Monson, 1996, pp. 78–79). As in this example, musical communication in jazz depends on all of the musicians knowing the "language" extremely well—not only the notes of the songs, but even knowing how a certain performer typically plays a certain song with a specific other performer. Peterson then told Monson:

> But you see what happens is, a lot of times when you get into a musical conversation, one person in the group will state an idea or the beginning of an idea and another person will *complete* the idea or their interpretation of the same idea, how they hear it. So the conversation happens in fragments and comes from different parts, different voices. (Monson, 1996, p. 78)

Monson, herself a jazz drummer and trumpet player, concluded her example by writing, "There is a great deal of give and take in such improvisational interaction, and such moments are often cited by musicians as aesthetic high points of performances" (p. 80).

Jazz musicians engage in this sort of conversational exchange in the improvised group activity known as "trading fours" or "trading eights," the number referring to the number of measures that a soloist is given to play before the next soloist begins. Because the chorus form is 32 measures, trading eights is a relatively rapid transition, and each solo is really only a mini-solo, with barely enough time for one or two phrases. Rather than develop their own musical ideas or starting a completely new idea, each musician continues in the spirit or mood established by the prior players, responding to and building on the prior musician's eight bars (Berliner, 1994, pp. 369–370). Rufus Reid told Berliner how he tries to weave the prior soloist's ideas into his own solo, but not always in an obvious way, and not always by direct quotation; he said it was more interesting to elaborate on the prior idea. Musicians constantly balance coherence and innovation, borrowing material from the previous phrase and then transforming it.

IMPROV THEATER

The material and substance of scene improvisation are not the work of any one person or any one writer but come out of the cohesion of player acting upon player.

—Spolin (1963, p. 19)

Improv groups perform short *games*, 5-minute scenes with a gimmick that marks the dialogue as different from everyday conversation, as well as *long form*, fully improvised one-act plays lasting 30 to 60 minutes. The games are perhaps the most popular with audiences and are more commonly performed than long form. More than 300 improv games, also known as *handles* or *formats*, have emerged from the improv community. Each game is defined by a set of rules, and the improvisation is guided and channeled by the rules. Each game is introduced by an MC who announces the name of the game, describes the game's format, and then asks the audience for a suggestion which will be used to start the dialogue—typically a location, a relationship, or an object. Most games are funny in part because their rules are noticeably different from those that apply in everyday conversation. Each game involves a specific number of actors, and many games assign a distinct type of role to each of the actors.

In chapter 1, I provided two examples of group interaction in everyday conversation—my nonverbal interaction with the nurse in the emergency room, and how listener and speaker eye gaze affect study group conversation. These examples demonstrate that people interact by creatively managing both verbal and nonverbal action. Many improv games exaggerate the parallel interactional modes of verbal and nonverbal symbols, as in the Dubbing Game. The Dubbing Game involves four actors: two actors who gesture and move their lips silently on stage, and two actors who ventriloquate and speak their words for them while standing at the side of the stage. One of them has been chosen to be the MC, who describes the game to the audience and asks for a suggestion to start the improvisation.

> **Example 2.1.** Off-Off-Campus, May 22, 1992 (from Sawyer, 2003). Bob is the MC. I indicate the timing of various gestures with the "at" sign character, @. As their offstage ventriloquists are speaking, the onstage actors gesture with their hands and nod their heads, in the exaggerated fashion of a silent film actor.

1	Bob	OK. We're gonna do	
		a scene in which	
		Gabrielle and I provide	
		voices for the bodies	
		of Ron and Sarah.	
		But we need a location	Bob and Gabrielle walk to
		and a relationship.	opposite sides of the stage
			during this line
2	Audience1	The Gap	
3	Audience2	A blind date	
4	Bob	OK,	
		a blind date at the Gap.	
			He claps loudly to signal the
			scene's beginning.
5	Ron		Walks to side of stage,
			mimes opening a drawer.
6	Sarah		Walks over toward Ron.
7	Gabrielle	I don't know,	
		I don't see any @ jean	@ Ron turns to Sarah
		jackets here as nice as	
		the one you've @ got on.	@ Sarah points at his chest.
			Ron preens, touching his
			jacket.

8	Bob	Oh, I guess I could try to put it on and try to walk out of the store without it going BEEP BEEP BEEP BEEP	
9	Gabrielle	(You should!)	
10	Bob	I actually was supposed to meet somebody here	At the onset of this line, Ron holds out his right hand as if he is holding something in front of Sarah
11	Gabrielle	Oh, well that's all really impressive, I'm sure you're meeting your father here or something.	Ron's arm moves down a little lower, but still is holding something out.
12	Bob	Oh no, no, I'm supposed to meet the kind of person that would wear this, you know, @ this tank top.	@ Ron extends his arm again
13	Gabrielle	Well that's, @ that's really slutty, that's disgusting. @ You know, you're really cute, I, uh	@ She takes it from him with both hands, @ and tosses it aside
14	Bob	Oh, wait, are you Enid, my blind date?	
15	Gabrielle	(laughs) Yeah, how did you know?	
16	Bob	Well, cause you were doing that weird thing with your ear, @ that I heard you could do.	@ she reaches hand up to her ear
17	Gabrielle	Aren't I beautiful, aren't I sexy and attractive? Oh, and I have	

"Enid" written on my
@ shirt   @ Sarah points at her hip,
                                           perhaps at a purse
pocket @ here,   @ lifts hand up to sleeve
See I wanted you to
recognize me.
18   Bob   I'm so excited, maybe
                we should dance?

                                           Ron extends his arms to
                                           Sarah, and they dance swing
                                           style, arm in arm.

As we see in this example, the offstage ventriloquists often voice things that are embarrassing for the onstage actors, such as "that weird thing with your ear" (turn 16), or physical actions the onstage actors must perform, like "maybe we should dance" (turn 18). This gimmick provides much of the humor of the game, because actors are trained to always accept whatever is proposed for their character. Actors refer to this guideline as the "Yes, and" rule: always accept what is offered in the prior turn, and then elaborate on it by offering something new to further develop the drama. Although the speaking actors make most of the offers, the onstage actor can be a nonverbal initiator, as well. In turn 10, Ron extends his hand as if he is displaying something to Sarah; in turn 12, Bob incorporates this gesture into his spoken turn, saying "I'm supposed to meet the kind of person that would wear this, you know, this tank top."

The Dubbing Game demonstrates the importance of nonverbal interaction in groups, since the onstage actors contribute a great deal to the scene through purely physical actions. By continually making ambiguous gestures, they provide clues for future action to the speaking actors. It likewise demonstrates the importance of both gesture and speech in conversation (cf. Goodwin, 1981; Kendon, 1990; McNeill, 1992). The rules of the Dubbing Game exaggerate the demands of everyday conversation, because gestures and speech are executed by two different actors. The gesturing actors have to respond very quickly so that their gestures are not too far off in timing from the corresponding spoken line. For example, in turn 17 Sarah points to her hip in an attempt to synchronize with Gabrielle's unfolding utterance, "I have Enid written on my shirt pocket here," and then when the word "shirt" is spoken, Sarah has to make a quick correction and point to her shirt pocket. The speaking actors also have to be attentive to moment-by-moment events; for example, they often have to alter their utterance through self-repair to provide the on-stage actor with adequate time to generate the appropriate gesture. For example, in turn 12, Bob initiates self-repair, "this, you know," to give Ron time to point to the indexed referent; when Ron does so, Bob continues his utterance, "this tank top."

THE IMPORTANCE OF GROUP INTERACTION

The above examples show that the conversational analogy is more than just a metaphor. I've shown that both musicians and actors accept and elaborate on each other's ideas during a group improvisation. These examples of group interaction in jazz and in improv both demonstrate the critical role played by communicative interaction among the performers. In the following sections, I further explore the role of symbolic interaction in group creativity. I begin by showing how these observations are related to a body of work on what is known as *interactional synchrony*. I then discuss the importance of the individual performer's *flow state*, and I extend this psychological concept to the group level, in presenting my concept of *group flow*. I conclude the section with a discussion of how different chemistry between different specific performers can affect both interactional synchrony and group flow.

Interactional Synchrony

These performances seem to work because the performers are closely attuned to each other; monitoring the other performer's actions at the same time that they continue their own performance, they are able to quickly hear or see what the other performers are doing, and then to respond by altering their own unfolding, ongoing activity. These examples of jazz and improv demonstrate a form of what is often called *interactional synchrony*. The term *interactional synchrony* was first coined and conceptualized by Condon and Ogston (1971), who analyzed videotapes of speakers and hearers frame-by-frame and found that "the speaker and hearer look like puppets moved by the same set of strings" (Condon & Ogston, p. 158). People can synchronize an incredible number of verbal and nonverbal behaviors in as little as 1/20th of a second (Condon & Ogston, 1967). Condon and Ogston (1971) believed it was impossible to predict exactly which body part would move; instead, they believed the key to synchrony lay in the rhythm and timing of behaviors (p. 161). The coordination of rhythms between two people has also been theorized using the concept of *entrainment* (Condon & Ogston, 1966), a term originally used by physicists to describe the mutual phase locking of two oscillators (Pikovsky, Rosenblum, & Kurths, 2001). In entrainment, one person's rhythms become attuned to another, almost like a tuning fork. Musicologists have analyzed similar phenomena using the concept of *groove* (Berliner, 1994; Keil & Feld, 1994; Monson, 1996).

These scholars emphasized the importance of focusing on the entire group. As Scheflen (1982) wrote, "If we observe only one person or one person at a time, there is no way we will observe synchrony or co-action or interactional rhythm" (p. 15). Neither an individual nor a cultural focus is sufficient, because synchrony is a complex systems phenomenon. These findings begin to flesh out the conversational metaphors of jazz musicians; they show that jazz groups are only like conversation conceived of as a jointly accomplished co-actional process. In contrast, many theories of conversation prominent in linguistics assume that conversation is a polite turn-by-turn exchange of ideas, bouncing back and forth like the ball during a tennis match. This view of conversation is sometimes called the *conduit metaphor* (Reddy, 1979). A full understanding of the conversational metaphor requires that one draw on co-actional theories of conversation rather than conduit theories, and I elaborate this view of conversation in chapters 3 and 4.

Interactional synchrony is thought to have a biological basis (Burgoon, Stern, & Dillman, 1995), and some have suggested that biologically based social disorders like autism and schizophrenia are based in a failure of synchrony (Scheflen, 1982, p. 16). Infants show evidence of interactional synchrony with their parents as early as 20 minutes after birth, and it appears in chimpanzees and even in interactions between dogs and their human owners. Interactional synchrony has been hypothesized to serve several important biological functions: for example, its early emergence in infancy may provide physical safety and comfort (Condon, 1980), and it helps to facilitate social interaction with parents (Cappella, 1991). My improv theater examples here, and the conversation examples in chapter 1, show that it is essential to communication and social skills (also see Condon & Ogston, 1971). However, there also seems to be an important cultural component to synchrony; synchrony is much harder to attain if the participants are from different cultures, because different cultures seem to have different interactional styles, and these differences can disrupt interaction timing (Burgoon et al., 1995, p. 23; Lomax, 1982).

A few researchers have examined the role of interactional synchrony in group musical performance. Several researchers have compared musical interaction in jazz to the interactional synchrony between mother and infant, noting many studies that show we are born with an ability to engage in rhythmically coordinated interpersonal interaction (Papaeliou & Trevarthen, 1994; Schögler, 1998, 1999–2000). Researchers have also examined interactional synchrony in groups that perform scored pieces from the European orchestral repertory (Weeks, 1990, 1996a, 1996b), and have documented the role of interactional synchrony in achieving changes in tempo (Weeks, 1990) or in recovering from mistakes (Weeks, 1996b). I further explore these studies in chapter 7.

By closely focusing on microsecond aural and visual actions, these studies have shown that group interaction cannot be understood by analyzing individual performers' actions in isolation. Rather, these studies have demonstrated that group interaction is a complex systems-level phenomenon, and that interaction among performers must be the primary focus. However, because these studies focus on such a small micro level, they represent only a first step in the study of interaction in groups. In group creativity, interaction occurs at many temporal levels, and includes social, cultural, and semiotic processes in addition to rhythmic ones (cf. Monson, 1995). In chapters 3 through 6, I extend this work on interactional synchrony to emphasize the many complex levels of symbolic interaction that play a role in group creativity.

Flow

Csikszentmihalyi's (1990b) term *flow* refers to a state of heightened consciousness that occurs in individuals during peak experiences:

> It is what the sailor holding a tight course feels when the wind whips through her hair, when the boat lunges through the waves like a colt—sails, hull, wind, and sea humming a harmony that vibrates in the sailor's veins. It is what a painter feels when the colors on the canvas

begin to set up a magnetic tension with each other, and a new *thing*, a living form, takes shape in front of the astonished creator. (p. 3)

Over two decades of research with people from many walks of life, Csikszentmihalyi (1990b) identified the common characteristics of the flow experience:

> The best moments in our lives are not the passive, receptive, relaxing times.... The best moments usually occur when a person's body or mind is stretched to its limits in a voluntary effort to accomplish something difficult and worthwhile. (p. 3)

When in flow, "people are so involved in an activity that nothing else seems to matter; the experience itself is so enjoyable that people will do it even at great cost, for the sheer sake of doing it" (Csikszentmihalyi, 1990b, p. 4). In flow, the individual feels a sense of control over their own actions, their self-awareness vanishes, and time feels warped.

Activities result in flow when the skills of the individual are perfectly matched to the challenges of the task (see Fig. 2.1). The letters and arrows in the figure represent the path a young pianist takes to gradually become a more talented classical pianist. After a few months of lessons, the young pianist has progressed to playing simple pieces from a book of instructional pieces, perhaps with a single melodic line in each hand (A1). Once the pianist has mastered this level, one of two things will happen. Either these pieces will become boring as his or her skills continue to improve (A2), or the piano teacher will assign a more advanced piece that is a more difficult challenge, and

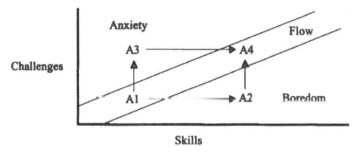

FIG. 2.1. Csikszentmihalyi's model of flow. Adapted from Csikszentmihalyi (1990b, p. 74).

the student will struggle and perhaps feel some anxiety (A3). Neither boredom nor anxiety are positive experiences, so the pianist is motivated to return to the flow state. If the pianist is bored, he or she will seek out a more challenging piece, shifting experience back into flow (A4). If the pianist is anxious about the increased challenge, he or she will practice to increase his or her skill level, again shifting experience back into flow.

This flow state is an important element in group creativity; individual performers in a group will be more likely to attain a flow state when their skills match the challenges facing them. As Berliner (1994) wrote concerning jazz, "improvisers experience a great sense of relaxation, which increases their powers of expression and imagination. They handle their instruments with athletic finesse" (p. 389). Improv theater actors almost all emphasize the high they get from the genre, and these comments seem to describe a classic flow state:

- "Improvisation swept us into another realm, another consciousness. . . . You forget yourself as the process takes hold. You sort of become part of the form itself. It's suddenly so natural, like going from crawling to walking." (Barbara Harris, in Sweet, 1978, p. 66)

- "Those great times when you're improvising where everything is so clear and you're just so connected and you just can sense where everybody is on the stage—that kind of brand new, everything is just happening space." (Pete Gardner, Sawyer interview, Feb. 25, 1994)

- "Once every six weeks you would be possessed. . . . That was thrilling, and you'd be drained and amazed afterward, and you'd have a sense of your possibilities. . . . You could actually become more than yourself and say things you couldn't have thought of and become people you didn't know . . . when you suddenly didn't have to think at all, that was the most, the *only*, exciting thing about it." (Mike Nichols on the excitement of performing with the Compass, in Sweet, 1978, pp. 77–78)

Groups attain flow by staying in the *improvisation zone* between complete predictability and going too far, between their shared knowledge about conventional situations, and doing something so inconsistent that it just doesn't make sense. Improvisational actors become highly attuned to this zone, and they are always trying to stay in the zone. The challenge of staying in the improvisation zone is responsible for the experience of flow that performers get from a particularly effective performance. Yet improvisation's unpredictability makes it a risky way to attain flow; it doesn't always happen, even in a group of talented, well-trained performers. Many improvising actors talk about both the high they get from a good improvisation, and the terror they feel when a performance is not going well. The unpredictability of group creativity can be frightening because failure is public, unlike creative genres like writing or painting. If a painter fails, he or she can paint over the canvas or perhaps even throw it away. Mark Gordon, a director of and actor in the Compass, said "It always felt to me like taking your pants off in front of an audience. A little terrifying" (Sweet, 1978, p. 110). Ted Flicker, director of the first St. Louis Compass and founder of the New York group The Premise, said "Unless you've actually tasted what improvising in front of an audience feels like, you can't *imagine* the horror of it" (Sweet, 1978, p. 162). Up to a certain point, this fear can contribute to the potential for a flow experience; but once it crosses a certain threshold, the actor moves from the flow zone into the anxiety zone.

The high of the flow of a successful performance is "something like a drug," the title of a book about the Theatresports league (Foreman & Martini, 1995). Improvisers keep doing it, in spite of the lack of money and fame relative to conventional theater, television, and movies, because of the high they get from the flow experience. Comparing improvisation to conventional theater, Andrew Duncan felt that the flow experience was much greater in improvisation. After leaving Second City in 1963, he said that "I really missed that kind of company—the community, working together, respect. . . . They were intense moments in your life that had meaning" (Sweet, 1978, p. 61).

Many Chicago improvisers are almost protective about what they view as a unique art form. Del Close, and many of his students that emerged from his ImprovOlympic theater, felt strongly that improvisation was an art form—particularly the long form genres—and that, like jazz, it took expertise and knowledge for an audience to fully appreciate the genre (Close, Sawyer interview, June 22, 1994). Actor Pete Gardner said,

> I have no aspirations. As far as improv goes, I don't want to sell it to people, to slick it down so it really works. I just want to keep screwing around with it and keep having fun with it and just enjoy the magic of it and the art of it. This is my one thing where I really find the art of it. (Sawyer interview, February 25, 1994)

Many improvisers have suggested that this is the reason the genre has thrived in Chicago, while it has languished in Los Angeles and New York—because actors in those cities are more career oriented, more focused on auditions and activities that will get them onto television or into movies.

Group Flow

> Tonight, things are going well. Tonight, watching them improvise is like watching an expert surfer. The surfer's incredible balance keeping him constantly poised on the crest of a wave; the cast, working from instinct rooted in hours of workshops and past improv sets, riding the crest of the moment. When they are on top, it is a sight to see. There is a thrill in watching them, a thrill born of the precariousness of their position and the ever-present threat that a misjudgment may send them hurtling into a wipeout.
>
> —Sweet (1978, p. xxxix)

There are many metaphors one can use to describe a talented group when they are "on," in interactional synchrony, performing well. One might say that they have a *good chemistry*, or that things are *clicking* or *in sync*. For example, Jimerson (1999) wrote about a pick-up basketball team, "we played quietly and efficiently. We rarely spoke and played effortlessly and effectively. As teammates, we were 'in sync' with each other" (p. 13). For just about any sports team, one can speak of the *group spirit*, the *team spirit*, or the *esprit de corps*. A commentator might say *they gelled as a unit* or that they displayed *good teamwork*. All of these metaphors focus on the entire group and on their performance together. Even if the individual performers are prepared and focused, a good group performance doesn't always emerge.

When a group is performing at its peak, I refer to the group as being in *group flow*, in the same way that an individual performing at his or her peak often experiences a subjective feeling of flow. The concept of group flow is related to Csikszentmihalyi's flow, but with a critical difference. Csikszentmihalyi intended flow to represent a state of consciousness within the individual performer, whereas group flow is a property of the entire group as a collective unit. When studying group creativity we need a way of characterizing the collective experience of the entire group. Based on my observations of performing groups, I have developed the concept of group flow to characterize those groups that are collectively in a flow state. Group flow has been neglected in studies of flow, which have focused on how individuals attain flow through their own actions (cf. Jimerson, 1999). In group flow, everything seems to come naturally; the performers are in interactional synchrony. In this state, each of the group members can even feel as if they are able to anticipate what their fellow performers will do before they do it.

Musicians use a wide variety of metaphors to describe group flow: riding a wave, gliding across a ballroom with a dance partner, or love-making (Berliner, 1994, p. 389). Jazz bassist Chuck Israels says, "If it's working, it brings you very close. It's a kind of emotional empathy that you develop very quickly. The relationship is very intimate" (Berliner, 1994, pp. 349–350). Curtis Fuller said, "when that's really happening in a band, the cohesiveness is unbelievable. Those are the special, cherished moments. When those special moments occur, to me, it's like ecstasy. It's like a beautiful thing. It's like when things blossom" (Berliner, 1994, p. 389). There is an open communicative channel among the performers; each performer is open and listening to the others, and each performer fully attends to what the others are doing, even as they are contributing to the performance themselves. Melba Liston said that "everybody can feel what each other is thinking and everything. You breathe together, you swell together, you just do everything together, and a different aura comes over the room" (Berliner, 1994, p. 392).

In musical groups, group flow requires a type of parallel processing; the musicians are playing nonstop, yet while they are playing they must simultaneously listen to their band members, hearing and immediately responding to what they are playing. "You have to be able to divide your senses ... so you still have that one thought running through your head of saying something, playing something, at the same time you've got to be listening to what the drummer is doing" (Sawyer interview, December 2, 1990). You can't relax your attention or else you will fall behind. Bassist Chuck Israels said: "From the very moment the performance begins, you plunge into that world of sounds ... and your whole consciousness changes" (Berliner, 1994, p. 348). Improvisational musicians often try to replicate this experience mentally as they practice alone. For example, a drummer might imagine a ground of bass lines as he plays (Berliner, 1994, p. 350).

Many groups require a preliminary warm-up period for the group flow to be established. In Chicago blues bands, the tradition is that the group plays the first set while the headlining lead singer, guitarist, or harmonica player remains backstage. This allows the group to get into an interactional synchrony, so that when the band leader comes on stage, he will have the benefit of a fully warmed up band. As jazz trumpeter Jimmy Robinson said about the rhythm section, "you just let them play to get the kinks out. After they'd got the feeling for one another and got themselves together, then the horns joined them" (Berliner, 1994, p. 357). Improv theater groups typically perform group exercises in a separate room near the theater while the audience members arrive and take their seats. Some of these exercises are high energy, and audience members occasionally hear strange shouts and pounding sounds filter into the theater as the group works toward a state of group flow.

Visual attention is important to both musicians and actors in establishing group flow. Jazz musicians typically watch each other closely as they are improvising, and this can help them to anticipate what will come next. For example, a pianist might raise his arms just before playing a block chord, or a saxophonist might take a larger than usual breath just before playing a particularly elaborate melody. Improvising actors also maintain eye contact and are attentive to each other's physical posture and mimed gestures, even when they are engaged in actions that in real life would not require eye contact (such as working side by side), and even though they must also remember to face at least partially toward the audience, so that their voices will project and the audience can hear the dialogue.

Group flow is an emergent property of the group. Group flow can inspire musicians to play things that they would not have been able to play alone, or that they would not have thought of without the inspiration of the group; "the highest points of improvisation occur when group members strike a groove together" (Berliner, 1994, p. 388). Group flow helps the individual performers to attain their own flow state. In a study of pick-up basketball games, Jimerson (1999) wrote that flow is caused by groups when it is "a result of their interaction with other people, [who] cooperatively maintain their flow, and respond to each other differently than they did before" (p. 35). When jazz musicians describe the subjective experience of performing in a group, they frequently refer to the important role played by the emergent group flow in propelling their own performance to ever higher levels: "Sometimes, I really feel that I am just the vehicle, the body, and that something is really singing through me, like I am not controlling everything that I am singing" (Carmen Lundy, in Berliner, 1994, p. 392).

The quality of a group performance is difficult to predict. Jazz musicians and improv theater ensembles alike have little idea how successful a performance will be; there are simply too many intangible factors that cannot be known until the performance begins. Franklin Gordon said, "It doesn't happen every single night ... but at some point when the band is playing and everyone gets locked in together, it's special for the musicians and for the aware, conscientious listener. These are the magical moments, the best moments in jazz" (Berliner, 1994, p. 388). In team sports, many games are scheduled between teams that are said to be far apart in ability; this difference in expected ability is reflected in the Vegas "spread," the amount that the favored team is expected to win by. But athletes always discount these numbers, because group performance on any given day or night is unpredictable. They say "that's why you play the game," and in fact, it's not that unusual for an underdog to win.

When a group is in a state of group flow, it's often the case that the individual members are in flow states, as well. However, this is not always the case; sometimes groups can perform effectively even though the participants may not enjoy it very much. This is a case of the more general group phenomenon—that properties of groups may emerge from individual action and interaction, and yet not correspond directly to any properties of any members of the group (Sawyer, 2002b). Group flow is an irreducible property of performing groups, and cannot be reduced to psychological studies of the mental states or the subjective experiences of the individual members of the group.

There are several anecdotes that reinforce my claim that group flow is an emergent group property, rather than a property of individuals. For example, a group may be in group flow even when the performers don't realize it. Improvisational musicians and actors alike often describe the experience of walking off of the stage at the end of the night, feeling that the performance had been really bad, and then hearing later that the audience had found it to be a stellar performance. This is not only an issue of expertise; even regulars and aficionados in the audience sometimes have different opinions of a performance than the performers themselves. Pete Gardner describes how the improvisers always valued shows in which everything connected well; but "the audiences absolutely love the shows where there was a mass confusion." He described an experience where one friend compared a slick show with a confused show, explicitly noting that the confused and messy show was "so much better" (Sawyer interview,

February 25, 1994). Inversely, most group performers can tell a story of at least one night's performance that they thought was particularly good, but later as they were discussing the performance with knowledgeable, trusted colleagues who had been in the audience, they discovered that it was not one of their best.

Many Chicago improvisers refer to group flow using the term *groupmind* (Halpern, Close, & Johnson, 1994). The perfect working of groupmind is a magical kind of high, akin to perfect teamwork in sports or even great sex; comedian Jim Belushi famously said that the high that comes from group flow was "better than sex" (Seham, 2001, p. 64; compare Berliner on jazz, 1994, p. 389). Actor Alan Alda referred to this state, saying "you're actually tuned into something that's inside the actor's mind and there's a kind of mental music that's played and that everybody shares" (Sweet, 1978, p. 326). Improv actors often speak of group flow as "a state of unselfconscious awareness in which every individual action seems to be the right one and the group works with apparent perfect synchronicity" (Seham, 2001, p. 64). Performers often talk about the groupmind in spiritual terms, and believe it channels "a truth beyond their own conscious reasoning" (Seham, 2001, p. 64).

In both jazz and improv, we find that groups performing at their peak are in a state akin to Csikszentmihalyi's flow, and I have called this group phenomenon group flow. Although I've quoted performers' perceptions of it and attitudes toward it, I've claimed that group flow is an emergent group property and is not the same thing as the psychological state of flow. It depends on interaction among performers, and it emerges from this process. The group can be in flow even when the members are not; or the group might not be in flow even when the members are. The study of group flow thus requires a fundamentally social psychology, and must proceed by examining the interactional dynamics among members during performance.

The Group Dynamic

Earlier, I described the state of group flow that groups attain when their performance is working particularly well. In this section, I talk about the dynamics between specific performers. All group performers have had the contrasting experiences of performing with someone where it clicks and there is often group flow, and also of performing with someone where it doesn't work at all and group flow is unlikely to occur. Some combinations of performers are more likely to attain group flow, others less likely, and this remains true across many different performances. Therefore this group dynamic has something to do with the personality styles and the interpersonal dynamics of these specific individuals, rather than the emergent processes of any single night's performance.

Certain pairs of actors always tended to work well together, and performers refer to this as *chemistry*. Actor Eugene Troobnick said that "We would find that we would tend to work with the same people in the improvisations. That's how Mike [Nichols] and Elaine [May] got together.... I had a special rapport sort of like that with Alan Arkin and Paul Sand" (Sweet, 1978, pp. 195–196). Mike Nichols echoed Troobnick's observation: "That was the difference between Elaine and me. She could do it with several people. I could always do it only with her. I never did a good scene of any kind with anybody else" (Sweet, 1978, p. 78). Severn Darden says about Barbara Harris: "The best work I ever did I did with Barbara. She was my favorite" (Sweet, 1978, p. 91).

Although some performers have preferences for a specific partner—like Mike Nichols for Elaine May—many actors can accept a range of partners that have a certain improvisational style. Bobbi Gordon said that "I was very good when I was working with somebody who really had an incredible idea for a scene and could take off. Then I didn't feel that the responsibility of making the scene work was on my shoulders" (Sweet, 1978, p. 110). Several people commented on how actor Andrew Duncan was able to make anyone in the 1960s Second City look good. Mark Gordon said, "Andy was not a funnyman. He was a *rock*, an unselfish rock. He was there for everybody" (Sweet, 1978, p. 117). Severn Darden said, "Andrew Duncan, among other things, I think, was the best straight man ever, which is extremely difficult improvising. You would go onstage with Andrew and he would make you look very good because it looked like you were making all the jokes" (Sweet, 1978, p. 93). Alan Arkin said that "he was in a lot of ways the glue that held the whole thing together" (Sweet, 1978, p. 222).

Some combinations in groups simply don't work well, despite the individual talents and the good faith efforts of the actors. Alan Arkin was critical of his work in the second St. Louis Compass with Anne Meara, Jerry Stiller, and Nancy Ponder: "I just felt it wasn't a well-matched group. The four of us weren't on the same wavelength" (Sweet, 1978, p. 219). Barbara Harris, speaking of the early Compass performances in Chicago, said "Shelley Berman, for instance, who is almost flawless by himself, could get into an improvisation which just wouldn't go, despite his talent" (Sweet, 1978, p. 70).

In jazz groups, as well, some combinations of musicians work well, while others don't. Some problems are caused by bad musicians, but others just by incompatible styles. Akira Tana observed that "meeting people on the bandstand is just like meeting people and interacting with them in other aspects of life. There may be certain idiosyncrasies in their musical personalities that conflict. It doesn't mean that they're bad players" (Berliner, 1994, p. 395). When a group finds that chemistry, some musicians believe it is a relatively rare thing; "the greatest things don't happen in bands often, because the chemistry between the combination of players doesn't lend itself to the most positive or the highest level of music. It seems like it's a stroke of luck or genius when everyone is matched perfectly and the music's really happening" (Don Pate, in Berliner, 1994, p. 395).

Musicians can fail to connect in many different ways. First, there are different rhythmic styles. All groups vary the tempo slightly through a performance, speeding up slightly as a solo builds to its climax, for example. Yet some musicians rush, others pull back, and some do both at different points in a song. Another problem with some musicians is that they play too much like a metronome, and they aren't able to subtly follow these tempo changes.

Second, there are overall volume preferences and specific preferences for changes in dynamics at certain points during a performance. Some musicians prefer a louder or softer pianist or drummer. Soloists need the rest of the band to be responsive to their cues with respect to volume; a soloist might want to play softly, but can't if the drummer keeps on playing loud, because then no one would hear the solo.

Third, different musicians have different ways of interpreting each genre, or may be strong in one genre but not another. Musicians can have honest differences of opinion about such things, and different groups will be more or less willing to meld genres and styles. Playing in a certain way often requires the rest of the band to play in a compatible way; if a pianist wants to play like Herbie Hancock, he needs the bass player and the drummer to play like Hancock's band; if they don't, his piano style won't really work, and he'll be frustrated (Berliner, 1994, p. 399).

Many improvisers emphasize that one of the most important roles of a director is to select a group of people that will gel together. Paul

Sills was said to have this ability "for putting a group of people together who somehow set each other on fire" (Arkin, in Sweet, 1978, p. 219). Jazz band leaders have the same responsibility (Berliner, 1994, pp. 417–420). Effective directors are capable of identifying group combinations that are more likely to achieve group flow; they have a rare ability to think simultaneously at both the individual level and the group level. They can see beyond the talents of individual performers in isolation, and envision how the group will work together.

STRUCTURE AND IMPROVISATION

Add too many rules and it's no longer improvisation and not much fun. But some goals or guidance seem to make it more likely that everyone will get to play and that the process will result in something interesting for an audience to watch.

—Seham (2001, p. 226)

Improv does not mean "anything goes." In jazz, each musician and each group must balance two competing tendencies: the expectation of creativity and inspiration, and the need to maintain coherence with both the tradition and the group. In the following sections, I first describe the conventions of group performance, and how beginning performers learn them. I then explore several different ways that these conventions influence group creativity—in the individual's balance of structure and improvisation, in emergent group riffs, and in rehearsal. These discussions reveal similar tensions between structure and improvisation at both the individual and the group level.

The Conventions of Performance

Berliner (1994, p. 417) described these two tendencies in terms of two competing social conventions: First, that jazz is democratic music, and all musicians should have the freedom to express themselves, and second, that players are mutually interdependent and should limit their individual freedom for the good of the group. Playing jazz is a team effort and "everybody has to do their specific job" (Leroy Williams, in Berliner, 1994, p. 418); "You're hired by people to make their music sound good and to complement them" (Akira Tana, in Berliner, 1994, p. 420).

Becker (2000) described these sorts of expectations as the *etiquette* of improvisation, drawing an analogy with the informal and implicit rules of good social conduct. For example, Becker reported from his own experience playing piano at jam sessions in Chicago. These jam sessions were late-night affairs, and many young trumpet and saxophone players would line up at the edge of the stage for their opportunity to solo. The first horn player would begin his solo at the beginning of the song form, and solo through the 32-bar song form repeatedly until running out of inspiration or energy; this could result in a solo anywhere from 3 to 10 times through the song form. One rule of etiquette that was uniformly followed in Becker's jam sessions was that each subsequent solo had to be the same length as this first solo. This rule of etiquette emerged informally to resolve two competing tendencies: A shorter solo would imply that the musician lacked musical inspiration and wasn't up to the same level as the first soloist; a longer solo would imply arrogance, as if he were trying to show up the first soloist.

Both Berliner and Becker noted that for jazz to work, the participants have to share a set of social conventions learned through a process of professional socialization. These conventions are typically not written down, but are the tacit practices of an oral culture. As Bastien and Hostager (1992) wrote, "jazz musicians have developed conventions that capitalize on the formal structure of the music to integrate the individual creativity of musicians into seamless, unitary, coordinated behavior" (p. 102). These conventions include a wide range of unwritten expectations: Musicians are expected to know a large repertoire of "jazz standards" and be able to play them without rehearsal; musicians are expected to know standard chord substitutions, to be able to hear a soloist use one, and to be able to follow along immediately; musicians are expected to be able to hear when a soloist is nearing the completion of a solo so that they can support the climax, and also so that the next soloist can begin without delay.

Other shared conventions are not musical per se, but have to do with the coordination of group activity:

1. The leader decides the song and the key of the song;

2. the soloist at a given time determines the style for the group, and the others are expected to support that decision and follow along;

3. each musician gets an opportunity to be the soloist (Becker, 2000, described the scene in Chicago, where each soloist had to take exactly the same amount of time as the first person to solo);

4. the 32-bar chorus is the basic unit of a solo;

5. no musician should embarrass other musicians by making them look bad with an unexpected surprise or by challenging them to do something they are not capable of doing (or as the directors of the ImprovOlympic theater put it in their book, "The best way for an improviser to look good is by making his fellow players look good," Halpern, Close, & Johnson, 1994, p. 37);

6. nonverbal communication cues, such as eye contact at key moments, that indicate important pending changes (Bastien & Hostager, 1992, pp. 95–96).

These rules, both explicit and implicit, both formal and informal, are what define a genre of improvisation. They emerge informally in a community of practice, over the years, with continual experimentation with what works and what doesn't work. In both improvisational theater and in jazz, performers must first be trained in improvisation in classes, and then socialized into the community of practice through rehearsals and, finally, performances in front of an audience.

Several creativity researchers have explored the role played by such rules and conventions in creative domains. In both the arts and the sciences, creative individuals must become familiar with what has come before, and only then can they begin to generate truly original products. Csikszentmihalyi (1988, 1990a) referred to the collective body of rules and conventions of a creative field as a *domain*. The domain includes the "raw materials" available to the creative individual, and the rules and procedures which can be used to combine them. Individual acts that do not satisfy the constraints of the domain are rarely viewed as "creative" by the *field*, the social group that defines a type of creative activity.

The domain and field components of Csikszentmihalyi's model seem to play an important role in jazz. Musicians frequently refer to leading jazz figures, key members of the field, in their discussions of jazz definition and method. Musicians often mention the importance of listening to albums of past jazz greats, to become familiar with the tradition and the "language." The "domain" of small group jazz would be the scales, harmonic patterns, and styles which make up the definition of jazz, and the "field" would be the musicians, critics, and jazz aficionados. Jazz musicians are deeply aware of the domain of jazz performance, primarily through listening to albums of jazz improvisation. Although many talk of being faithful to the music, to the jazz domain, there is also a recognition of the importance of breaking with tradition, of going beyond the domain definition. As with other scientific and artistic creative fields, creativity consists of innovation within constraints.

Sawyer (2003, chap. 5) identified a wide range of conventions followed by improvising theater ensembles. For example, all improvisers learn basic games like freeze tag, and techniques like tapping an actor on the shoulder when you want him or her to leave the scene. These games are the "standards" that all improvisers learn through their training. As with jazz, the neophyte observer who does not know about these structures thinks there is no structure. David Shepherd described his first experience watching Paul Sills' improvisation workshops: "There was no structure, and people were creating constantly. Actually, it turned out the structure was the games. But then I didn't know games. So it was this hidden structure" (in Sweet, 1978, pp. 2–3). The domain of improvisational theater could even be said to include all of popular culture, as shared by the actors and the audience members. In Example 2.1, the actors would not be able to communicate at all if they did not share a great deal of knowledge about what kinds of service encounters occur in retail clothing stores.

Although actors must learn these conventions before they can engage in effective improvisation, the conventions are not constraining so much as they are *enabling*—they enhance the creativity of the group and increase its improvisationality. Thus the conventions do not have the effect of making improvisational performances more structured and scripted; they paradoxically have the opposite effect, of making the performance more collaborative, more improvised, and more emergent (Sawyer, 2003). The rules and conventions result in greater group creativity than if those conventions did *not* exist.

Learning How to Improvise

All forms of group creativity seem to involve a similar developmental process, as aspiring performers gradually learn how to participate in creative groups; a performer must learn the conventions of the domain first. A universal problem that all learners must face is how to resolve the tension between learning the necessary structures and conventions underlying improvisation, and yet learning how to improvise artfully and collaboratively with them.

Contrary to a popular conception, jazz improvisation is not the creation of something out of nothing; it is not the case that anything goes. Even the freest improviser improvises within a musical tradition, and a large part of learning to improvise is learning that tradition (Alperson, 1984; Berliner, 1994). Jazz musicians become aware of the structures and conventions of the domain by *listening*. The verb "to listen" has unique connotations in the jazz community, including elements of "exercise" and "meditate." Listening provides the musician with the knowledge of the domain, and simultaneously with the knowledge of how to expand beyond the domain; one musician said "It's vital for me to listen as much as possible, because that's where the true studying begins, on stylistic stuff, so, if I don't listen, it's good because I'm creating something different, but in order for me to really do something that's an extension of this, I really have to be well-versed in the background, I can't ... otherwise it's something else, its not really this thing called jazz" (Sawyer interview, November 11, 1990).

Young jazz musicians often begin to learn by listening to famous albums and copying the performances note-for-note. This helps them to develop a personal repertoire of phrases, but the result is often that young improvisers sound recognizably like whoever they have been copying from. Trumpet players sound like Miles Davis or Wynton Marsalis; saxophonists like Coleman Hawkins or John Coltrane. Of course, it takes a high level of skill to get to the point where one can sound like a famous musician. But this is nonetheless only the first step in a lifetime of learning how to improvise in a group. Young musicians who have wonderful technique on their instruments—who can play extremely fast and flawlessly—often tend to be poor improvisers, because they lack feeling, and because they haven't yet learned how to communicate musically with the group (Berliner, 1994, p. 792n17). Berliner (1994) wrote that "students face enormous challenges in mastering both their respective instruments and the complex musical language for which, until recently, there have been few written aids" (p. 51). Musicians cannot learn jazz simply from books at home; before attaining competence, an aspiring musician must attend uncountable jam sessions, and probably has played in many different beginner bands, a learning process known as "paying dues" (Berliner, 1994, chap. 2). When alone at home, many musicians listen to favorite jazz albums and improvise along with the stereo.

In improvisational theater as well, the ways that actors learn reveal the ensemble nature of the art form. Whereas a jazz musician can partially replicate the group at home—by playing along with an album—improvisational actors cannot practice at all without a group of fellow improvisers. Improvisational theater classes emphasize spontaneity and listening. Beginners are placed in group settings immediately, but instead of being asked to improvise a complete scene right away, they are presented with simple group exercises that force them to listen and respond spontaneously. Training is fundamentally ensemble-focused from day one.

Improvisers are taught many rules explicitly, and these could be thought of, in Becker's terms, as rules of etiquette. For example, earlier in this chapter I described the most basic rule of improvisation: "Yes, and . . ."—in each turn of dialogue, an actor must agree to the dramatic reality proposes by the previous actor, and then must propose his or her own elaboration to the dramatic reality. When an actor rejects the proposal of the prior turn, improvisers refer to it as *denial*—the actor is denying the dramatic reality proposed by his or her partner on stage, and this is the cardinal sin of improvisation. The "Yes, and" rule has the effect of encouraging the collective creation of performance, because it insists that every performer's contribution be incorporated equally, and it prevents any one actor from dominating or "playwriting" the performance, a second cardinal sin.

These improv rules increase the improvisationality and the emergence of the performance. A second rule that actors are taught is "Don't ask questions." Rather than asking "What time is it?" an actor should say "Oh my God! It's 5:30!" The question does not offer new information, thus in a sense violating the "Yes, and" rule that actors should always extend the dramatic scene. If the other actor answers "It's 5:30," the scene has ended up where it would have been if the first actor had just stated that to begin with; the question wastes a turn of dialogue. It also limits the creativity of the actor who is asked, who is now highly constrained in the range of dialogue possibilities available. In contrast, the statement both offers new information, moving the scene forward, and at the same time leaves the next actor a wider range of creative possibilities.

A third important lesson that beginning improvisers must learn is "Don't write the script in your head." When faced with the uncertainty of improvisation, beginners have a tendency to want to establish structure and script as quickly as possible. This can lead them to try to guess how the other actors will respond to the utterance they are considering, and thus to already be thinking ahead to their own next turn. Not only does this lead to too much conscious planning and thus a delay before speaking; it also prevents the beginner from listening closely to the partner's response and responding to it. Beginners must be trained out of this tendency before they can become effective improvisers. For example, in one simple game called "The Word at a Time Story," several actors stand in a line at the front of the stage, all facing the audience. The goal of the game is to collectively create a story for the audience. The right-most actor speaks a single word to begin a sentence, and the actor to his left speaks the second word of the sentence; the sentence is constructed word by word as the focus moves down the line of actors. Actors are encouraged to speak quickly so that the group's sentence sounds like a single speaker, rather than pausing to think up a clever word. If a syntactically complete sentence has been formed, the next actor may choose to begin a new sentence. The sequence of sentences should tell a story; and the resulting story emerges from the individual actions of all players and cannot be planned or "written" by any one of them.

This exercise teaches actors to respond quickly, without too much conscious planning. It forces beginning actors not to write the script in their head because there is simply no way to do that effectively even if they wanted to; one word cannot impose a direction on the entire group. It teaches actors about collaboration and emergence—the way that the performance emerges from the collective actions of all actors together, rather than being imposed or chosen by any one of the actors.

Thus group creativity requires conventions and structure, even in the most improvisational genres. I've briefly described the conventions found in jazz and in improv. Performers must learn these conventions before they can improvise expertly with a group. This training cannot be accomplished alone, by reading a book or listening to a lecture; it is a fundamentally participatory and social process of learning.

Different Genres and Degrees of Structure

The improvisational theater scene in Chicago is a rich, vibrant, creative culture, and any given weekend one can choose from among a wide range of improvisational styles, from the open-ended freely structured performances associated with fully improvised 60-minute "long form" plays, to the more reliable, and more consistently humorous, short games. In the 1990s, these extremes were represented by the ImprovOlympic theater, which pioneered the open-ended long form style, and ComedySportz, which developed a relatively rigid structure that was designed to be a stylized sports event. The founder of ComedySportz, Dick Chudnow, referred to it as "comprovisation" to emphasize that it is not pure improvisation, but is primarily comedy (Seham, 2001, p. 87). Although not Chudnow's intention, the word also seems to combine "composition" and "improvisation," which is appropriate because the ComedySportz structures shift the performances toward a more structured, more precomposed style of group creativity.

Improvisation is unpredictable; neither the performers nor the audience know how good a given performance will be. This makes it a risky performance genre. Sheldon Patinkin, one of the early Chicago improvisers who later became a director of Second City, said that "if one out of four or five improvisations worked at all, it was terrific. And our audience *knew* that. The regular audience for the improvs knew the chances were good they were going to see a night of disaster" (Sweet, 1978, p. 236). But these actors continued to perform improvisations in spite of the risk of failure, because they were so much more fun than a more structured performance: "I found the spot improvisations the most fun, even though they were the riskiest. They never really failed. Even if they didn't always work, they didn't fail" (Anne Meara, in Sweet, 1978, p. 165). The most skilled performers prefer to perform the riskiest genres of improv, as predicted by Csikszentmihalyi's theory of flow; their high degree of skill requires a correspondingly high degree of challenge to attain a flow state.

The more free-form, unstructured genres of improvisation tend to exhibit a wider variability in quality. ImprovOlympic chooses greater freedom and a correspondingly higher amount of risk, whereas ComedySportz chooses a set of more rigid structures that reduce risk. The choice is influenced by personality and performance style, but also by financial considerations, because the less risky genres of improvisation are more accessible, and more likely to work consistently and professionally in a public performance setting. For example, jazz musicians who perform *free jazz* face this problem. It is the most unstructured genre of jazz, dispensing even with the 32-bar standard chorus form and often not choosing a key or a time signature in advance of the performance, and it has proven unpopular with all but a small group of aficionados. Club owners are much more likely to book a more conventional jazz ensemble, one that performs the standard repertory of 32-bar songs, many of which even naïve members of the audience may recognize.

Because of this riskiness, it is hard to translate improvisation into marketable, mainstream entertainment; for example, it has proven to be particularly difficult to make improvisation work on television. To increase the odds, many groups have experimented with introducing several kinds of structure to minimize improv's risks. Several long-form improv groups have begun to impose an overall structure on their performances; for example, in Sitcom, the ensemble identified a range of common television sitcom plots and events, and developed an outline and structure to guide their 30-minute improvisations (Sawyer, 2003). In ComedySportz, unlike in most ensembles, actors are allowed to repeat their successful jokes and bits (Seham, 2001, p. 87). Many improvisation-based cable TV shows have come and gone; the only one to survive more than one season has been *Whose Line Is It Anyway*, a show with a structure based on the ComedySportz format.

Yet even in the more structured genres of improvisation, some degree of innovation, creativity, and interaction is recognized as essential. A full understanding of an ensemble genre would allow us to explain what degree of innovation is allowed, what elements of the genre definition are more rigid or are more open to negotiation, and in which emergent contexts this negotiation can occur.

Individual Structures and Innovation

Musicians practice and perform the same songs repeatedly, and can often express themselves more effectively when they have a predeveloped set of musical ideas available (Gioia, 1988; Johnson-Laird, 1988). Gioia (1988) noted that this phenomenon is common among musicians, and drew parallels with the precomposed lines and couplets common in oral poetry traditions and first identified by Lord (1960) in *The Singer of Tales*. Gioia (1988) wrote that "the daunting task of improvisation, whether in music or poetry, can scarcely be achieved without some reliance on these memorized phrases" (p. 53).

However, if this process is carried too far, the spontaneous, improvisational nature of the performance is compromised. Jazz musicians frequently discuss an internal tension between their own personally developed patterns or structures and the need to continually innovate at a personal level, to continue growing musically. Musicians continually strive to innovate within these structures: "In the jazz thing, things tend to be based purely on structure, but we do everything in our power to make it take off from there, and really make it into something more than just the structure" (Sawyer interview, November 11, 1990).

The pianist Keith Jarrett says that he cannot rehearse in advance of an improv concert, because hearing himself play will interfere with his musical voice. He says, "I have the need not to hear piano music before I improvise on the piano. So what does that mean? It means I can't practice. So what does that mean? Sometimes, it's been a month or two that I have not touched the piano and then I go and do a concert" (Solomon, 1997, p. 35)

These precomposed patterns have a way of growing in importance through a musician's career, and can sometimes expand to fill an entire solo. In a review of a performance by pianist Ray Bryant, Hollenberg (1978) wrote:

> How much is improvised? Tonight, Bryant played *After Hours* in a note-for-note copy of the way he played it on the *Dizzy, Rollins, and Stitt* album on Verve some fifteen years ago.... Similarly, Bryant concluded each set tonight with a gospelish blues (in C, of course) that was, note-for-note, the same both times.... Some of the freest sounding pieces of the evening were the most mechanical. (p. 42)

Bryant is not alone in using precomposed solos; many famous jazz improvisers have occasionally repeated solos note for note, including Jelly Roll Morton, several of Duke Ellington's soloists, and Oscar Peterson (Brown, 1981). Where Hollenberg was critical, Brown (1981) was more forgiving, saying "that a given solo has been well worked out in advance should not be taken as a denigration of the solo or the player" (p. 22).

Improv theater often relies on precomposed phrases. The improvised Italian renaissance theater *commedia dell'arte* used *lazzi*, comic bits and memorized poetic speeches. Although these phrases and speeches were not invented in the moment, they could be recombined in an infinite number of ways, and thus still required improvisational skill. Contemporary Chicago improvisers quickly rediscovered the benefits of employing scripted routines. In speaking about the early Compass Players, Mike Nichols said that "for every one of those times [where improvisation inspired you] there were, let's say, ten when you relied on certain tricks and certain things you'd done before and certain gimmicks you knew always worked" (Sweet, 1978, p. 78). Shelley Berman referred to the "trickiness" of doing this, because the audience assumed they would see a fully improvised performance: "You get so that you're very tricky. You act like it's an improvisation when the fact is you know goddamn well what your tricks are going to be, where you've got your safeties. Many's the time that happened" (Sweet, 1978, p. 134).

Most of the audience cannot know how much of the performance is a repeated scripted bit, because they will only see one performance of the show. Likewise, most jazz audiences cannot tell the difference between a truly improvised melodic phrase, and a well-worn lick that the musician has played a hundred times before. Hollenberg only noticed the repetition in Bryant's performance because he was an aficionado and had listened to a 15-year-old album so many times that he had memorized the original solo; and because he had attended both sets (unlike most of the audience) and was expert enough to recognize the similarities in two solos that occurred hours apart. Most of that same audience could not have known. In fact, many pop and rock guitarists play memorized solos in concert, and those fans that notice rarely care, because in those genres pure improvisation is not as valorized as in jazz.

Yet even though they can usually get away with it, most improvisers work hard to avoid falling back too heavily on these structures. Improvisers often talk about the freedom that improvisation offers, emphasizing it over the structures that can guide group creativity: "Actors aren't liberated enough.... Actors' liberation is very important. We've always been, in a sense, preaching it. Improvisational theater stands on that" (Paul Sills, in Sweet, 1978, p. 16). But freedom can be frightening, particularly in live performance, and "the more frightened you get, the more you pull back and tend to do your set pieces" (Anne Meara, in Sweet, 1978, p. 166).

Improvising musicians and actors value mistakes because they force a performer out of their precomposed patterns: "Sometimes you get technically good with the chords, you can start to feel constrained; if you reach that point, it would be freeing, to free your ears to play a note, that normally wouldn't belong there" (Sawyer interview, December 2, 1990). "Mistakes" perform the valued function of interrupting the prearranged ideas and forcing an innovative alternative. In improv theater, if the group stumbles in some way, a talented ensemble quickly moves to cover up the mistake and to weave it into the unfolding drama. "You didn't let them catch onto your mistakes. You almost tried to constantly pretend that you knew what was going on" (Pete Gardner, Sawyer interview, February 25, 1994). But Gardner did not believe that mistakes should be avoided; rather, he fondly remembered shows when "we let the seams of the show show themselves a little bit more." It's more exciting to perform with groups that take chances, because "they stretch me in ways I probably wouldn't naturally go"; and such groups are the ones that are more likely to make a mistake. Groups that are too concerned with being slick, with being well received by the audience, may make less mistakes but the performance will ultimately be less exciting and less creative.

This tension between structure and innovation must be handled by all improvisational performers, whether theater actors or jazz musicians. And not only individual actors, but also entire groups, display this tendency for structured patterns to emerge and be repeated from performance to performance, as I show in the next section.

Group Riffs

At the beginning of the chapter, I described a rhythmic exchange that was commonly performed between pianist Geri Allen and drummer Art Blakey. The exchange occurred during many of Allen's solos; although these were for the most part improvised, the patterned exchange occurred so frequently that another drummer, Ralph Peterson, recognized this "group riff" and was able to invoke it in his own comping behind Allen's solo on another occasion (Monson, 1996, pp. 77–80). Berliner (1994) reported that many legendary groups develop similar group riffs, and that these often become part of the shared culture of the jazz community: "In groups that perform together frequently, players sometimes develop a core of common patterns that they periodically reintroduce in performances to stimulate interplay" (Berliner, 1994, p. 364). Thus, if one musician plays a recognizable portion of one of these legendary group riffs, the other musicians in the group can join in by playing the other complementary parts of that same famous group riff, showing that they are listening, that they recognize the reference, and reinforcing their sense of a common musical tradition by working together to perform a "group quotation" (Berliner, 1994, p. 368).

These group riffs usually don't develop only in rehearsal; they also emerge during live performance. In the Creole Jazz Band, Joe Oliver and Louis Armstrong would improvise new lines in unison, sometimes by silently demonstrating fingering patterns to each other during breaks (Berliner, 1994, p. 384). But more often, these riffs evolve over multiple performances; something clicks between musicians during a group performance, and they note it and talk about it after the performance, and agree to continue doing it in future performances (Berliner, 1994, p. 384). This doesn't always require explicit discussion; "by playing the tunes every night in a certain way, it becomes an arrangement, actually a better arrangement than if it had been written out" (Philly Joe Jones, cited in Stewart, 1986, p. 187). Dave Brubeck said of one of his recordings, "Almost everyone who has heard this album, including Joe and Gene, our own rhythm section, has had difficulty separating the composed from the improvised sections. I take this to be a real compliment, because good jazz composition sounds as though it were really improvised, and good improvisation should sound as though it was as well thought out as a composition" (Brown, 1981, p. 31).

Many improv theater groups perform scripted sketches in addition to their improvisations, and many of these scripts originate in a particularly successful improvised scene. A scene that worked particularly well may be improvised again the next night, and refined through successive rehearsal improvisations. Several theater groups use improvisational processes in rehearsal as a way of generating script ideas—including Chicago's Second City, and the British film director Mike Leigh. The natural tendency of improvisation to result in the emergence of collective group patterns can thus be used productively to develop scripted material.

The emergence of group riffs, and even of entire group compositions, shows that group creativity is not only an individual process; collective products can emerge as a result of group interaction. These group creations cannot be attributed to the creative insight of a single individual. Rather, these creative products emerge from the collective activity of the group, through interaction, in the excitement of live performance. The complex interplay of performers drives the group, and the group itself becomes a creative agent, originating novel creative ideas that can only be thought of as group property.

Yet over the life cycle of a group, more and more group riffs emerge, and eventually they can begin to interfere with spontaneity, just as individual musicians can fall into a rut of playing their own riffs rather than improvising freely. Concerning the life cycle of bands, Berliner (1994) wrote, "when [a band's] modes of interaction become increasingly predictable and artists begin to feel as familiar with the performance styles of other players as with their own, the band's collective ability to conceive new ideas in performance may diminish overall" (p. 441). In theater, this can happen even before the show starts, from too many rehearsals, or "over rehearsing." Actor Pete Gardner described an experience of overrehearsing with a show in Chicago: "We over rehearsed, we rehearsed four months, five months! We weren't surprising each other—we were doing what we knew." Gardner referred to "the pros and cons of knowing the other actors really well—in some ways, you've seen everything that they've done and you're occasionally surprised, but on the other side there is a sensitivity that comes with knowing each other" (Sawyer interview, February 25, 1994).

Just as individual performers must constantly balance the tension between the usefulness of personal riffs and the expectation of innovation and improvisation, groups must collectively resolve a similar tension between the natural tendency of groups to create emergent group riffs, and the desire of a group to keep it fresh, to continually innovate, and to continue to be true to the improvisational essence of the genre. Thus there seem to be parallel processes of emergent creativity at both the individual and the group level. In a sense, these processes are compositional, because they result in something like a scored or scripted piece. However, unlike composition, neither the individual nor the group has the intention of composing a product; rather, it emerges unintended from the improvisational process of performance.

Rehearsal

Actors in improvisational theater, like the dancer, musician, or athlete, require constant workshops to keep alert and agile and to find new material.
—Spolin (1963, p. 39)

Almost all performing groups rehearse; most of the rehearsal precedes the opening of the first night's performance, but some groups continue to rehearse during the week, in between performances. Some teachers even assign their students "homework thinking and journal writing" to help them expand their "improv vocabulary" (Seham, 2001, p. 227).

Even seasoned improvisers continue to practice ensemble skills in rehearsals. At the beginning of many rehearsals of the groups I performed with in Chicago, the players stood in a circle on the stage, with each player facing all of the others. They then engaged in a series of common exercises, designed to hone listening skills. For example, in one simple game, a player is chosen to speak a nonsense word—"zip," "zap," and "zowie" are common—while pointing at another player. The indicated actor then has to speak a different nonsense word and point, in turn, to a third player. The goal is to get the sequence moving as quickly as possible, forcing each player to attend closely as the "focus" bounces around the circle. This same exercise is used both in beginning improv classes and in expert ensembles.

Alan Arkin, describing the origins of the first Chicago improv group, the Compass, said "we did exercises forever with [director Paul] Sills, trying to find new forms that would work. Trying to find new ways of improvising. Trying to break down the acting process into elements and doing exercises for the specific elements" (Sweet, 1978, p. 219). Mark Gordon, talking about the early Compass, echoed Arkin's memory: "I realized that we needed to do a lot of group exercises that would make people work together so they could read each other as quickly as possible" (Sweet, 1978, p. 111). Ted Flicker, the director of the first St. Louis Compass in 1957, emphasized the importance of rehearsal, saying "If I were putting together a company today, I would spend a good ten or twelve weeks working with the people on this technique before opening, and keep working every day as well as performing every night for the next three months. The freer the form, the greater must be the underpinnings of discipline" (Sweet, 1978, p. 161).

Jazz musicians and improv theater actors alike both report that rehearsals help the group develop interactional synchrony and group flow. How does rehearsal help a group to attain it? Why does rehearsal improve the ability of a group to perform? Why do groups that have worked together in the past perform more effectively than newly composed groups? Many improv groups emphasize the importance of *trust* in one's fellow players (e.g., Halpern et al., 1994). Rehearsing together allows the actors to get to know one another, and to learn whether or not they can trust a certain actor to follow the "Yes, and" rule, and not to deny their offers. Pete Gardner described the benefits of rehearsal; it results in "a sensitivity that comes with knowing each other"; with strangers, "you wouldn't be as attuned and you wouldn't be hearing the differences in their voices as they're changing and as they're saying things" (Sawyer interview, February 25, 1994).

Berliner's analysis of jazz also emphasized the experience and familiarity gained about specific musicians in rehearsal. Musicians learn "specific knowledge of the concepts or approaches of different musicians—reflected in their recurring vocabulary patterns, the logic underlying phrase construction and motive development, and long-range storytelling strategies" (Berliner, 1994, pp. 363–364). After a rhythm section becomes used to a soloist, it can "follow their train of thought and complement it," said drummer Akira Tana (Berliner, 1994, p. 364). Knowledge about a specific musician can accumulate over a career, not only over a month of rehearsals. After 30 years of performing with bassist Richard Davis, pianist Roland Hanna knew "what he might play from one note to the next . . . and I know he may be making a certain kind of passage. I've heard him enough to know how he makes his lines. . . . We train ourselves over a period of years to be able to hear rhythms and anticipate combinations of sounds before they actually happen" (Monson, 1991, p. 139).

On the other hand, some leaders limit rehearsal because they prefer to have the raw spontaneity that can emerge when there are no established interactional habits. Rehearsal enables interactional synchrony to be established more quickly, but it also makes the group performance more predictable. Miles Davis told his musicians, "I pay you to practice on the bandstand," and believed that this made the music as "fresh" and "honest as it can possibly be" (Davis, 1986). Many band leaders limit rehearsals and tell their band members to not talk about the performance; they believe that this forces musicians into maximum spontaneity.

One 1990s improv group in Chicago, the Improv Institute, had a policy of never rehearsing, and the two actors that owned the theater brought in a different set of fellow actors every night. They were worried about the possibility that structure and repetitiveness would creep in if they kept performing with the same people. Without rehearsals, and without any opportunity to become more familiar with the personal quirks and patterns of other actors, they believed that the performances would be more spontaneous, more unpredictable, more fresh. The trade-off was that the performers did not have the time to develop trust and interactional synchrony.

Conscious and Nonconscious Processes

> *To really achieve the magic is to trust yourself more and more and more of
> having no control and just whatever comes out of your mouth, as ridiculous
> as it may be, is exactly what we're supposed to have said, and just keep
> trusting yourself that it's going to work.*
>   —Pete Gardner, Chicago improviser
>   (Sawyer interview, February 25, 1994)

In the earlier sections, I described different aspects of the tension between structure and innovation during group performance. These discussions show that improvisation is a complex skill that takes years of
training and rehearsal to master. How do performers balance these
competing forces—on the one hand, the desire and expectation to
spontaneously improvise and interact with the group, and on the
other hand, the need to impose structuring constraints to reduce the
risk of failing completely? How can performers get into a flow state—
listening to other performers while they are performing, and integrat-
ing their partners' actions into their own unfolding activity, while at
the same time acting within the conventions of the genre?

From the reports of both musicians and actors, it is clear that these
difficult tasks cannot be managed nor directed consciously. A prominent feature of jazz and improv is the complex interaction of both conscious and nonconscious processes during an improvisation. During a
performance, improvisers move along a continuum between two
poles: at one extreme, consciously directing their actions, and at the
other, acting in a "heightened state of consciousness" in which the
conscious mind seems removed from the process, and their action
seems to come from a deeper place. Both musicians and actors emphasize this aspect of performance:

> *Jazz:* I find what I'm playing is sometimes conscious, sometimes sub-
> conscious, sometimes it just comes out and I play it; sometimes I hear it
> in my head before I play it, and it's like chasing after it, like chasing after
> a piece of paper that's being blown across the street; I hear it in my head,
> and grab onto it, and follow it; but sometimes it just comes out, it falls out
> of my mouth. . . . When you start a solo, you're still in thinking mode; it
> takes a while to get yourself out of thinking mode . . . and you start giving
> yourself a little line to follow along, and you start following along that
> line, and if it's a productive thought, way of expressing yourself, you
> keep following it, and after a while it's like getting farther and farther into

your mind, a way of burrowing in; and if you find the right thread to start with, intellectually, and keep following it, feeling it, you can turn it into something. (Sawyer interview, December 2, 1990)

Improv: [Viola's training] workshop frees the intuitive in order that spontaneous moments are possible. You have to cross that abyss before you can hit the state of improvisation. . . . It's only when you don't know, in your head, what to do that this happens. Only at that moment when there is no alternative but to follow your intuitive, and then you just *do.* That's the spontaneous moment. (Richard Schaal, in Sweet, 1978, p. 310)

As these quotations demonstrate, improv performers express a preference for a mental state during performance in which the intellectual, conscious aspect is minimized. Improvisers believe that their performances are better when they are maximally nonconscious. Yet performers realize that some conscious awareness is always essential: The inner performance state must be balanced with a simultaneous awareness of the other performers, and of the conventions, etiquette, and expectations of the genre: "It's all a matter of listening to the people you're playing with. . . . This is a real difficulty—you have to be able to divide your senses, but still keep it coherent so you can play, so you still have that one thought running through your head of saying something, playing something, at the same time you've got to be listening to what the drummer is doing" (Sawyer interview, December 2, 1990). There is a constant tension between fully conscious and fully nonconscious performance, and each performer must continuously resolve this tension to achieve a balance appropriate to the moment.

In group performance, some of the most creative inspiration emerges from the nonconscious mind: "Sometimes I catch myself playing things that I like, or ideas that came from somewhere and I can't exactly see where" (Sawyer interview, November 26, 1990). Because group creativity takes place in real time, unlike many other forms of creativity which allow for an indeterminate period of time for elaboration, a form of dialogue occurs between the performer's nonconscious and conscious. Many musicians describe the experience of being surprised by what they play, or they discuss the importance of not being consciously "in control."

Many creativity researchers have noted that both conscious and nonconscious processes are important to the creative process. This duality has been referred to as analytic vs. intuitive creativity (Simonton, 1988) and primordial vs. conceptual cognition (Martindale, 1990). Simonton viewed this as a dimension of cognitive style, and suggested these are relatively constant personality traits; Martindale used the duality to present a dialectic historical view of creative change. The constant interaction and balance of the two modes which must be maintained during group creativity is not well-described by either of these models (I discuss this further in chap. 7).

When a performer's nonconscious mind provides a new idea, the more conscious level filters and evaluates these ideas. The conscious level, although busy monitoring other performers or attempting to stay aware of the genre demands and constraints, can also contribute ideas to the ongoing improvisation. In contrast to creativity in the arts and sciences, which can be viewed as a largely conscious process with only occasional inspiration from a nonconscious source, in group creativity the nonconscious contribution is reported to be salient, continuous, and essential.

THE AUDIENCE AS COLLABORATOR

> *The Second City audience, having a greater investment in the event, is more generous. After all, what is being performed up there came out of the audience's own vocalized concerns. The audience is a collaborator, and so, for its own sake as well as for the cast's, it wants the improvs to succeed. By the act of taking the audience into its confidence, the company has largely broken down the wall dividing participants and observers.*
>
> —Sweet (1978, p. xxxix–xl)

In most Western genres of music—including both orchestras and rock concerts—the audience is not allowed to interact with the performers, except for highly circumscribed actions like applauding or cheering. The audience is perhaps even more constrained at a scripted theater performance. But anthropologists who study performance cross-culturally have found that this is rather unique; interaction between audience and performer is commonly found in anthropological studies of performance, and the audience–performer bond is different in every culture and every genre (Bauman & Sherzer, 1974; Brenneis, 1990; Duranti & Brenneis, 1986). In our culture, the more improvisational performance forms tend to minimize the audience–performer barrier.

In involving the audience, Chicago-style improvisation is quite different from the Actor's Studio style of improvisation known as "the Method." In the Method, the purpose of the improvisation is to create an experience for the actor in rehearsal. In contrast, in Chicago improvisation, the intent is to create an experience for the audience: "The main thing is to give something to the audience" (Alan Arkin, in Sweet, 1978, p. 218). Mike Nichols also said that "I think what shaped it was the audience. I'd done improvisations with Strasberg, but none of us had ever been in a situation of having to improvise with the pressure from the audience. . . . The pressure from the audience taught everyone to answer the unspoken question the audience asked—'Why are you telling us this?' " (Sweet, 1978, p. 75).

Improvisational performance forms have never attained the same level of popular and mass success as scripted, directed performance forms, such as popular music, television sitcoms, and movies. Nonetheless, improvisation manages to find an audience; that audience is typically composed of a large percentage of aficionados, fans that are relatively knowledgeable about the performance genre. At many jazz and improv performances as much as half of the audience may be composed of people who have themselves performed this performance genre.

One of the distinctive features of Chicago improv is that the cast asks the audience for suggestions for their upcoming scene. An MC steps to the front of the stage and says, for example, "I need a location for the next scene!" Audience members shout out different locations, and the MC picks the first one, perhaps "an airport," repeats it, saying "We take you to an airport," and the action begins immediately. This results in performances that reflect the audience's interests and concerns, as Ted Flicker noted: "The thing that makes improvisational theater so fascinating . . . is that each company takes on its own character and the character of its audience. For me, the only reason for doing theater, as opposed to making films, is that in the theater you have live people. . . . The *real* kick was in talking to an audience, taking what they said to you—how they reacted to you—and returning it to them through the prism of your vision of the world" (Ted Flicker, in Sweet, 1978, p. 160). In improvisation, in contrast to conventional theater, "You all of a sudden were making a direct connection with your audience from your innermost feelings, because there was no time to prepare or fabricate or give anything that was less than true. . . . The audience was watching you, watching your mind think. . . . There was nothing you could hide, and the audience recognized that" (Jerry Stiller, in Sweet, 1978, p. 174).

Several of the founding figures of Chicago improvisation tell a similar story: On nights when the group creativity is in flow and the performance is a success, the audience typically does not believe that it was really improvised. They assume that the group secretly had some script, or at least a fairly well-structured outline, that they were following. Consequently they don't believe that they really saw an "improvisation." On nights when the group creativity is not working so well and it's a flop, the (naïve) audience reaction is to say "improvisation could never work anyway, what a stupid idea!" So in other words, improvisational ensembles couldn't win; it was always very difficult to convince audiences of the uniqueness of improvisation (what the art form really was) and that it could work well (Sawyer interview with Del Close, June 22, 1994). Jacob Moreno (1973), who created the first improv group in Vienna in the 1920s, told the same story. Moreno, like the 1950s Chicago improvisers, began to ask for audience suggestions at the beginning of the night, to convince the audience that the performance is indeed unscripted. But even this technique doesn't convince everyone; some audiences find it very hard to believe that true improvisation could really work, or that actors would take the risk of attempting it in front of an audience. Chicago improviser Severn Darden noted that "It's very hard to get New Yorkers to suggest anything. They're sure, they're convinced, that every suggestion you take is planted. Nothing will convince them otherwise. But most audiences are convinced of that. The audience generally doesn't believe we take their suggestions seriously" (Sweet, 1978, pp. 96–97).

Music critic John Corbett argued that jazz "requires a different kind of listening in which the listener is active, a *participant-observer* of sorts" (Corbett, 1995, p. 233). Seham (2001) wrote that "many ImprovOlympians equate their work with the kind of free-form jazz that puzzles the neophyte listener but is enjoyed all the more by aficionados" (p. 43). Sid Smith (1995), a theater critic, wrote that the ImprovOlympic "is comedy in jazz riff" (p. 24). Seham (2001) wrote that ImprovOlympic fans are "mostly cognoscenti—friends or relatives of the performers, other improvisers, and sophisticated improv aficionados" (p. 57).

Improvisational genres require a relatively knowledgeable audience. Regarding the early Second City, Alan Arkin said, "The audience came to a show knowing, suspecting that thirty or forty percent of what they would see might not work in an improvisational set.... They understood the process and were very excited. It was like verbal-physical jazz. I think we had the same kind of audience which appreciates good jazz musicians" (Sweet, 1978, p. 225). Pete Gardner reported the same percentage: "Improv is 60/40. You know it's going to be sixty percent success and forty percent doesn't work" (Sawyer interview, February 25, 1994). Why does the audience keep coming if it fails so often? "I think the sense of watching something which might or might not work was interesting for the audience in the beginning. What was going to happen?" (Barbara Harris, in Sweet, 1978, p. 68)

Many jazz performers regard only jazz performed in a club atmosphere, with a live audience, as "true jazz." Interaction with the audience is considered a key component of the resulting creative product. Musicians often state that the performer is a "channel" from the music to the audience. Knowledgeable jazz audience members sometimes respond to creative moments with applause, shouts, and whistles (Berliner, 1994, p. 456). However, some musicians are ambivalent about the audience, stating that the performance is more creative when the musician is not influenced by the audience. Some jazz musicians prefer to ignore the audience as much as possible so they can focus on their own inner voice and on the musical interaction with their fellow band members; for these musicians, the audience is a distraction. Among jazz musicians, "playing to the audience" has a pejorative meaning, of grandstanding or going for cheap, easy applause from relatively naïve audience members. Many audiences are not very sophisticated, and improvisers often perform for audiences that know nothing about jazz and treat the music "like the wallpaper" (a musician quoted in Berliner, 1994, p. 457). Bands often prepare their performance with a knowledge of the level of sophistication of the audience. For a relatively unsophisticated audience, a band sometimes decides to limit the length of its solos, so that more of the performance will be the melodies that the audience will recognize (Berliner, 1994, p. 459). Some audiences shout compliments at the wrong moments in the performance, or in a way that is overdone or artificial, and this can distract the musicians from their performance (drummer Paul Wertico, in Berliner, 1994, p. 463). Audiences are most intrusive in bar settings when they are drinking and socializing, treating the music as an appropriately sophisticated soundtrack to their evening on the town, but not treating it with the respect that the musicians feel it deserves.

Audiences at different types of events have different expectations and expertise. A performance context likely to have a more knowledgeable audience than the usual group performance is the *open jam*, usually on a weeknight at a club, where visiting jazz musicians are invited to share the stage. Such events often do not gather steam until most clubs in town have closed, so that musicians can stop by after their paying gig is through; by this time the less knowledgeable members of the audience are already home in bed, and the club is filled primarily with other musicians. At the opposite extreme of audience expertise is the *society gig*, where the band is being paid to perform for an event such as a wedding: "With some of these open sessions, we try and make things new, try and not play them the same way, but in a society gig, you have to play things real [straight]. . . . Ironically, we have a tendency to talk about things more at the open sessions, like before a song; at a society gig, there's a standardized format, and we really don't have to talk about it" (Sawyer interview, November 11, 1990).

Improv theater groups also have to contend with different venues and audiences with different levels of expertise. In 1990, Second City started a Business Theater wing, which designed customized performances for local corporations (Seham, 2001, p. 114). In the mid 1990s, Chicago ComedySportz successfully marketed their group to corporations for parties and training sessions. Corporations like Intel and Kraft Foods required performances with a "mainstream style" (Seham, 2001, p. 111). These venues encouraged a short-form, game-oriented style of improvisation, one that reduced the risks of failure and kept the energy level and the comedy level high; cutting-edge styles like long form or scene improvisation were not performed for corporate parties.

Thus in jazz and in improv theater, we see a range of degrees of audience involvement, and their involvement roughly corresponds to the formality of the setting and the audience's level of expertise. In those settings that are more informal, with a more knowledgeable audience, the performers interact more closely with the audience, and the audience truly becomes a collaborator in the group's creativity.

SUMMARY

In this chapter, I drew on interviews with professional jazz musicians and improv theater actors to identify and describe some of the key characteristics of group creativity. I grouped these into three areas: group interaction, structure and improvisation, and interaction with the audience.

In conclusion, I highlight several important points that arise from this chapter. First, group creativity is qualitatively different from individual creativity, and it must be analyzed as a collective social phenomenon. It cannot be reduced to psychological analyses of the creative processes of the individual performers; in group creativity, the performance emerges from individual action and interaction, and the whole is greater than the sum of the parts. We saw group processes in rehearsals, in the emergence of group riffs in performance, and in the unpredictability of group flow. The study of group creativity requires a fundamentally social and interactional approach.

Second, interaction and communication among the performers is the essence of group creativity. Interaction was central in my discussions of interactional synchrony, of group flow, and of group dynamics. And it is specifically the *symbolic* nature of music and verbal art that is most important in this creative interaction. Group creativity's essence is symbolic interaction, and a theory of group creativity must have symbolic interaction at its core.

Third, jazz and improv are not designed to generate a product at the end of the performance. In some other genres of group creativity, there is a specific external goal; for example, a brainstorming session or a project-team meeting may have a specific goal in mind. But in these extremely creative genres of group creativity—improvised, public, and on stage—there is no goal external to the performance. Rather, the process is the product; the on-stage interaction among the performers is the only outcome that the group is working toward.

All three of these points emphasize that studies of group creativity must focus closely on the moment-to-moment process of symbolic interaction among the performers, and on how performances emerge from interactional processes. This continuing process of creative interaction is the focus of the rest of this book. In the next chapter, I present the basic outlines of a theory of symbolic interaction in group creativity. In chapter 4, I explore some influential philosophical treatments of artistic creativity that compare it to conversational interaction: the aesthetic theories of John Dewey and R. G. Collingwood, which both emphasize that all creativity involves social and interactional processes. Chapters 5 and 6 extend chapter 3's theory of the interactional processes that occur in group creativity, and demonstrate how a focus on symbolic interaction and creative communication can provide insight into a wide range of groups, and can help us to identify interesting similarities and differences between music, theater, and collaboration.

3

Interaction and Emergence:
An Interactional Semiotics

In chapter 2, I identified many common features of group creativity in jazz and improv theater. I grouped these according to three broad themes: interactional process; structure and innovation; and the audience. In this chapter, I present a model designed to help us better understand the group phenomena described in chapter 2. The model describes how a performance emerges from interaction among performers. In developing this model, I draw on several fields that study interaction, including semiotics, sociolinguistics, conversation analysis, sociocultural psychology, small group dynamics, and creativity theory. I first developed early versions of this model in the mid 1990s, inspired primarily by jazz improvisation—by my experience as a jazz pianist, my interview study of jazz musicians (Sawyer, 1992), and the work of Paul Berliner (1994) and Ingrid Monson (1991, 1996). I then applied and elaborated the model in two book-length empirical studies of group creativity: a study of conversation in children's sociodramatic play in the preschool classroom (Sawyer, 1997b), and an ethnographic study of the verbal artistry of Chicago improvisational theater groups (Sawyer, 2003).

Because my goal is to develop a model that describes both music and verbal art, I rely heavily on semiotics—the study of sign systems in the abstract—and theories of group dynamics that do not rely heavily on features unique to language. Although semiotics often focuses on language—perhaps the most complex sign system—it has also been applied to many other sign systems, including music, culture, ideology, fashion, and advertisements. However, group interaction has been almost completely neglected in the study of sign systems. For example, when a recent issue of *Semiotica* (1987, Vol. 66, nos. 1/3) was devoted to the semiotics of music, none of the articles addressed the phenomenon of improvisational performance, nor of group creativity. As Tagg (1987) noted in his contribution to this volume, these analyses focused on Western musical forms with highly developed notational systems, and therefore resulted in a static, structuralist approach to music, neglecting the indeterminacy of performance. In this chapter, I address this neglect by drawing on other scientific traditions that emphasize group performance, resulting in what I refer to as *interactional semiotics*—a micro-interactional model of group creativity based on traditional semiotic concepts, particularly Peirce's notions of indexicality as extended by Jakobson and Silverstein.

The 1987 volume of *Semiotica* appeared at the end of a 30-year period of growing popularity of the use of linguistic, semiotic, and structuralist models in the analysis of music. Comparisons between music and language began to appear in the 1950s (Bright, 1963; Nettl, 1958; Springer, 1956), and in the 1960s, Lévi-Strauss' structuralist analysis of myth (1955, 1969) inspired the application of structural methodology to musical analysis. Ruwet (1967, 1972) was the first to apply this method to musicological analysis, and Nattiez (1975, 1977, 1990) was an influential elaboration of this approach. Ruwet's method involved segmenting melodies strictly according to internal repetition and recurrence, without regard to musical content, and then analyzing musical transformations and substitutions in an attempt to identify paradigmatic sets and syntagmatic rules of combination. Ruwet used a method of two-dimensional transcription inspired by Lévi-Strauss's canonical Theban myth chart, in which the vertical columns represented paradigmatic "equivalence sets." Soon after Ruwet's initial presentation of this approach, structuralist and semiotic approaches to music analysis became so common that by 1980, a series of extensive review articles and critiques were available (Feld, 1974; Hatten, 1980, 1990; Powers, 1980; Suhor, 1986; Tunstall, 1979). These later studies focused on structuralist analyses of musical genres, both Western and non-Western, frequently adopting a transformational/generative grammar approach, exemplified by Becker and Becker's (1979) generative grammar for the Javanese gamelan genre *srepegan*.

Perhaps because these approaches originated with linguists and semioticians working in a structuralist tradition, they did not attempt to analyze performance in improvisational genres.

Several scholars have applied the generative grammar approach to jazz improvisation (Johnson-Laird, 1988; Perlman & Greenblatt, 1981; Steedman, 1984). The parallels are perhaps most explicitly laid out in a 1981 article titled "Miles Davis meets Noam Chomsky" (Perlman & Greenblatt, 1981); the authors drew analogies between the deep structure of a sentence and the harmonic chord structure of a jazz standard, and between the words of a sentence and the melodic fragments, or "licks," that musicians weave into their solos. Johnson-Laird (1988) developed a computer program that could improvise jazz solos, and his design was likewise based on parallels with generative theories of language.

Yet in these efforts to compare music and language, the interactional influences among performers characteristic of group creativity has been completely neglected (some notable exceptions are found in the recent literature on jazz, including Berliner, 1994; Monson, 1991, 1996; Rinzler, 1988; and Sawyer, 1992). This neglect is partly attributable to the fact that structuralists focus on monophonic music; as Ruwet (1972) acknowledged, "it would clearly be very difficult to apply the same procedure to polyphonic structures" (p. 116), and polyphonic interaction in group creativity is resistant to structuralist analysis. As Powers (1980) noted—equating structuralist models of language with all linguistic theory—"the more any musical practice is subject to constraints of ensemble performance, the less easily amenable it will be to quasi-linguistic analysis" (p. 42). Using a similar logic, Tarasti (1993) argued that the generative approach could not be applied to improvisation: "[generative] rules do not take into account that improvisation does not only concern a product, object, text but involves the act of improvisation, the activity itself" (p. 65).

Structuralist models are inadequate to group creativity for the same reason they have been inadequate to describe the practices of social life; this is the crux of the poststructuralist critique, and many poststructuralists have attempted to address the improvisational nature of social interaction, although they have not turned their attention to group creativity per se (e.g., Bourdieu, 1977; de Certeau, 1984; Cicourel, 1974; Foucault, 1972). For example, Bourdieu's (1977, pp. 8–17) practice-based critique of structuralism hinted at the importance of improvisation in social action: Practice is "the 'art' of *necessary improvisa-*

tion" (p. 8). Bourdieu (1977) defined his important concept of *habitus* in terms which might apply to a jazz quartet: "Objectively 'regulated' and 'regular' without being in any way the product of obedience to rules, they can be collectively orchestrated without being the product of the organizing action of a conductor" (p. 72).[4]

The theory of group creativity that I present in this chapter is an elaboration of these practice-based critiques of structuralist and semiotic approaches to music and language. Chapters 1 and 2 provide several reasons why group creativity cannot be explained using structuralist models. For example, it is unpredictable, with each moment emerging from the prior flow of the performance; it is collective, with individual performers influencing each other from moment to moment; and it is emergent, with the group manifesting properties greater than the sum of the parts.

In 1932, G. H. Mead explained why social scientists have particular difficulty in studying emergence: the difficulty is that once the emergent—the ensemble performance—is complete, the analyst attempts to "rationalize" it, showing (incorrectly) that it can be found "in the past that lay behind it" (1932, p. 14). Mead's observations have an uncanny predictive validity when one examines the ensuing history of research in both musicology and conversation analysis. Rather than exploring the improvisational, contingent nature of group creativity, most research has focused on structuralizing models. In the cognitive sciences and in conversation analysis, common models have included scripts, frames, discourse grammars, and conversational routines. In folkloristics, such approaches originate in formalist or structuralist methodologies (see critiques in Bauman & Briggs, 1997; Hanks, 1996). In musicology, many studies of improvisational performance have retained a "compositional" approach to improvised performances, often using techniques developed for the analysis of notated text artifacts (for critiques see Berliner, 1994; Blacking, 1981; McLeod & Herndon 1980).

These approaches fail to answer key questions about group creativity: How does an improvised performance, a socially constituted and contingent process, differ from a creative product such as a musical score? How can the analyst represent the improvised and collective aspects of group creativity? Tools appropriate for the composi-

---

[4]Although note that Bourdieu misinterprets Chomsky's notion of "rule" to be conscious, intentional obedience to a precept, or the forced imposition of such obedience, whereas Chomsky used *rule* to refer to a scientifically valid descriptive regularity.

tional analysis of creative products seem to lead the researcher away from these defining, unique elements of group performance.

Building on poststructuralism and on Mead's symbolic interactionism, recent theorists of linguistic interaction have argued that talk cannot be understood as a static transcript, but must be viewed as fundamentally in play during interaction (Gumperz, 1982; Schegloff, 1990; Schegloff & Sacks, 1973). Chafe (1997), invoking a musical metaphor and discussing the "polyphony" of everyday conversation, wrote that "we need to avoid reifying our transcripts, keeping always in mind that they are an artificial freezing of phenomena which are in constant change" (p. 52). Gumperz (1982) criticized structuralizing perspectives for inadequately representing the indeterminacy actually present at each moment of an interaction:

> Although we are dealing with a structured ordering of message elements that represents the speakers' expectations about what will happen next, yet it is not a static structure, but rather it reflects a dynamic process which develops and changes as the participants interact. (p. 131)

These recent theorists emphasize the *pragmatics* of language—how language is used in social settings. A central theme of this chapter is that group creativity in music and verbal performance is a collaboratively emergent social process, and its analysis requires a focus on interaction, practice, and pragmatics. In contrast, structuralist studies of music focus on the semantics and the syntax of musical signs. A semiotics which attempts to understand music by analyzing static compositional products will fail, and for the same reasons as has a structuralist linguistics which focuses on competence rather than performance, on contrived sentences on a page rather than transcripts of real talk.

I do not discuss musical semantics—the meaning of music—which represents another line of study (Lidov, 1980; Meyer, 1956; Noske, 1977). Such studies have often focused on what might be called "lexical" signs, which in practice have been phrases segmented out of a monophonic line, when in fact music can be segmented at many hierarchical levels, within multiple hierarchical interpretations, with equal validity (as I note in the discussion of *units of ideation* in chap. 7). To the extent that a sign's referent is dependent on the context of usage, that referent cannot be identified based on any invariant meaning, or *sense*, of the sign. As the contextually dependent—"deictic" or "indexical"—properties of a sign token increase, the sense component of that token tends to decrease, in relation to determining the token's interactional effectiveness. Group creativity is extremely indexical: as Tarasti (1993) observed, "improvisation of an utterance is always deictic" (p. 67).

In the next section, I begin by reviewing how music scholars have contrasted improvisation and composition. This contrast raises several issues related to the structure–practice and syntax–pragmatics oppositions. I then review theories of the indexicality of sign usage developed by linguists. Finally, I present my model of group creativity, elaborating on these theories of the indexicality of sign usage. This model focuses on semiotic mediation in interaction, and is meant to be applicable to any group interaction that is mediated by signs; for this reason, it is more general than the biologically based theories of interactional synchrony discussed in chapter 2. I close with a discussion of how the model applies to musical interaction in ensembles, again emphasizing the indexicality of interactional processes.

IMPROVISATION AND COMPOSITION

Because so much structuralist analysis has focused on composed music rather than improvised music, I begin by comparing the two. Some theorists argue that improvisation is no different from composition, or is perhaps a form of "spontaneous composition" (Alperson, 1984); these conceptions would seem to imply that structuralist approaches designed for composed music might transfer readily to improvisational music. Other theorists argue that improvisation is qualitatively different from composition, and it is these latter perspectives that I draw on as I emphasize the need for an interactional semiotics of group creativity as situated practice.

Musicologists have almost exclusively studied compositions; studies of improvisation have been remarkably absent from the Western musicological tradition. In 1938, Ernst Ferand published what Nettl (1974) characterized as "[a text that] continues to be the only large, scholarly book on the subject of musical improvisation" (p. 1). Yet historians of music believe that musical performances in classical Greece were improvisational, and that improvisation played an important role in liturgical music from the fourth century through the Baroque era (Grout, 1980). Even in the European tradition, some scholars believe that our current conception of music as being best exemplified in composed scores extends back only to the 16th century (Dalhaus, 1982, pp. 10–11).

Since Nettl's 1974 article, improvisation has become more prominent in ethnomusicology, due to a greater awareness of the world's music traditions, and to the increasing respectability of jazz. There have been several recent studies of a wide range of improvisational genres; in addition to jazz (Berliner, 1994; Monson, 1991, 1996), European and American writers have written widely on the Indian *raga*, the Javanese *gamelan*, the Arabic and Turkish *maqam*, the Persian *dastgah*, and group African drumming. Despite the recent availability of these ethnographies, musicology has remained focused on compositional, largely Western genres of musical performance, or on what turn out to be the least improvisational genres found in other cultures.

A few cognitive psychologists have examined jazz performance, and they have often done so by contrasting the immediate improvisationality of jazz with the unlimited revision possibilities afforded by composition. Johnson-Laird (1988) and Sloboda (1985) both argued for models of improvisation which are based on the view that cognitive processing capacity is minimal during a real-time performance, and thus improvisational creative forms must evolve to constrain the amount of decision making necessary during a performance. They both contrasted this situation with composition, where effectively unlimited processing capacity is available, allowing more complex musical structures to be created. These researchers characterized the jazz idiom as one which of necessity includes strongly constraining genres, song forms, and individual styles.

The term *improvisation* has been used within musicology to describe a variety of genre types. Nettl (1974) suggested that composition and improvisation were not qualitatively different: Rather, he proposed a continuum among musical genres, from more improvised to less improvised. Nettl viewed this continuum as representing rapid composition at the improvisational end, and slow composition at the compositional end, pointing out that many well-known Western composers, such as Schubert, composed in bursts of "quick, spontaneous creation." Nettl (1974) described this continuum as one representing "varying degrees of independence for the performer in working from a model" (p. 7; also see Alperson, 1984). In support of this position, Nettl presented a variety of ethnographic evidence that, in some cultures at least, performers doing what we would consider improvisation do not have a subjective sense of being creative or innovative, but instead claim they are simply performing a culturally specified composition.

Nettl's discussion was an important step in elaborating the relations between improvisation and composition. Yet his discussion overlooked a critical distinction between composition and performance: the presence or absence of a score (see chap. 5). Scripts and scores, when inscribed using an orthography, are inherently compositional: They are ostensible products that are the result of a creative process with a history. In contrast, in group creativity, the relevant continuum is more appropriately considered to be from *ritualized* performance to *improvisational* performance. Although sharing many formal parallels with compositions, ritualized performance genres are not ostensible products created by a single composer: they are shared social facts, reproduced anew in each performance. In many ways, ritualized genres parallel Saussure's notion of *langue*, the shared, relatively stable social fact of language.[5] In contrast to ritual, everyday conversation—Saussure's *parole*—may be considered near the improvisational end of this continuum. This suggests another reason why structuralist approaches are not appropriate for an analysis of improvisation: these attempts to draw parallels between music and language have analyzed improvisational forms of music by using linguistic models originally developed for *langue*, nonimprovised verbal behavior.[6] Powers (1980) hinted at the need for theorists of music and language to focus on improvised performance: "the less a musical practice lends itself to freely improvised musical discourse, the less amenable it will prove to quasi-linguistic analysis" (p. 46), because improvised music is more like conversation than is composed music.

---

[5]In developing his concept of *langue*, Saussure was influenced by Durkheim's theory of social facts, and I use this term intending to invoke Durkheim (see Sawyer, 2002a).

[6]The unstated assumption has been that scored compositions are analytically similar to *langue*. Yet there are complex theoretical issues which underlie this assumption: the structuralist conception of *langue* was not based on the analysis of text artifacts like scores or the printed word, but of a postulated "deep-structure competence" which nonetheless retains the characteristics of spoken language, rather than a printed artifact. The confusion of this distinction was one of Derrida's (1978) critiques of structuralism. Ruwet (1967, 1972) attempted to address this by drawing the analogy between linguistic "competence" and the underlying compositional structure of a score; yet there are complex and indeterminate relationships between the deep structure of a piece of music, and the compositional structure of the score itself.

INDEXICALITY AND THE POETIC FUNCTION

Most structuralist analyses of music are focused on composition rather than improvisation. Yet improvisation is qualitatively different from composition because it requires a focus on practice, emergence, and interaction. In this section, I turn to theoretical traditions that can help us to develop an *interactional* semiotics of group creativity. The material in this section is perhaps the most difficult in this chapter, but it is a necessary preliminary to the remainder of the chapter, which presents the theory of group creativity that I use in the remaining chapters.

A few scholars of jazz improvisation (Berliner, 1994; Monson, 1991, 1996) have argued that the traditional musicological focus on compositional structure is inadequate to capture the essence of interactive musical performance. This approach in ethnomusicology parallels the recent shifts I described in chapter 1 in linguistic anthropology, conversation analysis, and sociolinguistics; these fields argue that talk cannot be understood as a static transcript, but must be viewed as fundamentally in play during interaction. In this section I continue this shift away from structure in both musical and linguistic studies by developing an interactional semiotics.

Recent theories based on Peirce's concept of *indexicality* can provide the foundation for a semiotic theory of improvisational interaction. In Peirce's trichotomy of signs, an *index* is a sign which requires an association between the sign and its object. The classic example of an index is the weathervane, which "indicates" wind direction. An index is not necessarily arbitrary, thus distinguishing it from the *symbol*, of which each token or instance is connected to its object only by a conventionalized rule and nothing else. It is also not isomorphic to its object, thus distinguishing it from the *icon*, which is connected to its object by similarity of sign-autonomous properties (Peirce, 1931, pp. 243–265, 274–307). Classic examples of icons are a photo or a map; both physically resemble their referent. The concept of index can also be applied to language use, in referring to linguistic signs, lexical or otherwise, that have a nonarbitrary relation to their object—usually some aspect of the sociolinguistic context. Within pragmatics, the most studied aspects of the indexical use of language are *deictics*, lexical signs whose referent is computable on the basis of an indexical relation the deictic token bears to its context of usage (Levinson, 1983). For example, the referent of a personal pronoun like "you" can only be determined by reference to the specific social context of its utterance. Expanding upon this notion of indexicality, one can observe other forms of indexical relations; for example, syntactic structures or prosodic contours which indicate that a certain referent has already been identified as the topic currently in play are themselves indexical of that referent as being the topic of the surrounding stretch of discourse. This general phenomenon has been referred to as *pragmatic presupposition* (Keenan, 1971; Levinson, 1983, pp. 177, 204–225) or *indexical presupposition* (Silverstein, 1976, 1979, 1993, pp. 36, 42).

Deictics such as personal pronouns are particularly interesting in this regard, because they function indexically on two parallel levels. On a *denotational* level, a personal pronoun such as "you" cannot be resolved to a referent outside of a specific context of use; thus the usage indexically presupposes that the denoted individual is present and is the addressee of the utterance. On an *interactional* level, some types of personal pronouns also indexically presuppose nondenotational aspects of the context. Keenan's (1971) example was pronominal selection in French: the use of *tu* conventionally presupposes that "the addressee is an animal, child, socially inferior to the speaker, or personally intimate with the speaker" (p. 51). As a conversational interaction proceeds, the indexical presuppositions established up to each moment (both denotational and interactional) act to constrain each speaker, since the speaker must maintain some minimum level of coherence with the speech styles and registers, and role relations already established.[7] Indexicality may also propose a future content or structure of an interaction; Silverstein (1993, pp. 36, 42) referred to this as *indexical entailment*, since it represents an indexical relationship to some presumed future direction of the interaction.[8] For example, in languages with a system of politeness registers (e.g., the T/V distinction in Russian), the selection of a given register by a first speaker in an interactional dyad indexically entails one way in which the status relations may play out during the interaction (Friedrich, 1971). Note once again the two-layered indexicality of such pronouns: The pronoun denotationally indexes its referent, but in addition, inter-

---

[7]Note the distinction between this *interactional coherence* and logical or denotational coherence of the topic, which is maintained (in parallel fashion to interactional coherence) through the use of logical/semantic presupposition and semantic entailment.

[8]Although Levinson (1983, p. 174) commented on "logical" or *semantic entailment*, he did not mention any use of the term *pragmatic entailment* in the literature; it seems to be a coinage of Silverstein (1976, 1993) who also used the term *indexical creativity*.

actionally indexes a certain kind of social event. These creative indexical entailments are nondenotational forms of indexicality, because they have nothing to do with identifying the referent of the pronoun; rather, they propose a genre or style for the interaction and a set of social roles to be enacted.

Both levels of indexicality are *metapragmatic* (Silverstein, 1976, 1993), because the object of these indexical signs is the pragmatic structure of the interaction. Note that both of the earlier examples use the *T/V* distinction; this points to a general property of socially creative, nondenotational indexicality—that indexical presupposition and entailment are often found in the same lexical items, and the analyst must speak of relatively creative sign forms, or relatively presupposing, such analysis being based on the context of use. As Silverstein (1979) noted, "the give-and-take of actual interaction depends on the constantly-shifting communicative negotiation and ratification of indexical presupposition vs. indexical creativity" (p. 207). Even though this nondenotational level combines both indexical presupposition and entailment, at the denotational level indexicality tends to be presupposing, rather than entailing. The fact that both levels of indexicality are often found in the same sign tokens, combined with the fact that the denotational level of indexicality tends to be presuppositional, leads many analysts to identify even the socially creative entailing functions of such signs as presuppositions.

This analytic error is an example of how the performances that emerge from group creativity are, in general, misunderstood to be a metapragmatics of presupposing, segmentable, denotationally functioning indexical signs. This type of analytic error was identified by Mead (1932) in his discussion of the *emergent*: After an act is performed, everyone assumes it was predicted by the prior flow of the interaction. In contrast, Mead held that the emergent is created through the balance of indexical presupposition and entailment. In a discussion of *linguistic ideology*, Silverstein (1979) noted that speakers tend to be unaware of the creatively indexical effects of sign forms, instead perceiving those effects to be derived from indexical presupposition (p. 232).

Peirce's notion of indexicality was further elaborated by Jakobson in his analysis of the *poetic function* of language. Silverstein (1984) pointed out that Jakobson's writings on indexicality and poetics (e.g., Jakobson, 1960, 1971) implied that some forms of indexicality are dependent on broader structuring principles of a text; for example, a word placed in line-final position has implicit indexical relations with other words in other line-final positions, which can vary depending on the overall structure of the poem. Much of Jakobson's work was focused on exploring continuities across poetic language and everyday speech.[9]

Most studies of metapragmatics are restricted to quoted speech, which Silverstein (1993) referred to as *reportively calibrating metapragmatics*, since the metapragmatic utterance determines, or "calibrates," the interpretation of a prior segment of the interaction. Silverstein (1984) used Jakobson's concept of the poetic function to explore a less-commonly recognized type of metapragmatics: *reflexive calibration*, when utterances function to calibrate their own pragmatic import. Silverstein (1984) used this concept to analyze a poetic structure of indexicality in everyday conversation, discovering through a micro-analysis of a transcript that much of the social interaction was played out through (nondenotational) indexical techniques. Sawyer (1997b) identified similar poetic structures in children's fantasy play dialogues. When an utterance or utterance sequence refers *reflexively* to its own pragmatic import, this often results from the poetic structure of the text, or the "configuration of indexicals":

> The very notion of configuration is, of course, the notion of a structure of parts and wholes each co-occurring part of which is in indexical relationships with all the others, directly or mediately through some schema of hierarchical concatenation. Such configurational metapragmatic indexicality becomes crucially important in reflexive calibration. (Silverstein, 1993, p. 48)

These configurations are realized in discourse through the poetic function of language:

> Formal units, as units of a poetic order of language structure, depend for their very definition and special kind of meaningfulness ... on the fact of their cardinal combinatory positions within the sequential order of actual, linear discourse. (Silverstein, 1984, p. 183)

---

[9]Note in particular Caton's (1987) review, focusing on the use of Jakobson's theories to study language use in cultural context. Several articles have provided excellent reviews of Jakobson. See Senderovich (1982) for a review of Jakobson's early work on poetics. More comprehensive reviews are found in Krampen (1981) and Stankiewicz (1983). Jakobson emerged from the Prague school of linguistics, and the relation between poetic language and everyday speech was central to the work of many of these linguists. See (Mukarovsky, 1964) for a related statement, and see (Pratt, 1977) for a critique.

Silverstein suggested that conversation derives much of its coherence and structure from this poetic organization. He suggested these poetic principles structure the flow of an interaction in much the same way that syntax structures sentences: "through principles that are inherently linear, yet abstract and formal" (1984, p. 185).

A MODEL OF GROUP CREATIVITY

The foregoing discussion of indexicality suggests that language use is fundamentally creative. This theoretical perspective inspired me to do the research that resulted in *Creating Conversations* (Sawyer, 2001a), a book that focuses on the creative aspects of language use. For example, Friedrich's (1971) analysis of discourse in the Russian 19th-century novel demonstrated how participants creatively use register and other indexical properties of language to define the social properties of an encounter. Other linguistic anthropologists have studied the variety of forms of conversational creativity observed cross-culturally. Many cultures have developed complex improvisational verbal forms, requiring significant creative skill, which are used in ritual (Fox, 1974), negotiation (Keenan, 1973), gossip (Brenneis, 1984), and greeting rituals (Goffman, 1971; Irvine, 1974). These genres of ensemble verbal art have been studied by sociolinguists (Gumperz & Hymes, 1972), linguistic anthropologists (Bauman & Sherzer, 1974), and folklorists (Fox, 1974; Lord, 1960). Although many scholars have attempted to apply linguistic models to musical analysis, none of them have applied these more culturally contextualized approaches; instead, they have limited their borrowings to structural or transformational/generative linguistics.

The model of group creativity in Fig. 3.1 is based the nature of the *semiotic mediation* (Mertz & Parmentier, 1985) of the interaction. In group creativity, interaction between performers is immediate, durationally constrained to the moment of creation, and is mediated by musical or verbal signs. The process of group creativity is coincident with the moment of reception and interpretation by other participants.

Each performance act is subject to a variety of interactional forces: the performer of the act, who contributes something new to the flow of interaction through indexical entailment; the other participants in interaction; the definition and constraints of the performance genre; the independent constraining force operating on the act which de-

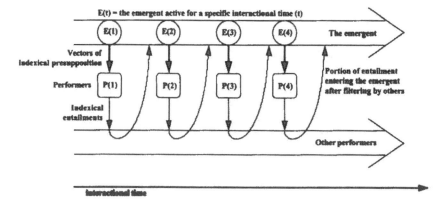

FIG. 3.1. Group creativity. No two-dimensional figure can adequately represent the complexity of real-time interaction; this figure should be viewed as one of many possible visual representations. The horizontal axis, time, represents the constantly changing nature of the emergent. No representation of the structure of the emergent is implied or intended.

rives from the flow of the prior interaction, and constitutes the indexical presuppositions of the act, Silverstein's *entextualization* (Silverstein, 1993) or Mead's (1932) *emergent*, the term I use here.

The emergent is structured but ephemeral, changes with each performance act, and emerges from the indexical presuppositions accumulated through the prior collective interaction. It is an emergent social fact; it is not determined by any single performer, and only partially constrained by the genre definition. For the interaction to continue as an intersubjective shared activity, the performers must work together in creating the emergent.

This description of group creativity is analogous to ordinary conversation (a nonmarked performance genre in most cultures), where the "performers" are the participants in the conversation. However, note that topic and the usual discourse analyses of topical coherence, topic shift, and the like represent only one facet of the complex social fact that is represented by the emergent. For example, an emergent may contain multiple topics, subtopics, and idiosyncratic interpretations of topics which are all in play and activated to varying degrees, the balance shifting with each utterance. In addition, the emergent contains all of the sociointeractional effects resulting from the flow of a conversation: relative role and status assignments, invocations of prior interactions, and voicings of recognized social roles or characters.

The requirements of intersubjectivity constrain each performer to contribute utterances which retain coherence with the emergent. This constraining force has been given various names by linguists who study pragmatics; perhaps the best known treatment is the *speech act theory* of Austin (1962) and Searle (1969), which speaks of the "illocutionary" and "perlocutionary" forces of utterances. Habermas (1987) defined *communicative action* using the former concept: "the type of interaction in which *all* participants harmonize their individual plans of action with one another and thus pursue their illocutionary aims *without reservation*" (Vol. 1, p. 294). Habermas associated "strategic action" with perlocutionary force. My notion of the emergent's constraining force makes no distinction between these two forces; critiques of speech act theory have convincingly demonstrated that the distinction cannot be maintained in practice (DuBois, 1992; Duranti, 1988; Rosaldo, 1982).

Some cognitive psychologists have studied the mental processes of solitary musical improvisation in jazz and classical musicians, and these researchers have noted that improvisation requires the cognitive ability to balance two competing tendencies: coherence and inventiveness. An improvising musician must both maintain coherence with the genre and the prior flow of the performance, while creating something novel. These are both necessary components of the improvisational process, and do not operate in isolation but rather continually interact with each other during the generation of the improvisation (Clarke, 1988). Of course, what counts as coherence may vary with each performance and across genres, and the degree of constraint of an emergent can vary significantly; but there are constraints on how rapidly the emergent can change, which in turn may be dependent on the genre definition and the surrounding social context. Through indexical processes that function metapragmatically, the emergent constrains a performance act on all levels mentioned above simultaneously: topic structure, relative role and status assignments, invocations of prior interactions or actions, and voicings of recognized performance roles and even specific well-known performances. At any given moment these different levels may be differentially constrained.

Using Mead's notion of the emergent, we can characterize the process of group creativity as follows. Performers are loosely constrained to operate within the performance genre. A given act is more strongly constrained by the emergent. The nature of this constraint is unique

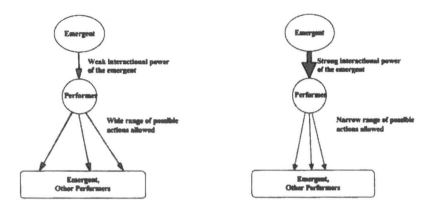

FIG. 3.2. Different constraints on the range of creative entailment.

and specific to the performance and the moment of interaction; at some moments the emergent is highly constraining and leaves only a small range of possible actions, whereas at other moments, the emergent is weakly constraining and performers have a wide range of possible actions (see Fig. 3.2).

In improvisational genres, each performer is expected to contribute something original to the evolving emergent in each act. Some of these indexical entailments project a high degree of constraining force, leaving the next performer with a smaller range of possible actions; these include many of those actions that are explicitly proscribed in improv theater, such as "writing the script in your head" or "endowing." Other actions project a weaker degree of constraint, leaving the next performer with a broader range of possible actions. These latter actions have the effect of keeping the emergent open and full of possibility, whereas the former tend to bring about convergence more quickly. In response to the performer's action, the other participants evaluate the act, and the subsequent interaction determines to what extent the indexical entailment resulting from the act affects the (still/always evolving) emergent. This "evaluation" is often immediate and often not consciously goal-directed (see chap. 7). A more skillful indexical entailment is more likely to enter the emergent, thus operating with more force on subsequent performance acts.

Thus, we have a continuing process: A performer, constrained by the collectively created emergent, originates an action with some indexical entailment; the other performers, through their responses in subsequent actions, collectively determine the extent to which this act enters the emergent; the new emergent then similarly constrains the subsequent performers. Throughout, the "meta-constraint" of genre definition controls many properties of this interactional process: how much indexical entailment is considered acceptable, how performer's acts are allocated, how performers create acts which retain coherence with the emergent.[10]

Example 3.1. Four actors stand at the back of the stage. Andy begins the scene.

(1) (Andy walks to center stage, pulls up a chair and sits down, miming the action of driving by holding an imaginary steering wheel)

(2) (Bob walks to Andy, stands next to him, fishes in pocket for something)

(3) Andy: On or off?

(4) Bob: I'm getting on, sir (continues fishing in his pocket)

(5) Andy: In or out?

(6) Bob: I'm getting in!
           I'm getting in!

(7) Andy: Did I see you tryin' to get in the back door a couple of stops back?

(8) Bob: Uh . . .

Bauman and Briggs (1997) noted that in creative linguistic interaction, not only is the topic under constant negotiation; the emergent context itself is subject to reflexive metapragmatic negotiation, a process they referred to as *contextualization*. All aspects of the performance situation must be considered part of the emergent. The improvisational theater dialogue in Example 3.1 illustrates many of the con-

---

[10]This theory has some interesting parallels with the theory of the "grounding process" proposed by Clark, Wilkes-Gibbs, and others (see Wilkes-Gibbs, 1995). The basic interactional moves in this theory are the *presentation* of a *contribution*, corresponding to the offer, and the *acceptance phase* in which the offer is collectively evaluated and filtered by the group. Their term for this process is *refashioning*: "in refashioning, the participants try to diagnose and repair the troublesome part of a presentation, and either expand, revise, or replace it until there is a version on the floor that they can accept" (Wilkes-Gibbs, 1995, p. 244). One (minor) difference is that grounding theory is focused on attaining mutual understanding and interpretation, and thus is less appropriate to the analysis of open-ended, creative improvisations in which intersubjectivity and ambiguity remain fluid.

cepts presented in the earlier discussion and in Fig. 3.1. Andy, taking the first turn, is able to act without creative constraints, other than those of the performance genre. His initial nonverbal act is to sit in a chair and mime the act of holding a steering wheel. This proposes the entailment that he is the driver and is sitting in a vehicle. However, this initial emergent is relatively minimally constraining (see Fig. 3.2); Bob had many possible acts available at turn (2) which would have retained coherence with this emergent. For example, Bob could have pulled up a second chair and sat down next to the "driver," and he would have become a passenger in a car. Andy's initial act does not indicate whether the vehicle is moving or not; it does not indicate the type of vehicle; it does not indicate the role of his character, nor the relationship with any other character. The entailment of Bob's act in (2) is also broad and minimally constraining, leaving Andy with an equal range of options for turn (3). In (3), Andy could have addressed Bob as his friend, searching for theater tickets. The range of dramatic options available on stage are practically unlimited: For example, at (2), Bob could have addressed Andy as Captain Kirk of Star Trek, initiating a TV-show parody. Andy's utterance (3) creates stronger entailments, and thus leaves Bob with a narrower range of possible action for (4). "On or off" would not be an appropriate statement for a car driver. It suggests that Andy is a professional driver of a bus (but also, note, is compatible with Andy driving a plane, boat, or spaceship). (3) also entails a relationship: Bob is a paying customer of Andy.

A few minutes of examination of any improvisational transcript indicates many plausible, dramatically coherent utterances that the actors could have performed at each turn. Improvisational interaction is highly contingent from moment to moment; a combinatorial explosion quickly results in hundreds of potential performances, branching out from each actor's utterance, and it is this wide range of possible trajectories that results in unpredictable emergence. In spite of the contingency and combinatorics, by (8) the actors have established a reasonably complex drama, a collectively created emergent that now has its own constraining force. They know that Andy is a bus driver, and that Bob is a potential passenger. Andy is getting a little impatient, and Bob may be a little shifty, perhaps trying to sneak on. In the remainder of the sketch, the actors must retain dramatic coherence with this emergent. Of course, each actor's turn will propose additional entailments, which will enter the emergent dramatic scene and influence subsequent performer's acts.

My focus on indexicality thus emphasizes the socially creative nature of musical and verbal art. Improvisational genres require innovations—creative entailments—from the performers; creativity rests in introducing novelty in the form of a new topic or subtopic, or shifting the role relationships of the participants to the speaker's advantage, while satisfying the indexically presupposing constraints of the emergent. Yet these entailments are subject to a social process of evaluation. When a performer introduces a new creative entailment, the entire group of performers collectively determines whether that entailment will be accepted into the emergent, ongoing performance. They collectively have the option of accepting the innovation (by working with it, building on it, making it "their own"), rejecting the innovation (by continuing the performance as if it had never occurred), or partially accepting the innovation (by selecting one aspect of it to build on, and ignoring the rest). This evaluative decision is a group effort, and cannot be identified clearly with any specific moment in time, nor with any single individual (see chap. 7). The performance may evolve for some time before it becomes clear what has or hasn't been accepted. For example, in a long-form improv performance, a suggested plot twist may not be clearly integrated into the play until 10 or 15 minutes after its introduction (Sawyer, 2003). In many cases the performers do not know what will happen until after it has happened, because no single individual has the authority to make these evaluative judgments. This uncertainty is due to the complex interplay of indexical presupposition and entailment of group creativity.

Johnson-Laird (1988) explored the cognitive constraints imposed by the need to continually balance coherence and inventiveness. Because improvisation occurs in real time, he hypothesized that the type of elaboration and innovation feasible with composition could not occur. This hypothesis was based on the observation that compared to a long-term compositional process, processing capacity during improvisation is relatively limited. Sloboda (1985) also based his comments on the processing capacity limitation notion. Many cognitive psychologists have similarly proposed that improvisational genres evolve over time in such a way that individual creative choice is limited.

Like these psychologists, I argue that a great deal is demanded of performers: They must listen, evaluate, and create simultaneously. However, although it is tautological to note that there is less processing capacity available in improvisation than in composition, because there is much less time available for creative mental processes to occur, the relevant question would be if this reduction in processing capacity is enough to constrain the resulting creative product. In fact, Tirro (1974) argued that the solos created during great jazz improvisations are as complexly structured as the notated compositions of the European tradition. And the contemporary genre of *free jazz* does not appear to conform to the "constrained genre and style" view of many cognitive psychology models (Pressing, 1988; Sloboda, 1985). In this genre, the stated goal is to have no rules or structure (although some residual or minimal structure is of course present in all activity). Extremely improvised genres, like free jazz and long-form improv, suggest that models based on an assumption of qualitatively different processing capacity during improvisation and composition may need to be revised.

INDEXICALITY IN MUSICAL ENSEMBLES

In contrast to structuralist approaches to music, my focus on interactional pragmatics is based on poststructuralist notions of practice and process. Music has no obvious referent, making a semantic study difficult; and the syntactic parallels between music and language, although present, are limited. Consequently, a pragmatic, interactional approach may be more promising.

In jazz, unlike conversation, there is no turn-taking behavior; all participants perform continually. Nonetheless, jazz musicians almost universally describe their interaction on stage as a conversation. In chapter 2, I presented many such quotations, and I excerpt one of them here:

> By talking to people up on stage through your music, you can start working on stuff you've never heard and never done ... you need people to play with ... when I do it, I'd find that there are these things coming out of myself, which I didn't even know were there, I'd never heard them, I didn't know where they came from. (Sawyer interview, December 2, 1990)

Jazz solo improvisation involves a significant interplay between the soloing band member (typically a brass wind instrument) and the rhythm section (typically drums, bass, and a harmonic instrument such as piano or guitar). Jazz is broad enough to allow for a full range of balance or lack of balance between the soloist and the other band members. In most jazz groups the soloist's performance has primacy, and the remainder of the band has the goal of echoing and surrounding this performance with accompaniment ("comping" for short). In contrast, a balanced cocreative performance style is demonstrated by a group in which the soloist's performance is less central, and the other band members' improvisational lines are participating in a more democratic dialogue. The subgenre of free jazz is known for its ensemble interaction and an extremely democratic style. Regardless of the degree of balance among performers, in all jazz styles each band member's improvisational performance contributes to the unfolding musical performance.

The concepts of *poetic structure* and of *indexical entailment* allow us to further elaborate the parallels between group creativity in music and verbal art, by drawing parallels with the nondenotational indexical properties of linguistic interaction. Jazz musicians collectively create an emergent with many similarities to Fig. 3.1. Each musician is constrained by the emergent, the set of *indexical presuppositions*, including the key of the piece, the song's harmonic structure, and the indexical entailments projected by the other players. In the presence of these constraints, jazz requires each performer to offer something new at each point, ideally something that is suggestive to the other musicians. A semiotic view of such ensembles must focus on indexicality as the primary interactional mechanism, as the denotationally entailing properties of language have no parallel in music.

Figures 3.1 and 3.2 capture many parallels between musical and verbal ensembles. Each musician performs in the presence of an intersecting set of constraints. These come from the social context of the performance (e.g., the type of audience), the genre of the piece, the structure of the song being played, and the immediate influence of the "musical emergent" resulting from the performance up to the current moment. In Peircean terms, all of these musical constraints are indexical, because they are relationships between a performance act and a context of action. The ensemble is constantly suggesting and elaborating musical motifs, concepts, styles, and moods, and sometimes implicitly referencing other songs or other performances of the same song. To remain musical, the performer is required to perform something that retains musical coherence with the emergent. Of course, the degree of constraint of any given emergent can vary significantly (as in Fig. 3.2); but there are constraints on how rapidly it can change, which in turn may be dependent on the genre or the social context of the performance. The emergent constrains a given performance act on several musical planes simultaneously: tone or timbre, mode and scale permitted, rhythmic patterns, specific motifs, stylistic references, and references to other performances or songs. At any given moment these different planes may be differentially constrained. Thus as with conversation—where a participant is required to maintain coherence with the linguistic emergent—a musician's creativity is constrained by the musical emergent.

Some musicologists have touched on these notions of indexicality and poetic structure. Lidov (1975, 1980) and Noske (1977) discussed similar issues in their analysis of opera, a multimodal genre that combines text and music. Lidov's (1980) approach to musical semantics suggests the performance can have "indexical and metonymic" effects, by which he meant a "biological stimulation which music actually conveys" (p. 388). Lidov (1980) also noted the validity of applying of Jakobson's notion of parallelism to musical segments (p. 388). In fact, as Lidov pointed out, there is a tradition in music analysis of arguing that the "narrative structure" of a musical composition—an indexically entailing effect resulting from poetic structuring—results in its emotional force (Langer, 1953; Meyer, 1956, 1973). The semiotic focus on indexicality and on the poetic properties of language can provide us with a framework for a rigorous elaboration of these classic observations.

CONCLUSION

In this chapter I presented a model of group creativity that was inspired by the properties of music and verbal art presented in chapter 2. I proposed that both verbal and musical performance collectively emerge from interactional processes which are contingent from moment to moment. I contrasted this model to structuralist approaches to performance which have focused on composed products like scripts and scores. Unlike the study of composed products, the analysis of group creativity requires a fundamentally interactional semiotics, one which emphasizes the indexical properties of sign usage, rather than a structuralist analysis focused on sense, segmentation, paradigmatic equivalence sets, or static notational systems.

I drew on Peirce, Jakobson, and Silverstein to develop an interactional semiotics appropriate for both verbal and musical ensemble performance. The model is also related to the pragmatism of G. H. Mead and John Dewey. For example, symbolic interactionism developed out of Mead's (1934) writings, and focuses on *social acts*, or *joint action* (Blumer, 1969): "the larger collective form of action that is constituted by the fitting together of the lines of behavior of the separate participants" (p. 70). Blumer (1969) emphasized that social action was an appropriate level of analysis for study, distinct from the individual level and the macrosocial level: "Both such joint activity and individual conduct are formed *in* and *through* this ongoing process; they are not mere expressions or products of what people bring to their interaction or of conditions that are antecedent to their interaction" (p. 10). The pragmatists emphasized the importance of focusing on emergent, interactional processes. In the next chapter, I explore Dewey's theory of emergence and interaction in art.

4

Group Creativity and the Arts

In chapter 1, I noted that group creativity has been neglected by many fields that study creativity and the arts. Instead of studying improvising groups, researchers have focused on *product creativity*: activities that result in objective, ostensible products—paintings, sculptures, musical scores—which remain after the creative act is complete (Runco & Albert, 1990; Sternberg, 1988; Sternberg & Davidson, 1995). These products are created over extended time periods, with unlimited opportunities for revision by the creator before the product is displayed. In contrast, in improvisation, the creative process *is* the product; the audience is watching the creative process as it occurs. Product creativity is found in artistic domains such as sculpture and painting, as well as scientific domains, where the products generated are theories, formulas, or published articles.

In this chapter, I explore the relationships between group creativity and product-oriented arts such as painting, writing, and music composition, by drawing on Dewey's model of "art as experience" and Collingwood's model of "art as language." Group creativity can contribute to our understanding of all creative genres, for two primary reasons. First, the creative process that goes on in the mind of a creator is generally inaccessible to the researcher, in part because it occurs in fits and starts, over long time periods. But a group performance is created in the moment, on stage, and can easily be observed by the researcher. Second, many group performance genres are fundamentally collaborative. Observing this collaboration on-stage is relatively straightforward, compared to the difficulties of observing the many forms of collaboration, sometimes over long periods of time, that contribute to the generation of a work of art.

THE PHILOSOPHY OF ART

In his studio, Picasso is painting free-form—without preconceived image or composition, he is experimenting with colors, forms, and moods. He starts with a figure of a reclining nude—but then loses interest. The curve of the woman's leg reminds him of a matador's leg, as he flies through the air after being gored by a bull—so he paints over the nude and creates an image of a bull and matador. But this leads him to yet another idea; he paints over the bullfight image and begins work on a Mediterranean harbor—with water-skier, bathers in bikinis, and a picturesque hilltop village.

The free-form inspiration continues. Five hours later, Picasso stops and declares that he will have to discard the canvas—it hasn't worked. But the time was not wasted—he has discovered some new ideas, ideas that have emerged from his interaction with the canvas, ideas that he can use in his next painting. Picasso says "Now that I begin to see where I'm going with it, I'll take a new canvas and start again."

This 5-hour improvisation was captured in the Claude Renoir film *The Mystery of Picasso*, using time-lapse photography (Picasso, 1982). I often show the Picasso film to my class on the Psychology of Creativity, because it helps to dispel some common myths about artists—that inspiration always precedes execution, that artists never edit their work, that everything that is painted is released to the world. Perhaps these myths arise from our tendency to focus on the products of creativity—the finished paintings, sculptures, and musical scores that critics review, that are left for future generations to analyze and interpret. This film gives us a rare opportunity to view, instead, the improvisational process of creativity—the real, lived experience of the artist, interacting and improvising in his studio.

Unlike product creativity—which involves a long period of creative work leading up to the creative product—in group creativity, the process *is* the product. We saw in chapter 2 that a jazz ensemble collaborates on stage to spontaneously create the performance. In chapter 3, I referred to this performance "product" as the *emergent*, because the performance emerges from the musical interactions among multiple band members; there is no director that guides the performance, and no script for the musicians to follow. And in improvisational theater, the actors collectively create an emergent dialogue; like jazz, this process is the essence of the performance. The purpose of such groups is not to generate a product; the performance emergent is the product. In contrast, in product creativity, the artist has an unlimited period of time to contemplate, edit, and revise the work. In five hours, Picasso generated three paintings, all of which were discarded; the creative process may eventually result in a creative product which will be displayed to an audience, or it may not. The process is almost always invisible to the public; however, occasionally a museum will display a collection of sketches and studies from an artist's studio, as a way of providing insight into the creative process that resulted in the final painting. The general public tends not to be very interested in such exhibits; they receive the most attention from fairly knowledgeable individuals.

Psychologists who study creativity have focused on product creativity; this focus is also found in the philosophy of art, a branch of philosophy known as *aesthetics*. Aesthetics has tended to focus more on art works than on the creative process. Most aestheticians have the same implicit bias as psychologists who study creativity: They focus on culturally valued art forms—the high arts like abstract painting or orchestral composition—to the almost complete neglect of performance.

Like both the psychology of creativity and the philosophy of art, many performance-oriented fields have neglected group improvisation, including folkloristics, ethnomusicology, and musicology (see chap. 1). The few treatments that exist have been ethnographic descriptions of musical and verbal performance genres. In music, in addition to a recent focus on jazz (Berliner, 1994; Monson, 1996), European and American writers have written widely on the Indian *raga*, the Javanese *gamelan*, the Arabic and Turkish *maqam*, the Iranian *dastgah*, and group African drumming. Studies of verbal improvisation are primarily found in the branch of linguistic anthropology called the *ethnography of speaking* (Bauman & Sherzer, 1974; Hymes, 1962). These researchers focus on public verbal performance in a variety of cultures; most of these performance genres incorporate improvisational elements.

In this chapter, I examine two influential theories in the philosophy of art, drawing on the ensemble phenomena described in chapter 2 to critique and elaborate these theories. When I began my study of group creativity, I was surprised to discover a complete absence of research on creativity in performance—neither improvisation nor scripted theater had been studied by psychologists. So I expanded my search to other disciplines, looking for theoretical models that might help me to understand the process of group creativity. When I began to study the aesthetics literature, I was drawn to theories that emphasize the communicative, interactional properties of art—such as those of John Dewey and R. G. Collingwood.

John Dewey (1859–1952) was one of the best-known and most influential of the American philosophers known as *pragmatists*. His work has had a significant impact on educational practice; Dewey founded the Laboratory School at the University of Chicago to develop and apply his inquiry-based and child-centered theories of learning. Although Dewey's theory of "experience" was an ambitious attempt to explain all of human experience—including science and nature—perhaps his most effective theoretical description of experience appears in his one book about art, *Art as Experience* (Dewey, 1934), a book that aesthetician Monroe Beardsley (1966) declared to be "by widespread agreement, the most valuable work on aesthetics written in English (and perhaps in any language) so far in our century" (p. 332; also see Jackson, 1998).

R. G. Collingwood (1889–1943), a historian and a political philosopher, was one of the most prominent members of the school of British idealism. The British Idealists were influenced by Greek classical political thought (especially by the political philosophy of Plato and Aristotle), by the philosophical system of German Idealism (Kant, Fichte, Hegel), and by the insights of the British philosophical tradition (Hobbes, Hume, Locke). Collingwood's extended discussion of aesthetics and creativity appears in his 1938 book *The Principles of Art*. Like British idealism more generally, Collingwood emphasized the practical consequences of philosophical work.

In this chapter, I argue that at the core of both Dewey's and Collingwood's writings is a theory of art as group improvisation. By focusing my discussion on improvisation, I bring out aspects of both theorists that have been neglected in most analyses. Of course, there is a lot in both theorists I do not mention—this is of necessity a selective reading. But I believe that this focus on group improvisation comes close to revealing the essence of both men's theories.

I begin by first revisiting the improvisational theater example from chapter 3, and I use that transcript to identify five important characteristics of improvised group creativity. Then, I focus on each of these five characteristics in turn, and for each, I argue that both Dewey's and Collingwood's writings emphasize exactly that aspect of the aesthetic experience. The focus on improvisation reveals many similarities between these very different philosophers; their theories unite on all five characteristics. And by applying each theory to the concrete case of group creativity, I show where each theory could benefit from elaboration, and suggest some properties of an aesthetic theory that would adequately address improvisation in groups.

There is no extant evidence that Dewey read Collingwood's work, or vice-versa. However, the exchange between Croce and Dewey in the late 1940s seems to suggest a connection, since Collingwood's theory is often associated with Croce (Croce, 1948; Dewey, 1948; also see Alexander, 1987; Douglas, 1970; Pepper, 1939). But this debate largely had to do with whether Dewey's theory is an idealist theory—rather than a pragmatist one—and whether Croce had correctly understood Dewey. By focusing on improvisation and communication, my approach in the following leads me down a different path from the traditional Croce–Dewey comparison.

IMPROVISATIONAL THEATER

In improvisational theater, an ensemble of actors creates a scene on stage, without any prearranged dialogue, with no character assignments, and no plot outline. Everything about the performance is collectively created by the actors, on stage, in front of the audience. The transcript in Example 4.1 (also in chap. 3) of the first 30 seconds of an improvised theater sketch, which lasted a total of about 5 minutes, helps to demonstrate the collective and contingent aspects of improvisation.

Example 4.1. Four actors stand at the back of the stage. Andy begins the scene.
(1) (Andy walks to center stage, pulls up a chair and sits down, miming the action of driving by holding an imaginary steering wheel)
(2) (Bob walks to Andy, stands next to him, fishes in pocket for something)
(3) Andy: On or off?
(4) Bob: I'm getting on, sir (continues fishing in his pocket)

(5) Andy: In or out?

(6) Bob: I'm getting in!
           I'm getting in!

(7) Andy: Did I see you tryin' to get in the back door a couple of stops
           back?

(8) Bob: Uh ...

In my discussion of this transcript in chapter 3, I emphasized that
at each turn, each actor has a wide range of possible actions available, and that each one of these possibilities would take the drama in
a different direction. Although each actor must speak a line that
remains consistent with what has come before, at each moment an actor can create many plausible, dramatically coherent utterances. Improvisational interaction is highly contingent from moment to moment, and the scene is built from the successive contributions of the
actors working together. It is in this sense that an improvised scene is
emergent, in both the classic coinage of the 19th century philosopher
George Henry Lewes (Lewes, 1875, p. 412), and in the contemporary
sense associated with connectionism and distributed cognition (Sawyer, 2002b). Lewes' concept of "emergence" was widely discussed in
the 1920s, largely by evolutionary biologists but also by philosophers,
and these discussions influenced G. H. Mead and John Dewey.

FIVE CHARACTERISTICS OF IMPROVISATION

In this section, I use five characteristics of improvisation to focus my
comparisons between Dewey and Collingwood (see Table 4.1). I introduce and interpret Dewey and Collingwood within this five-charac-
teristic framework. Although in each case, they developed a theory of
all art, and specifically of product creativity, both based their aesthet-

TABLE 4.1
Five Characteristics of Improvisation

(1) An emphasis on creative process rather than creative product
(2) An emphasis on creative processes that are problem-finding rather than problem-
    solving
(3) The comparison of art to everyday language use
(4) The importance of collaboration, with fellow artists and with the audience
(5) The role of the ready-made, or cliché, in art

ics—even if only implicitly—on a theory of the creative process as improvisation.

I. Emphasizing Creative Process Over Product

In Chapter 1, I argued that *process* was one of the key defining properties of group creativity. Yet those who study the arts have historically tended to focus on art products, rather than on the processes that generate them. This is true not only of art historians and of psychologists, but also of aesthetic philosophers. Some argue against a consideration of creative process on principle; for example, in arguing against one form of critical intentionalism, Beardsley (1965) argued that understanding the creative process "makes no difference at all," and that he did "not see that this has any bearing upon the value of what [the artist] produces" (p. 309).

However, a few influential art critics have emphasized that art works cannot be understood without considering process. Clement Greenberg's influential position on modern abstract art was that "the avant-garde imitates the processes of art" rather than imitating nature (Greenberg, 1986a, p. 17); the subject of the art is "the disciplines and processes of art and literature themselves" (p. 8). For Greenberg, the *processes* of art of a given stage in history are the proper subject of art for the following stage.

The distinction between creative process and resulting product was one of the central themes of American pragmatism. Dewey (1934) based his aesthetic theory on the distinction between *art product* and *work of art*: "The *product* of art . . . is not the *work* of art" (p. 214). The work of art is a psychological process; it is "active and experienced. It is what the product does, its working" (p. 162). Dewey's (1934) theory of art as experience lends itself naturally to an extension to the performing arts and to improvisation:

> In seeing a picture or an edifice, there is the same compression from accumulation in time that there is in hearing music, reading a poem or novel, and seeing a drama enacted. No work of art can be instantaneously perceived because there is then no opportunity for conservation and increase of tension. . . . It follows that the separation of rhythm and symmetry from each other and the division of the arts into temporal and spatial is more than misapplied ingenuity. It is based on a principle that is destructive . . . of esthetic understanding." (pp. 182–183)

Collingwood also made a similar distinction the core of his aesthetic theory: "The painted picture is not the work of art ... [however,] its production is somehow necessarily connected with the aesthetic activity, that is, with the creation of the imaginative experience which is the work of art" (Collingwood, 1938, p. 305). Collingwood also made a strong claim that the visible, ostensible product is essentially irrelevant to art proper: "A work of art may be completely created when it has been created as a thing whose only place is in the artist's mind" (p. 130).

Collingwood's theory is not quite adequate to the phenomenon of staged improvisation, because of his insistence that the real work of art occurs only in the head of the artist. When he mentioned live improvisation (in passing), he insisted that it is only incidental to real art: "When a man makes up a tune, he may and very often does at the same time hum it or sing it or play it on an instrument.... He may do these things in public, so that the tune at its very birth becomes public property. ... But all these are accessories of the real work. ... The actual making of the tune is something that goes on in his head, and nowhere else" (p. 134). In this insistence, Collingwood made the same error that he later attributed to "individualistic psychology" (see below); in group creativity, the essence of the creative process is social and interactional, and cannot be reduced to the inspiration or mental process of any single actor.

In contrast, Dewey's pragmatist framework led him to emphasize action in the world and the practical effects of that action, and for these reasons he did not focus on what is "in the head" of the artist. So although both philosophers argued for a shift away from a focus on products to a focus on process, they differ on the importance of action in the world, and this difference reflects the pragmatist basis of Dewey's thought and the idealist basis of Collingwood's.

2. Problem Finding and Problem Solving

The film of Picasso improvising at his canvas is particularly striking, because most of us never see an artist in action—we only see finished paintings in galleries and museums. But Picasso is not unusual—this improvisational style, called *problem finding* by creativity researchers, is used by most successful painters, as the psychologists Jacob Getzels and Mihaly Csikszentmihalyi discovered in a 10-year study of MFA students at one of the country's top art schools, the School of the Art Institute of Chicago (Getzels & Csikszentmihalyi, 1976). A "problem finding" painter is constantly searching for their visual problem while painting—improvising a painting rather than executing one. In contrast, a *prob-lem-solving* style involves starting with a relatively detailed plan for a composition and then simply painting it; "problem solving" because the painter defines a visual problem before starting, with the execution of the painting consisting of "solving" the problem (see chap. 7 for additional discussion of these two styles).

An improvisational performance is also, of necessity, a problem-finding process—albeit a collective one. For comparison, consider a traditional theater performance, perhaps a play by Shakespeare, where the actors start with a script, with memories of past performances by other companies—the long tradition of Shakespearean theater. This type of performance is at the problem-solving end of the spectrum, because the "problem" is well-specified: to create a successful performance of the script. In contrast, in improvisation the actors have to create everything; the dramatic elements emerge from the dialogue, in a problem-finding process that is collaborative and emergent.

The modern psychological distinction between problem finding and problem solving is strikingly similar to Collingwood's distinction between *art* and *craft*. In so many words, Collingwood (1938) stated that a craftsman is problem-solving, whereas an artist is problem finding:

[Craft] involves a distinction between planning and execution. The result to be obtained is preconceived or thought out before being arrived at. (p. 15)

In contrast:

Art as such does not imply the distinction between planning and execution (p. 22).... [The work of art] is something made by the artist, but not made ... by carrying out a preconceived plan, nor by way of realizing the means to a preconceived end. (p. 125)

This kind of "making" that is not craft is *creating*; "To create something means to make it nontechnically, but yet consciously and voluntarily" (Collingwood, 1938, p. 128). And creation doesn't have to be physical or ostensible; "a work of art may be completely created when it has been created as a thing whose only place is in the artist's mind" (p. 130). However, it is hard to imagine Picasso's beach scene emerging without his interaction with the paints and the canvas. And more generally, creators in a wide range of fields emphasize that they have many of their insights while they are working with the materials of their craft (John-Steiner, 1985).

Although Dewey's pragmatist theory emphasizes action in the world, Dewey (1934) also agreed that real art is problem finding, and that a problem-solving approach will not lead to real art: "A rigid predetermination of an end-product ... leads to the turning out of a mechanical or academic product" (p. 138). An art work will only be great if the artist finds a problem during the process of creation: "The unexpected turn, something which the artist himself does not definitely foresee, is a condition of the felicitous quality of a work of art; it saves it from being mechanical" (p. 139).

It's not surprising that two very different philosophers would develop a problem-finding theory of art in the 1930s, after several decades of abstract, nonrepresentational painting. As Greenberg (1986a) observed of artists in the Middle Ages, "Precisely because his content was determined in advance [by commission of a patron] ... the artist was relieved of the necessity to be original and inventive in his 'matter' and could devote all his energy to formal problems" (p. 18). Perhaps only in Greenberg's avant-garde could a problem-finding painter like Picasso become one of the greatest painters; before the onset of abstract art, problem-solving artists were almost certainly more dominant.

Art critics have debated the role of spontaneity in modern art, in part because of this historical and cultural locatedness. The abstract expressionists were famous for their supposedly improvisational painting styles—Harold Rosenberg called them "The American Action Painters" to describe their nondeliberate approach to the canvas—yet Leo Steinberg criticized this term, noting that Kline and de Kooning made their paintings with deliberation, carefully working them toward the appearance of spontaneity. Steinberg (1972) hinted that there is something distinctly American about this valorization of the problem-finding style: "It appealed once again to the American disdain for art conceived as something too carefully plotted, too cosmetic, too French" (p. 62). In the 1998 book *The Culture of Spontaneity*, Belgrad explored and elaborated the cultural and historical locatedness of the post-World War II "impulse to valorize spontaneous improvisation" (p. 1). In this era of cultural studies, no one should be surprised that not only our art, but also our aesthetic theories, are consistent with and emerge from broader cultural values.

3. Art Is Like Everyday Language Use

In chapters 1 and 2, I showed that jazz musicians and improvising actors alike compare their ensemble interaction to conversation. This insight is at the core of the theories of both Dewey and Collingwood. But for both Dewey and Collingwood, art is like language only in a certain sense; it is like language as used in everyday social settings—the *pragmatics*, rather than the *syntax*, of language. Thus, both theories are compatible with the theory of chapter 3, and its emphasis on the pragmatics of symbolic interaction. Collingwood, in particular, went to great lengths to criticize views of language that, if anything, became more dominant in the ensuing decades; Collingwood argued that art is *not* like the language of the grammarians of the 1930s—who he criticized for focusing on the product, rather than the activity, of speaking, and for dividing language into words and grammatical relations. Collingwood also argued that art is not like the language of the logical positivists—who he criticized for analyzing sentences as propositional statements, and analyzing their truth value. Instead, he presented a pragmatist, socially contextualized theory of language as *utterance*, as *gesture*, as *act*.

Collingwood's "art as language" discussion has not received much attention, even in the recent defense of Collingwood by Aaron Ridley (1997; but see Hagberg, 1995). I am impressed with Collingwood's (1938) critique of his contemporaries—the grammarians (pp. 254–259) and the logicians (pp. 259–268). Because both of these schools became foundational elements of Chomskian linguistics in the 1950s, Collingwood's arguments prefigured the critiques of Chomskian linguistics that emerged in the 1960s and 1970s in anthropology and sociolinguistics. And the theory of art presented in Book III displays remarkable overlap with contemporary sociocultural theories of creativity that emerged in psychology only in the 1980s.

Collingwood's theory of language prefigured an important tradition in the late 20th century study of language—the analysis of language use and language function that today includes conversation analysis, sociolinguistics, and the study of language use in cultural context. These contemporary approaches were indirectly influenced by American pragmatism, through its social psychological descendant, symbolic interactionism, which took as its object of study group creativity.

In pragmatist fashion, Dewey (1934) often compared aesthetic experience to everyday conversation: "Acts of social intercourse are works of art" (p. 63). They each are interactional, and have a temporal dimension. Dewey (1934) wrote "Moliere's character did not know he had been talking prose all his life. So men in general are not aware that they have been exercising an art as long as they have engaged in spoken intercourse with others" (p. 240). Thus the connection with improvisation: In many ways, everyday conversations are also improvised (Sawyer, 2001a). Especially in casual small talk, we do not speak from a script; our conversation is collectively created, and emerges from the actions of everyone present. In every conversation, we negotiate all of the properties of the encounter—where the conversation will go, what kind of conversation we're having, what our social relationship is, when it will end. In fact, improvisational theater dialogue can best be understood as a special case of everyday conversation (Sawyer, 2003).

When everyday conversation is improvisational, it shares many properties with Dewey's theory of aesthetic experience; this theory depends on his characterization of experience as improvisational and yet structured. Dewey (1934) defined experience as *interaction*, with people or with the physical environment: "experience is the result, the sign, and the reward of that interaction of organism and environment which ... is a transformation of interaction into participation and communication" (p. 22). For Dewey, language and music both shared the structure of experience, and music, because of the obvious temporal dimension, was of all the arts the most representative of his aesthetic theory (p. 184). Although Dewey did not mention improvisation explicitly (except parenthetically comparing "jazzed music" to movies and comic strips, p. 5), his metaphoric descriptions of experience, often emphasizing rhythm, would seem quite familiar to jazz musicians: "all interactions ... in the whirling flux of change are rhythms. There is ebb and flow ... ordered change" (p. 16).

Thus although the two theorists come from different traditions, they both share a communication theory of art. Dewey (1934) repeatedly stated that communication is the essential property of art: "Because the objects of art are expressive, they communicate. I do not say that communication to others is the intent of an artist. But it is the consequence of his work" (p. 104). And although Collingwood's theory of art is generally known as an "expression" theory of art, I think it is more accurately called a communication theory of art, because for Collingwood (1938), *art proper* is that art which "produces in [the audience] ... sensuous-emotional or psychical experiences which, when raised from impressions to ideas by the activity of the spectator's consciousness, are transmuted into a total imaginative experience identical with that of the painter" (p. 308). This usage of "experience" is quite compatible with Dewey's.

Both Dewey and Collingwood were careful to point out that by calling art a language, they did not want us to make the mistake of privileging verbal or linguistic communication as any kind of ultimate language. Dewey (1934) argued that it is a mistake to privilege spoken language, and to think that because art expresses things, those things can be translated into words. "In fact, each art speaks an idiom that conveys what cannot be said in another language and yet remains the same" (p. 106). Dewey wrote, "Because objects of art are expressive, they are a language. Rather, they are many languages" (p. 106). Each art has its own medium, and each one is like a different language, with our spoken language being just another one of the modes of communication. Nonetheless, "Art is the most universal form of language ... it is the most universal and freest form of communication" (p. 270).

Collingwood and Dewey both made explicit the implications of their theories: That all language (as they define it) is aesthetic. Collingwood (1938) emphatically stated, "Every utterance and every gesture that each one of us makes is a work of art" (p. 285). And he acknowledged that his theory of art entails that many everyday activities—not only the "high arts"—are aesthetic. As Alan Donagan (1962) wrote: "Collingwood's definition entails that you must recognize as works of art, on the one hand, every racy and lively contribution to conversation ... and on the other, every scientific and philosophical treatise" (p. 130).[11] Also commenting on Collingwood, Peter Ingram (1978) observed, "In engaging in linguistic activities in a creative way, we are all artists. There is no distinction between the 'artist' and the ordinary man" (p. 56).

4. The Importance of Collaboration

In group creativity, collaboration between performers is an essential aspect of the creative process. No one can generate a performance alone; the performers have to rely on the group to collectively generate the emergent performance. In group performance, these col-

___

[11]On page 131, Donagan (1962) wrote that Collingwood didn't accept that all discourse was art until after he wrote the earlier *Essay on Philosophical Method*. This was always Croce's point, but Collingwood had earlier rejected it.

laborations also involve an audience; for example, in improv theater the actors always ask the audience members to shout out suggestions to start each scene, and many groups pause scenes in the middle to ask for audience direction. More fundamentally, like all humor, the actors assume that the audience shares a large body of cultural knowledge and references. In this sense, the audience indirectly guides their improvisation (see chap. 2).

In a 1968 lecture, Leo Steinberg (1972) emphasized the role of the audience in saying, "I suspect that all works of art or stylistic cycles are definable by their built-in idea of the spectator" (p. 81). Collingwood (1938) made a fairly extreme statement that the audience is not only an influence, but should be considered to be a collaborator with the artist:

> The work of artistic creation is not a work performed in any exclusive or complete fashion in the mind of the person whom we call the artist. That idea is a delusion bred of individualistic psychology.... This activity is a corporate activity belonging not to any one human being but to a community. It is performed not only by the man whom we individualistically call the artist, but partly by all the other artists of whom we speak as "influencing" him, where we really mean collaborating with him. It is performed not only by this corporate body of artists, but (in the case of the arts of performance) by executants ... and ... there must be an audience, whose function is therefore not a merely receptive one, but collaborative too. The artist stands thus in collaborative relations with an entire community. (p. 324)

Dewey (1934) made much the same point, claiming that even when an artist is alone, there is a public and social aspect to his creativity: "Even the composition conceived in the head and, therefore, physically private, is public in its significant content, since it is conceived with reference to execution in a product that is perceptible and hence belongs to the common world" (p. 51). Dewey drew on the language metaphor to emphasize this point: "Language exists only when it is listened to as well as spoken.... Even when the artist works in solitude ... the artist has to become vicariously the receiving audience" (p. 106).

For both Dewey and Collingwood, the artist's creation can only be interpreted by reference to the community for which he creates, and this is a logical outcome of their emphasis on art as a communicative language. Collingwood (1938) argued that in art proper, the artist is playing a special role for his community: "[The artist] takes it as his business to express not his own private emotions ... but the emotions he shares with his audience. ... What he says will be something that his audience says through his mouth. ... There will thus be something more than mere communication from artist to audience, there will be collaboration between audience and artist" (p. 312). This is why Collingwood felt that artistic activity is the property of an entire community, not of an individual creator: "[The artist] undertakes his artistic labor not as a personal effort on his own private behalf, but as a public labor on behalf of the community to which he belongs" (p. 315). Dewey (1934) also emphasized that art is a communal process, not an individual or psychological one: "[Art] is not an isolated event confined to the artist and to a person here and there who happens to enjoy the work. In the degree in which art exercises its office, it is also a remaking of the experience of the community in the direction of greater order and unity" (p. 81).

Thus both philosophers prefigure those contemporary theories of creativity that emphasize social and cultural context. For example, Csikszentmihalyi's (1988) *systems model* includes three elements: the individual, the *field* of influential "gatekeeper" individuals, and the *domain* of materials and symbols that define a genre or discipline. Like Collingwood, Csikszentmihalyi and other contemporary creativity researchers have criticized purely psychological conceptions of creativity as overly "individualistic" (also see chap. 5).

Both Dewey and Collingwood emphasized the collaborations between the artist and their audiences, rather than the collaborations between artists that are the essence of group creativity. However, Collingwood (1938) did acknowledge the importance of collaboration among a community of artists, criticizing the "individualistic theory of authorship" and even recommending that copyright law be changed (p. 325), writing "All artists have modeled their style upon that of others, used subjects that others have used, and treated them as others have treated them already. A work of art so constructed is a work of collaboration" (p. 318).

In group creativity, collaboration is essential to the performance. And unlike the rather more abstract form of collaboration discussed by Dewey and Collingwood, in group creativity collaboration is undeniably a fundamental part of the creative process, and it can be observed and analyzed.

5. The Role of the Ready-Made in Improvisation

All improvisers know that improvisation does not mean that any-thing goes—improvisation always occurs within a structure, and all im-provisers draw on *ready-mades*—short precomposed motifs or clichés—as they create their novel performance. In the theater transcript in Ex-ample 4.1, the interaction requires a great deal of shared cultural knowledge—the two actors use well-known cultural symbols, whether visual (hands on steering wheel), gestural (Bob fishing in his pocket), or verbal ("On or off?"). The actors did not invent these symbols; they are ready-mades that the actors and audience already share.

Ready-mades are even more important in jazz improvisation. Some of the most famous jazz improvisers relied on a large repertoire of stock phrases; one of the most creative improvisers of all time, Char-lie Parker, drew on a personal repertoire of 100 motifs, each of them between 4 and 10 notes in length (Owens, 1995). Jazz musicians fre-quently discuss an internal tension between their own personally de-veloped patterns—called *licks*—and the need to continually innovate at a personal level (see chap. 2). Musicians practice and perform the same songs repeatedly, and can often express themselves more effec-tively when they have a predeveloped set of musical ideas available. However, if this process is carried too far, the improvisational nature of the performance is compromised. Jazz musicians are aware of the tension between the need to develop ideas in advance and the poten-tial for a gradual evolution toward patterned rigidity.

The role of ready-mades was discussed—pejoratively—by both Dew-ey and Collingwood. Collingwood's (1938) contrast between "art proper" and "false art" is largely based on the presence or absence of clichés or ready-mades. False art is when the creator uses a "ready-made 'language' which consists of a repertoire of clichés to produce states of mind in the persons upon whom these clichés are used" (p. 276). These ready-mades already exist: They were created by real artists as part of art proper. But if they are re-used, it be-comes false art: "artistic activity does not 'use' a 'ready-made lan-guage,' it 'creates' language as it goes along" (p. 275). False art simu-lates art by borrowing and recombining clichés from formerly created real art: "The dead body ... of the aesthetic activity be-comes a repertory of materials out of which an activity of a different kind can find means adaptable to its own ends. This non-aesthetic activity ... uses means which were once the living body of art. ... It is not art, but it simulates art" (p. 276).

Dewey (1934) was equally pejorative about clichés: "No genuine work has ever been a repetition of anything that previously existed. There are indeed works that tend to be mere recombinations of elements selected from prior works. But they are academic—that is to say, mechanical—rather than esthetic" (p. 288). For Dewey, perception of art only occurs when the perceiver actively, aesthetically, creates his own experience. "Otherwise, there is not perception but recognition" (p. 52). Recognition usually results from clichés: "In recognition we fall back, as upon a stereotype, upon some previously formed scheme." Greenberg's (1986a) classic distinction between avant-garde and kitsch stands or falls on the same point: kitsch uses as "raw material" the "fully matured cultural tradition," borrowing "devices, tricks, stratagems, rules of thumb, themes" (p. 12).

The idea that every component of a work must be completely new is unique to the West. For example, in Javanese Gamelan music, a composition is not supposed to be completely original; a Javanese composer is expected to build a new piece by reworking traditional materials, combining existing melodic fragments that have already appeared in many other compositions (Sutton, 1987, p. 83). The number of fragments, or *gatra* patterns, is limited; and each *gatra* of a given piece is found in many other pieces in the tradition. Sutton wrote that "as one gains knowledge of the repertory, almost every passage of every piece seems to come from other pieces" (p. 75) and that "all *gendhing* are variations of each other" (p. 83). This conception of composition, apparently excluded by both Dewey and Collingwood, is common in oral traditions.

Like improv theater and jazz, all art relies on ready-mades of one sort or another. The sociologist Howard Becker (1982) pointed out that shared *conventions* are always used by artists to aid in communicating with their audience. Csikszentmihalyi (1988) made much the same point when he argued that all creators rely on a *domain*, a shared body of conventions, techniques, and historical knowledge, as they create novel works. Thus Collingwood's standard for art proper is unrealistically high: No one can ever be 100% original. In fact, Collingwood (1938) acknowledged this later, saying that all artists have to speak in a language that they learn from the community: "The musician did not invent his scale or his instruments.... The painter did not invent the idea of painting pictures or the pigments and brushes with which he paints them.... [Artists] become poets or painters or musicians ... by living in a society where these languages are current" (pp. 316–317). The problem is that Collingwood never made clear where the line is: What counts as using language aesthetically, and what counts as using too much cliché? Still later, Collingwood seemed to say that artists should use *more* ready-mades, and should be free to borrow from other artists: "We must get rid of the conception of artistic ownership.... If an artist may say nothing except what he has invented by his own sole efforts, it stands to reason he will be poor in ideas" (p. 325).

Collingwood's distinction between art proper and false art is essentially a distinction between *more improvisational* art, and *less improvisational* art. False art is less improvisational because it relies on ready-mades—clichés—as an economic shortcut. Collingwood's theory can thus be extended, by analogy with group performance. Performances cannot be dichotomized into "improvisational" and "scripted"; all improvisers draw on ready-mades—short riffs or clichés—as they create their novel performance. Does the repeated use of 100 personal riffs suggest that Charlie Parker's performances were "false art," as Collingwood implies? If we have to exclude Parker—one of the most creative and talented improvisers of this century—from art proper, then what improvisational performance would qualify?

Dewey (1934) also acknowledged that every period and culture has conventions, and that the shared communal experience of a people is always in the work of art: "Every culture has its own collective individuality ... this collective individuality leaves its indelible imprint upon the art that is produced" (p. 330). And "The subject-matter is charged with meanings that issue from intercourse with a common world. The artist in the freest expression of his own responses is under weighty objective compulsions" (p. 306).

Thus there is an unresolved tension in both Dewey's and Collingwood's aesthetic theories: What is the role of conventions, clichés, and ready-mades? How exactly can one draw the line between true art and imitative art? A version of either theory that relied on a black-and-white distinction would be brittle and internally inconsistent. Aesthetic theory must acknowledge that all art relies on ready-mades to some extent; that in fact, one must think in terms of a continuum between art proper and false art—between art which relies on no conventions whatsoever, and art which relies on a relatively large number of them. This continuum parallels a continuum in group creativity—the continuum between fully improvised performance, through partially embellished performance, to highly ritualized and scripted performance (see chap. 6).

TOWARD AN AESTHETICS OF GROUP CREATIVITY

By focusing on group creativity, I identified five common themes in the aesthetic theories of Dewey and Collingwood. Essentially, both of them developed theories of art as ensemble improvisation, by focusing on creative process, problem finding, collaboration, and communication. And by identifying the common themes of these two philosophers, I have begun to suggest some ways to elaborate a theory of group creativity.

At the same time, my comparison of these philosophers leaves several areas that need elaboration, that aren't sufficiently addressed by either philosopher, and that the phenomenon of group creativity makes especially clear.

1. *Process Versus Product.* Both Dewey and Collingwood developed theories that compare all creativity to a conception of language that I have interpreted as group creativity. But despite these many similarities, product creativity is not identical to group creativity—after all, the former *does* result in a product. The painter has to interact with physical materials, has many opportunities to revise his or her work, and even may discard it entirely upon completion. A theory of product creativity would have to build onto the theory of group creativity in this direction: To explore if, and how, this edit-and-revise process changes the nature of the work—the "experience," in Dewey's terms. Although the core creative processes may be the same, there are sure to be some differences (I explore these further in chap. 5).

2. *Problem-Finding Versus Problem Solving.* At the beginning of an improv scene, there is no dramatic frame; but within a minute or so, many parameters are already established. By turn (8), we know that Andy is a bus driver, and that Bob is a potential passenger, who may not be able to afford the bus fare (see Example 4.1). At this point, the actors have created a problem for themselves, and they have to spend the rest of the scene solving that problem. In fact, in most creative genres, the creative process is a constant balance between finding a problem and solving that problem, and then finding a new problem during the solving of the last one; Picasso's film is a good example of this constant tension. Getzels and Csikszentmihalyi (1976) observed that artistic styles fell on a continuum between relatively problem

finding and relatively problem solving; but all the artists they studied, regardless of where they fell on the continuum, had to find and then solve a problem to generate a completed painting. The theories of Dewey and Collingwood make too sharp a division between the two, seeming to claim that if *any* degree of planning or predetermination is involved, then it's not real art.

3. Collaboration. The theories of Dewey and Collingwood focus on collaboration between the artist and the audience, rather than collaboration among a community of artists or performers. Of course, both men believed that all members of a community are artists, and both made explicit claims to this effect—that in truly perceiving a work of art, the perceiver becomes just as much an artist as the creator of the work. Yet Dewey and Collingwood do not explain the constant, spontaneous, immediate communication that results in the collaborative emergence of an ensemble performance. A painter may have an image of the eventual audience while he works, but this is quite different from having another musician play a rhythmic pattern that was not expected, and using that pattern to find new inspiration for where to go next.

The problem is that neither Dewey nor Collingwood developed an adequate theory of symbolic interaction. Such a theory would include descriptions of how intersubjectivity is achieved through communication, how group behaviors are emergent from individual actions, and the interactional semiotic mechanisms of situated language use. The theory presented in chapter 3 is an initial attempt to address such properties of interaction. Once such a theory is in place, then perhaps one could make an argument that the nature of the communication between a painter and the museum-goer is the same as that between ensemble performers—and say exactly how it's similar in some ways, and different in others (this is the topic of chap. 5). A sufficient communication theory of art would need to be capable of making these distinctions.

4. The Role of Ready-Mades. Collingwood, in particular, was overly simplistic on this point. Most jazz musicians can't imagine the possibility of never playing a phrase or motif that had ever been played before—that's not the way jazz works. Jazz is heavily motif-based, but that does not diminish the creativity of the performers.

Even the most overused verbal clichés can require creativity in use. In the early 1990s, a common cliché was to add the single word, "NOT," after a friend's utterance that you thought was patently false. But you can't insert "NOT" just anywhere; it takes creativity to know when an utterance can appropriately be followed by this single word, and one often laughs at a particularly creative instance (Sawyer, 2001a). Collingwood's distinction between art and craft cannot be maintained without resolution of this issue.

The focus on group creativity suggests some fruitful areas for further study. Although not prevalent in Western cultures, cross-cultural study indicates that performance genres employing elements of improvisation are quite common worldwide (see chap. 6). The focus in aesthetics and creativity research on product creativity is not surprising, given that our purposes are often to understand the histories of our own creative genres, and to identify and encourage creativity in our own societies. However, aesthetic theories that are restricted to product-oriented domains may be Eurocentric, and seem to imply that oral cultures are somehow less creative, or less respectable, or less deserving of analysis. Theories that claim to be directed at underlying universals in the psychological and social processes of creativity must be cognizant of all manifestations of creativity, including both product and performance creativity.

Both Dewey's and Collingwood's theories suggest that the psychological and social processes operating in group creativity and in product creativity may be more than superficially similar. Both authors were writing in the same time period that the Russian psychologist Lev Vygotsky developed his now-influential theories of mind as internalized social interaction (although Vygotsky was not widely available in English until the 1960s). Vygotsky's (1978, 1986) model of thought as internalized interaction also suggests that the individual artist or scientist always works with an internal mental model of the field and domain processes (Csikszentmihalyi & Sawyer, 1995; Moran & John-Steiner, in press; see chap. 5). Dewey and Collingwood both argued that artists who do not internalize such a model are not likely to generate products judged as creative.

In addition to its usefulness to aesthetic theory, a focus on group creativity helps to elaborate the claim that everyday life is aesthetic—a claim made by both Dewey and Collingwood. Everyday small talk is, of course, a group improvisation, perhaps accounting for Dewey's many conversation metaphors. We all know that many everyday settings involve improvisational interaction and creativity, including teaching, collaborating, parenting, and leadership (Sawyer, 2001a; see chap. 7). In spite of Dewey's strong claims for the aesthetic value of everyday experience, neither psychology nor aesthetics has had much to say about the creativity of everyday life. Many of us have intuitive notions that one teacher may be more creative than another; but how can we explain creative teaching as product creativity? A view of creative teaching as a set of recorded techniques—products like curriculum, lesson plans, or weekly goals—is not coincident with our memories of creative teachers, or for that matter creative parents, leaders, or managers. A teacher or a manager who sticks to a predetermined script will be unable to respond effectively to the unique needs of each situation.

In this chapter, I focused primarily on two books: Dewey's *Art as Experience* (1934) and Collingwood's *The Principles of Art* (1938). Could these two books—published 4 years apart in the 1930s—be partly responsible for the postwar "culture of spontaneity" (Belgrad, 1998)—Black Mountain and beat poets, bebop musicians, abstract expressionists, modern dance, installation art, the emphasis on composition as process in poetry and prose writing? All of these forms of improvisation emphasized "the process of the subjective artist as well as the content of his objectified art—through improvising, the creator becomes a performer" (Brustein, 1963, p. 28).

In 1940, Clement Greenberg wrote that literature was the "dominant art" of the time, and that avant-garde painting—the "chief victim of literature"—was defined by its "revolt against the dominance of literature"—in practice a turn to formalism and away from propositional content (Greenberg, 1986b, p. 28). Greenberg argued that the avant-garde turned to music as its model, a purely formal art that would allow an escape from literature. If Greenberg were writing today, he would perhaps observe that performance is the dominant art of our time. The visual arts have been heavily influenced by the creative potential of performance art, resulting in installation-specific pieces, or multimedia works that integrate video images or taped sounds. The critic Michael Kimmelman wrote in 1998, "Art today often seems to aspire to the conditions of theater and film" (p. 32). Performance may be taking over the role of "dominant art" that Greenberg once assigned to literature. If so, we have even more motivation to study group creativity and its place among the arts.

5

Group Creativity as
Mediated Action

In this chapter, I explore connections between group creativity and product creativity, building on chapter 4's claim that everyday social encounters involve a kind of creativity. I begin by observing that product creativity involves interaction over time. One creator develops a novel product, and the product is then communicated to other creators who work in the same area. The subsequent creations of these other individuals then respond to, and elaborate on, this product; this process results in *diachronic interaction*, a creative dialogue over time, with the "conversation" mediated by products rather than by spoken language. I compare this historical interaction to the more immediate symbolic interaction that occurs during group creativity. Because interaction among participants is immediate—and in music, simultaneous and in parallel—it is *synchronic interaction*.

I identify several parallels between group creativity and historical change in product domains, based on the nature of mediated action in both. In group creativity—synchronically mediated action—interaction between creating agents is immediate, durationally constrained to the moment of creation, and is mediated by linguistic or musical signs (as in Fig. 3.1). The process of creation is coincident with the moment of reception and interpretation by other performers and the audience. In product creativity, interaction between creating agents occurs over time, the interaction is mediated by ostensible creative products (in the case of linguistic creativity, text artifacts such as novels or po-

	Synchronic (Performance)	Diachronic (Product)
Type of interaction	Immediate (single reception)	Delayed (multiple receptions)
Mediation	Ephemeral signs	Ostensible products
Creative process	Coincident with product	Distinct from/generates product

FIG. 5.1. Defining contrasts of synchronic and diachronic creativity.

ems), and the process of creation is distinct temporally and spatially from the receipt and interpretation of the product by other individuals (see Fig. 5.1).

I begin the chapter by discussing sociocultural psychology, and how it relates to the model of group creativity presented in chapter 3. I then discuss recent approaches to product creativity which emphasize the social processes involved. This discussion suggests that group creativity could be viewed as the diachronic creative process in microcosm. Following the presentation of this model, I discuss six *interactional dimensions of contrast* which apply to both group creativity and to historical change in product domains. By formally characterizing the similarities and differences between group creativity and product creativity, the semiotic mediation model of chapter 3 suggests some novel perspectives on the creative process, with implications for the analysis of diachronic change in scientific and artistic fields.

SOCIOCULTURAL PSYCHOLOGY AND GROUP CREATIVITY

Sociocultural psychologists have identified group creativity in many social interactions, including informal conversation, classroom collaboration, and workplace teams (Rogoff, 1990, 1998; Wertsch, 1998). In all of these social encounters, a collective creative process involving semiotic mediation results in an emergent, ephemeral interaction. Socioculturalists have shown that many social interactions are characterized by emergence, unpredictability, and a high degree of contingency: Although a retrospective examination reveals a coherent interaction, each social act provides a range of creative options, any one of which could have resulted in a radically different performance.

Sociocultural psychologists draw on the symbolic interactionist tradition in their focus on *actions* or *events* as the basic units of analysis. Sociocultural theorists have also drawn on semiotics, sociolinguistics, and the writings of Vygotsky (1978, 1986). These psychologists have attempted to expand psychology to take into account how meaning is generated in social contexts. In this approach, "the irreducible unit of analysis of *mediated action* must serve as the focus ... [the focus is on] an inherent tension between uniquely situated acts on the part of an individual or individuals on the one hand and the socioculturally provided mediational means on the other" (Wertsch, 1992, p. 279).

The focus on action is an attempt to avoid a conceptual separation between individuals and their contexts (Rogoff, 1990, 1998). In an attempt to avoid the individual–environment boundary implied by the term *internalization*, Rogoff (1995) proposed the term *participatory appropriation* to describe how children, by participating in interactions with the physical and social environment, develop social and cognitive skills. Socioculturalists focus "on the *process* (rather than the products) of creative planning.... Planning is inherently a creative process that involves foresight as well as improvisation" (Baker-Sennett, Matusov, & Rogoff, 1992, p. 95). For example, in Rogoff's approach to *collaborative planning*, she conceptualized this activity as a collectively generated creative product (Rogoff, 1995; Baker-Sennett, Matusov, & Rogoff, 1992).

The sociocultural approach suggests that the study of group creativity has implications for psychology more generally. Socioculturalists emphasize that all group interaction displays emergent qualities (Sawyer, 2002b). In social interaction as in group creativity, an "emergent" is generated by the symbolic interaction of the group. The emergent is ephemeral, changes with each utterance, and emerges from collective interaction. It is a social fact, not determined by any single individual. The emergent constrains participants on many levels; for example, in a conversation, the emergent constrains each individual speaker with its topic structure, relative role and status assignments, invocations of prior interactions, and voicings of recognized social roles or characters (see Fig. 3.2).

Sociocultural psychologists have emphasized collective action through a methodology that focuses on analyzing group processes and socially situated events. Their empirical studies have revealed that all social interactions display improvisational elements; many of these studies have focused on emergence and collaboration in classrooms and in families. Such interactions are unpredictable, contingent, involve complex communication processes, and result in the emergence of group phenomena that are difficult to analyze in terms of the participating individuals (Sawyer, 1997a). Socioculturalists have studied how group collaboration emerges from the interactions and contributions of the participants. The sociocultural tradition suggests that group creativity is rather common and accessible; in contrast to creativity in privileged domains in the arts and sciences, all humans have some ability to participate creatively in groups.

PARALLELS WITH DIACHRONIC CREATIVE INTERACTION

I use the term *diachronic creative change* to refer to historical processes mediated by products, and the term *synchronic creative change* to refer to the microinteractional flux of group creativity, which I described in chapter 3 using the concepts of emergence and creative entailment. Socioculturalists have emphasized the parallels in the nature of the social processes involved in both, by focusing on collaborating groups and emphasizing how those groups generate collaboratively created, emergent outcomes. In learning contexts, knowledge is the emergent outcome; in organizational contexts, problem solutions are the emergent outcome. In the following, I take a slightly different approach; I contrast the *timescales* of the two, and the nature of their *mediating artifacts*—synchronic interaction is mediated by ephemeral signs, and diachronic interaction is mediated by ostensible products.

This representation of group creativity as mediated action displays interesting parallels with recent creativity theories, known variously as *systems* or *ecological* theories, which focus on the sociointeractional aspects of the creative process. Several researchers have noted that creativity is fundamentally dependent on the social interaction of a group of individuals. Most of these theories acknowledge the influence of Campbell's (1960) "evolutionary" model of scientific discovery. Campbell applied the basic evolutionary paradigm of *variation, selection, retention* to the process of scientific creativity. This metaphor has been extended in the *systems view* of creativity (Csikszentmihalyi, 1988, 1990a), the *ecological model* (Harrington, 1990), and the *inter-*

actionist model (Woodman & Schoenfeldt, 1989). For example, Harrington (1990) examined the "cocreative process" in product creativity. As I noted in chapter 4, Collingwood (1938) stated the essence of these approaches, writing that "The work of artistic creation is not a work performed in any exclusive or complete fashion in the mind of the person whom we call the artist. That idea is a delusion bred of individualistic psychology. . . . This activity is a corporate activity belonging not to any one human being but to a community" (p. 324). Much earlier, Auguste Comte (1842/1854) noted that all creativity is collaborative to some degree:

> No partial intelligence can so separate itself from the general mass as not to be essentially carried on with it, even if it be, as an extreme case, that of a wise physician compelled to live among madmen. . . . The most profound thinker will therefore never forget that all men must be regarded as coadjutors in discovering truth (Vol. 2, p. 522)

Comte is known as the father of sociology, and the systems view is essentially a sociological perspective. However, within the psychology of creativity today, it is generally associated with psychologists like Csikszentmihalyi (1988, 1990a; Csikszentmihalyi & Sawyer, 1995) and Gardner (1993). Like the socioculturalists, Csikszentmihalyi proposed that creativity cannot be operationalized at the psychological level alone; rather, individual creativity must be defined with respect to a system which includes not only the individual, but also social and cultural factors which influence the creative process and help to define creativity.[12] Csikszentmihalyi separated these influences into the *field*, the social group of individuals participating in this type of creative activity, and the *domain* (see Fig. 5.2). The domain is constituted by the set of ostensible products created by members of the field, and selected by the field to enter the domain through a collective, social decision-making process. The creative process involves the generation of a novel product by the individual; the evaluation, or "filtering," of the product by the field; and the retention of selected products by adding them to the domain. Thus the creative process involves a continual cycle of person → field → domain → person, which is mediated by ostensible, more or less permanent creative products.

---

[12]See Sawyer (in press) for additional elaboration of the parallels between contemporary creativity theory and sociocultural theory.

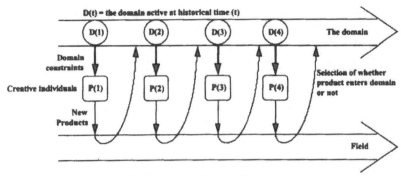

FIG. 5.2. Diachronic (historical) interaction.

Although this model is an effective framework for analyzing creativity in product domains, it does not directly address group creativity, because there are no ostensible products to mediate creative interaction. For example, although Csikszentmihalyi's model focuses on social forces, it does not adequately represent the constant musical interaction between the members of a creating ensemble. Harrington's (1990) focus on creative ecosystems and interpersonal influences is compatible with this characteristic of group creativity; but his discussion focused on the longer term, diachronic interaction characteristic of scientific and artistic creativity. The synchronic nature of interaction during group improvisation is distinct from the type of social interaction that occurs over time in product domains; the real-time nature of the interaction within the creative group is a distinguishing feature of group creativity. To adequately characterize group creativity, socially oriented theories of creativity must incorporate a theory of synchronic symbolic interaction.

To the extent that recording technology allows the creation of objective artifacts from performance texts, the systems model can be used to represent historical changes in performance genres. For example, in jazz, the field would be composed of the musicians, the listening consumer, the magazine critics, and the club patrons, whereas the domain would be the set of albums available, and perhaps books and articles written about performances.[13] However, models of dia-

---

[13]Gioia (1988) emphasized the importance of albums for this reason, suggesting that "the existence of the recording industry was necessary if jazz were to develop at all" (p. 64) and that "it has been the recording, rather than the live performance, that has propelled the development of jazz" (p. 65).

chronic creative change do not address what occurs at the interactional level of group creativity, when creative interaction is mediated by ephemeral sign systems.

Group creativity plays a role in the generation of many creative products. In many product domains, the creative process involves collaboration and brainstorming. This is particularly true in scientific laboratories (Crease, 1993; Csikszentmihalyi & Sawyer, 1995; Dunbar, 1995), in complex multimedia productions like movies and music videos (Becker, 1982), and in complex organizations (Weick, 2001). These creative processes involve group creativity, like any other social interaction. Some socioculturalists have studied sociointeractional processes in groups that are organized with the explicit goal of generating a created product. The group processes found in a scientific laboratory have been explicitly compared to performance (Crease, 1993). In this sense, many product domains involve both synchronic (ensemble) interaction and diachronic (historical) interaction. Thus the study of group creativity can help us understand how social and interactional processes contribute to product creativity (also see chap. 7).

The flow of creative interaction in a group is processually isomorphic in diachronic and synchronic creative interaction; a juxtaposition of Figs. 3.1 and 5.2 reveals the parallels. The primary distinction is that diachronic creative interaction is mediated by products, which constitute a domain, and group creativity is mediated by the discursive signs of language or music, and by the emergent. Csikszentmihalyi's domain concept corresponds to the (historically determined through diachronic creative change) genre constraints of chapter 3's model. Following Csikszentmihalyi's terminology, one could refer to the emergent as a "microdomain." Of course, this microdomain is at all times subject to macrodomain (i.e., genre) constraints. One could also think of the participants in the group as a "microfield," since they play an analogous role: Through a collective social process, they determine which creative entailments (or "microproducts") enter the emergent.

PARALLEL DIMENSIONS OF SYNCHRONIC AND DIACHRONIC CREATIVE INTERACTION

I have argued that both the synchronic interactions of group creativity and the diachronic interactions of product creativity are forms of semiotically mediated action. The juxtaposition of Figs. 3.1 and 5.2 suggests that analogous interactional processes may be involved.

Synchronic interaction	Diachronic interaction
Receptivity of emergent to novelty	Receptivity of genre to novelty
Permanence of creative entailment	Permanence of domain change
Range of possible indexical entailments	Range of possible innovative products
Size of ready-mades	Size of ideational configurations
Involvement of audience	Involvement of field
Degree of creative involvement of performer	Degree of creative involvement of creator

FIG. 5.3. Interactional dimensions of contrast.

Based on the parallels between Figs. 3.1 and 5.2, I identify six contrast dimensions for semiotically mediated creativity; this list is intended to be representative rather than exhaustive. Each dimension can be applied to both synchronic and diachronic creative interaction. The dimensions discussed are summarized in Fig. 5.3.

For both group and product creativity, each dimension partially constitutes the difference between *maximally structured* and *minimally structured* interaction. I refer to maximally structured performance as *ritualized*, and minimally structured performance as *improvisational* (I further discuss this contrast in chap. 6). I follow Kuhn's (1960) terminology in referring to maximally structured product domains as *paradigmatic*, and minimally structured domains as *nonparadigmatic* (preparadigmatic or revolutionary).

Receptivity to Novelty

In group creativity, this dimension represents the ease with which a novel creative entailment can be added to the emergent. In product creativity, this dimension represents the ease with which a novel creative product can be added to the domain.

Maximally improvisational performance genres, while always manifesting recognizable style and genre constraints, are by definition receptive to innovations, and in fact might be said to require innovations. Among American musics, the emergents created during jazz improvisation are perhaps the most receptive to novelty. Ritualized performance genres are more firmly defined and are more difficult to change than loosely structured improvisational genres; cultural conventions often define novelty as a departure from a reified form, and thus inherently bad. This is equally the case with primitive forms of ritual (e.g., Bauman & Sherzer, 1974; Caton, 1990; Kaeppler, 1987) as with the Western orchestral repertoire. However, even ritualized performance genres experience slippage in form, of which the members of the culture are sometimes unaware; for example, the Rotinese couplets described in Fox (1974), or gradual and subtle changes in orchestral style that have been brought into focus by the original music movement.

In product domains, the existence of a set of ostensible products or text artifacts, with objective existence apart from any single interactional context, limits the possibility of diachronic change. Slippage cannot occur in the same fashion when a product is available for reference.[14] These products, independent of any single context of interaction, constitute the domain studied by creativity theory. The permanence of these objects across interactions results in the historical nature of interactional processes in diachronic creativity. Nonetheless, as with group creativity, product domains vary in their receptivity to novelty. Modern nonrepresentational art perhaps represents an extreme of receptivity; contrast this with the ecclesiastical art prior to the Florentine Renaissance, in which content and form were largely specified by the domain.

Permanence of Change

In group creativity, this dimension represents the duration that a creative entailment, once having entered the emergent, remains in the emergent to the extent that it influences the other performers subsequent to the entailing event. In product domains, this dimension represents the duration of historical time that a novel creative product remains in the domain, influencing later creative individuals.

In a ritualized ensemble genre, an innovative entailment, once accepted, is likely to remain in the emergent across a long subsequent

---

[14]Although it is a current theoretical issue in text studies to what extent there is slippage in the presence of a text artifact. Derrida (1978), for example, seemed to argue that the existence of text artifacts does not qualitatively change the interactional processes involved (diachronically or synchronically).

period of interaction. In contrast, in a more improvisational genre, because innovative entailments are accepted more readily, subsequent entailing events will subsume or "push out" earlier entailments more quickly.

In paradigmatic product domains, a product must satisfy numerous criteria before it is accepted into the domain by the field. Because changes are less frequent, each product that successfully enters the domain is likely to stay in the domain, perhaps until the next revolutionary period. In nonparadigmatic product domains, the criteria for product acceptance are much less certain and provisional. Because novel products are being accepted at a higher rate, the domain is changing more rapidly, and each product is likely to lose its relevance more quickly.

The "permanence of change" dimension has interesting implications for diachronic change in ensemble performance domains. Although there are no products to fix the domain objectively, there is nonetheless change over time. Inasmuch as ritualized performance genres are more resistant to novelty, once an entailment is accepted during a performance, it is more likely to remain in the genre for a long period of time, influencing later performances within the genre. In contrast, an innovation in an improvisational genre is less likely to have an effect beyond its performance event. Saussure's (1959) classic analysis of language argued that specific linguistic interactions have very little effect on diachronic change; this is characteristic of improvisational performance genres. His observation suggests that everyday language use is one of the more improvisational performance genres in our culture; changes occur over historical time, but are not under the control of any one individual, and may not even be noticed by the community of speakers. Saussure focused on synchronic linguistics, and his influence in the early 20th century contributed to a neglect of diachronic "domain" elements such as the influence of the culture's linguistic ideology and the hegemony of standard register (Silverstein, 1979). Although perhaps inadequate to describe reified linguistic registers associated with high social status, which are more ritualized and seem to display more stability over time, Saussure's view is effective in describing low registers such as informal conversation, in which domain changes are relatively short-lived. In literate cultures, writing and other notational systems were applied first to more ritualized genres: High registers (in both music and language) were more likely to be recorded, and the upper social classes were more likely to be able to read these text artifacts. The most ritualized performance genres are the first to be transformed, through transcription, into product domains.

Range of Possible Innovation

Ritualized ensemble genres, by virtue of their rigidity, do not provide as many opportunities for individual performers to act in creative ways. As a result, the potential for an innovative creative entailment fades asymptotically (the indeterminacy of performance causes there to be always some interactionally entailing effect). Rather than indexical entailment, texts in ritualized ensemble genres display a high density of multilayered poetic tropes which constrain the interactional originality of the performer on several interactional and functional levels simultaneously. These tropes simultaneously constrain the potential interpretations of the coperformers and the audience. Tambiah (1985) suggested that this "pragmatic dimension" of ritual may be its defining characteristic, as it serves a social and cultural function largely independent from individual intentionality. Because of the multilayered poetic organization of ritualized texts, such genres restrict individual performers' abilities to influence the emergent through innovative creative entailments. One result of such indexical poetics is that the possible audience interpretations of the performance are relatively constrained.[15]

In contrast to ritualized performance, more improvisational genres provide for interactional creativity by providing individual performers with a broad range of possible indexical entailments at each moment. Much of the interest for the audience rests in the complex interplay of competing indexical entailments and presuppositions emanating from and impinging on individual performers (as shown in Fig. 3.2).

---

[15]For Tambiah, *ossification* of ritual occurs when the multilayered tropes of the ritual begin to constrain the possible interpretations and meanings of the ritual. Tambiah suggested that this is the natural historic tendency of all ritual forms: progressively to lose *semantic* content, which is replaced by these *pragmatic* constraints on interpretation. In contrast, in a period of revival, the semantic content of the ritual form becomes salient, and the ossified tropic layers are deconstructed. If Tambiah were correct in suggesting that there is a universal tendency toward ossification, performance genres which have retained improvisational elements over long periods of time would be of particular interest.

Change in product domains can be conceived using these same semiotic concepts. Paradigmatic domains constrain innovation by more rigidly specifying the materials, techniques, and subjects considered appropriate for the domain. Nonparadigmatic domains, by virtue of the absence of a clearly specified paradigm, allow the individual to create a wider range of possible products. As implied by the juxtaposition of Figs. 3.1 and 5.2, the innovative component of an original creative product can be thought of as a "diachronic entailment."

Size of Ready-Mades and Density of Decision Points

Some improvisational ensemble genres (e.g., Javanese *gamelan*, Rotinese parallel oratory, Slavic epic poetry) require the performer to construct the performance using pre-existing units, which will be recognized by any member of the culture as being part of the performance genre. The creativity of the performer rests in innovative combinations of these *ready-mades*. In such genres, the ready-mades cannot be changed, and new ones cannot be created by the performer. These performance genres manifest a *lower density* of decision points than a genre without ready-mades, in which the performer can make an innovative decision at virtually every note (referred to by Powers, 1980, as "modal genres"). Jazz and *ragas* are of this latter type.[16]

In theories of product creativity, the *unit of ideation* corresponds to the notion of ready-mades. In a nonparadigmatic product domain, these units are less complex, and have fewer layers of hierarchical chunking. Paradigmatic domains provide the individual scientist or artist with larger prespecified units, whether established theories, laboratory methods, or visual themes. This is the benefit of establishing a paradigm: The use of these progressively more complex units, collectively embellished and integrated by the individuals working in the field, provides each individual with greater cognitive efficiency. Sociologist Howard Becker (1986) described his creative process in these

---

[16]In jazz, several writers have noted that each individual performer tends to develop a personal set of ready-mades which are repeatedly used (see chap. 2). However, a dimension such as "degree of use of personal ready-mades" is orthogonal to this dimension, since these ready-mades are not culturally specified or constrained, but are idiosyncratic creations which may be changed or replaced by the performer.

terms: "I am always collecting such prefabricated parts for use in future arguments. Much of my reading is governed by a search for such useful modules" (p. 144).

This dimension roughly corresponds to the distinction in creativity theory between *problem finding* and *problem solving* creative processes (Getzels, 1964; Csikszentmihalyi & Sawyer, 1995). The decision points in an improvisational performance correspond to the moments of problem finding during the product-generating creative process, and the execution of ready-mades corresponds to periods of problem solving. Exploration of this dimension during improvisational performance could provide a better understanding of how problem finding and problem solving creative processes are combined in product domains.

Involvement of the Audience or Field

Brenneis (1990) suggested that the relatively passive role of European audiences may have caused Western researchers to neglect the pervasive importance of the audience in musical genres of other cultures. The same observation has been made with respect to verbal art (Duranti & Brenneis, 1986). The improvisationality of a performance genre is generally proportional to the degree of audience involvement. In some performance genres, the audience–performer barrier is fluid; this is generally the case with unmarked conversational interaction, because the listener is expected to contribute with appropriate body posture, eye gaze, and verbal back channeling. In more improvised genres, the performers are more aware of themselves as responding to the audience; in some genres, for example the Sufi devotional songs or *qawwali*, the performers believe that they are acting as vehicles for the spiritual state of the audience (Qureshi, 1986, 1987). The cultural function of ritualized performance also includes a desired effect on the audience members. However, in improvisational genres that effect is chosen spontaneously and collectively by the performing group, and that choice can be partially influenced by the audience's reactions. As such, we would expect to observe the indexical entailments of the performers acting not only on coperformers, but also on the audience.

In product domains, there is significant variation in the degree to which other members of the field influence an individual's creative

process. Many scientific domains are characterized by frequent communication and collaboration (Crease, 1993; Csikszentmihalyi & Sawyer, 1995). Even working in isolation, an individual is usually aware of
the reception his creations are likely to receive. The comparison with
group creativity suggests that nonparadigmatic domains would be
characterized by more collaboration and informal communication,
whereas paradigmatic domains would allow for more isolation and
less awareness of the social field of one's peers.

Degree of Creative Involvement of the Individual

Musical and verbal ensemble genres can be characterized as either
defining and constraining the role an individual can play, or allowing
for individual personality and creativity to determine the nature of
the role. Highly ritualized systems of linguistic interaction, such as the
nine Javanese "politeness" registers (Errington, 1985; Geertz, 1972)
maximize the social constraints on role performance, limiting the ability of the individual to make a creative statement. Improvisational
genres, by permitting a wider range of potential creative entailments,
allow a more personality-dominant type of performance. As musical
genres approach the improvisational extreme of the continuum, the
act of creation becomes progressively more coincident with the act of
performance.

Because of the presence of multiple individuals' entailments,
emergents often have a *heteroglossic* character (Bakhtin, 1981); i.e.,
multiple voices are simultaneously in play in group emergents. A
heteroglossic emergent provides the potential for complex individual
acts that combine voices in novel interactive patterns. Bakhtin argued
that a person's speech was always a voicing of someone else's
speech; even so, in heteroglossic speech environments there are always creative possibilities inherent in the blending of multiple voices.
Note that ritualized interactional genres tend to limit an individual's
speech to a single appropriate voice.

Product domains project different degrees of constraint on individuals active in that domain. Kuhn characterized paradigmatic domains
as highly constraining on individuals, requiring more of a problem-
solving orientation, while nonparadigmatic domains are less constraining, and require a problem-finding orientation. Nonparadigmatic
domains also demonstrate a heteroglossic character: Because the do-

main has not unified around a single coherent paradigm, there are usually multiple competing "subdomains" and "subfields" active. Much of the problem finding and innovation during nonparadigmatic periods involves these heteroglossic combinations.

CONCLUSION

In this chapter I have explored the connections between group creativity and creativity in the arts and sciences. I built on the philosophical discussions of chapter 4 by elaborating some implications of the theoretical model of chapter 3. I used that model to compare and contrast microinteractional processes in group creativity with macrohistorical changes in product creativity. I noted that both were forms of mediated action; group creativity is *synchronic* interaction mediated by ephemeral signs, such as language, music, or gesture, whereas product creativity is *diachronic* interaction mediated by products. Based on similarities between my model of group creativity (in Fig. 3.1) and systems theories of product creativity (in Fig. 5.2), I postulated a "microdomain," the emergent, and a "microfield," the coparticipants in interaction, paralleling the concepts of domain and field in the analysis of product creativity. The isomorphism inherent in the nature of mediation suggested six dimensions of contrast which characterize both group creativity and product creativity.

Although I have focused on creativity, the connection to sociocultural theory suggests that all human activity displays elements of group creativity. The recent focus on mediated action, sociocultural action, and situated cognition within psychology suggests that the psychological processes operating in group creativity and product creativity may be more than superficially similar (cf. Sawyer, in press). Vygotsky's model of thought as internalized interaction (1978, 1986) suggests that the individual artist or scientist always works with an internal mental model of the field and the domain (Csikszentmihalyi & Sawyer, 1995; John-Steiner, 1985). Artists and scientists who do not internalize such a model are not likely to generate products judged as creative. Likewise, during a group performance, each participant must maintain internal models of the microdomain—the emergent—and the microfield—the other participants. Jazz musicians say they must be extremely aware of the emergent musical structure as it evolves from moment to moment, in order to contribute coherent and yet innovative musical ideas. And jazz musicians universally say they play better with musicians they have played with before, indicating the importance of the internalization of the microfield (Berliner, 1994; Monson, 1991, 1996; Sawyer, 1992).

The study of both group creativity and product creativity as forms of mediated action may have implications for a wide range of socially contextualized activities. For example, this approach may allow us to formalize folk notions of creativity in social domains where existing creativity theory has been inadequate, such as teaching, collaborating, parenting, and facilitating/leadership. Many of us have intuitive notions that one teacher may be more creative than another; but macro-domain analyses of creative teaching are dependent on visible, recorded products, such as curriculum specifications and the requirements for teacher certification. A view of creative teaching as a set of recorded techniques which are passed on in schools of education is not coincident with our memories of creative teachers, or for that matter creative parents, leaders, or managers. The parallel dimensions of contrast outlined earlier suggest why it is so difficult to improve these domains: The more improvisational a group genre is, the more difficult it is to effect change on a macrodomain level. Teaching and managing require improvisationality to be effective; a teacher or a manager who sticks to a predetermined script will be unable to respond effectively to the unique needs of each situation. This could help to explain why improving creativity in domains such as teaching or managing remains such an elusive goal. In chapter 7, I further explore group creativity in education and in organizations.

The comparison of group creativity and product creativity has several implications for psychology. The creative process and the psychology of creativity have proven to be difficult to study directly due to the long timeframes involved, and due to the fact that the germination of a single creative thought in some fields can take several years. This has led to methods of study which are historical (Gruber & Davis, 1988), based on analysis of the final product (Getzels & Csikszentmihalyi, 1976), or are psychometric. Some of the most valuable studies have focused on the social processes of scientific practice (Crease, 1993; Dunbar, 1995; Latour & Woolgar, 1979; Suchman, 1987), however, these studies are based on time-consuming ethnographic and observational methodologies.

To the extent that group creative performance can be viewed as the creative process in microcosm, observation of group creativity could provide valuable insights into creative fields in which the creative process takes too long to observe directly. For example, the study of improvisation as a visible creative process could be helpful in understanding aspects of the individual creative process which are salient in group creativity, but elusive in product creativity. These include the relative importance of intuitive and analytic creativity within different domains, the psychological balance of structure and innovation, and the differential interaction of levels and units of ideation and selection. Socioculturalists have made the same observation with regard to studies of cognitive processes more generally; whereas it is quite difficult to observe the moment-to-moment processes of thought occurring in an individual's mind, thinking that is embedded in a collaborating group is a publicly accessible symbolic interaction (e.g., Engeström, 1994; also see chap. 7).

Diachronic change in creative fields is also difficult to study. A complete theory of creative change should be able to answer questions such as: How does a domain integrate innovations? When are innovations judged appropriate despite their breaking the rules? Is there a relationship between certain structural characteristics of creative domains, and the types of innovation permitted? Is there a relationship between the structural characteristics of creative domains, and the types of individuals who are successful in the domain? If group interaction can be viewed as a microcosm of the interactional processes that occur in product creativity, many new avenues of empirical study would be available.

A focus on semiotic mediation has always been central in studies of sociocultural action. For example, those studying sociocultural processes in planning and cognition have used primarily ethnographic approaches and have closely focused on transcripts of conversation. Linguistically mediated interaction can be studied empirically using analytic methods from fields such as discourse analysis, folklore, and anthropology. These methods are well-established in the study of verbal and musical performance forms in non-Western cultures, and could provide a starting point for this study.

I conclude by noting that I have spoken of group creativity and product creativity as if they are mutually exclusive. However, most creative human activity involves elements of both group creativity and product creativity. Many group performances are based on a created product, and some group performances are designed to generate a final product.

For example, a string quartet involves group interaction even though it is performed from a score, and the score is a composed product that results from product creativity. Yet, the score is not the same thing as the work; the score must be performed by a group to be realized as a created product. In literary theory, this is the sense in which a "text" emerges from the interaction of a reader with a "text artifact" (Fish, 1980; Silverstein, 1993, 1997). For example, Barthes (1979) made a distinction between *work* (a text artifact) and *Text* (capital "T" in original), and Fish (1980) advocated a shift in focus from what texts mean to what they do, making the text "an *event*, something that *happens* to, and with the participation of, the reader" (p. 25). In aesthetic theory, this is sometimes referred to as a distinction between *type* and *token* (e.g., Margolis, 1980; Wollheim, 1980), following an established philosophical usage in which a token is a realized "instance" of a type, an abstract entity or property of a kind that can be instantiated. (In chap. 4, I showed that this distinction between text and text artifact, type and token, was central to both Dewey and Collingwood.)

And group performances sometimes result in the creation of products. In chapter 2, I described how group riffs emerge from the repeated performances of jazz ensembles, and how improv theater groups sometimes use improvisation in rehearsal as a way of developing scripted material. Even when there is no notational system, an ensemble genre becomes product-like when a repeated, ritualized form evolves. These regular forms are independent from any particular performance, or *decontextualizable* (Bauman & Briggs, 1997), and thus have some of the properties of products like scores and scripts. But because there are no fixed ostensible products, these ritualized forms are qualitatively different from performance based on a composition. Thus my contrast between group creativity and product creativity is related to the contrast between improvisation and composition, an issue that has been explored by several musicologists (see chap. 3).

In the improvised genres of group creativity that I focus on in this book, there are no ostensible products remaining after the performance. In jazz and improv theater, most performances are not recorded and the performers cannot interact through fixed products. In such genres, historical change is not mediated by created products; historical mediation by ostensible products is unique to product domains, where the product is generated by, and comes temporally after, the (collaborative) process. In improvisational creativity, the process *is* the product.

Because there is no fixed ostensible product, even ritualized performance forms are qualitatively different from product-based performance. Yet once a ritualized form has emerged over historical time, it nonetheless affects the group's creative process. In the next chapter, I examine the contrast between relatively improvised and relatively ritualized performances, in performance genres where there is no notation system and thus no product to mediate successive performances.

6

Degrees of Improvisation
in Group Creativity

I closed the last chapter by observing that some group performances, although unscripted, are nonetheless highly structured and may be repeated on multiple occasions with relatively little variation. Many unwritten musical traditions are relatively fixed, and do not involve improv as in a jazz ensemble. Yet every performance of an unscored traditional song involves some degree of group creativity—there is always variation in performance even when the traditional style and song are well-known to all the performers.

My goal in this chapter is to further explore differences between group interactions that are relatively improvised and those that are relatively fixed. Linguistic anthropologists have proposed several schemas to allow researchers to characterize different types of verbal interaction within a single framework (Caton, 1990; Hymes, 1962, 1972; Jakobson, 1960; McDowell, 1983; Silverstein, 1993; Tambiah, 1985). These models analyzed a variety of culturally situated linguistic forms, from everyday conversation to ritual, in an attempt to develop frameworks which could characterize the shifts in social purpose which covary with the underlying structures of different forms of language in context. Some musicologists have likewise proposed overarching frameworks to compare more and less improvisational genres (Nettl, 1974).

In this chapter, I elaborate these frameworks by exploring the *degree of improvisationality* of group creativity. By "degree of improvisationality," I refer to the fact that some genres of group creativity are highly improvised, with relatively few constraints or pre-existing bits or ready-mades, while others are relatively *ritualized*, so much so that they almost seem to be scripted. In chapter 5, I explored this dimension of group creativity with the purpose of drawing parallels with similar dimensions of contrast found in product creativity domains. Instead of a single dimension from improvised to ritualized, I proposed that there are a range of *contrast dimensions* for group creativity. In this chapter, I elaborate my discussion of the six contrast dimensions identified in chapter 5 and add five new contrast dimensions along which different types of performance can be contrasted. These 11 contrast dimensions are derived from the model presented in chapter 3. Rather than opposite ends of a continuum, improvisation and ritual represent points maximally opposed in a multidimensional space.

In the first section of this chapter, I briefly describe the 11 contrast dimensions (see Fig. 6.1). This discussion elaborates a theme from chapter 5: that group interactions can be located on a range of contrast

	Ritualized	Improvisational
1*	Ossification	Revivalism
2	Low creative involvement	High creative involvement
3	Indexically reflexive	Indexically entailing
4*	Narrow genre definition	Broad genre definition
5	Large ready-mades	Small ready-mades
6	Low audience involvement	High audience involvement
7*	Not ensemble oriented	Ensemble oriented
8	Resistant to novelty	Receptive to novelty
9	Changes long-lasting	Changes short-lived
10*	Notation	No notation
11*	High cultural valuation	Low valuation

FIG. 6.1. Contrast dimensions for musical and verbal performance. An asterisk indicates that this contrast dimension is new here and was not one of the six that appeared in chapter 5.

dimensions that roughly parallel the degree of improvisationality of the interaction. These 11 dimensions are not intended to be exhaustive; there may be other additional dimensions not discussed here. In the second section of the chapter, I discuss six different ethnographies of performance genres, three each of both music and of verbal art. The three genres of musical performance that I have selected include one that is highly ritualized, one that is highly improvised, and one intermediate genre; the three genres of verbal art also include one improvised, one ritualized, and one intermediate. I conclude by showing that both music and verbal art show similar patterns when analyzed using the 11 contrast dimensions. Thus this approach to group creativity reveals some intriguing similarities between music and verbal art, similarities not identified by approaches that focused on the syntax or semantics of musical and verbal language.

STRUCTURAL DIMENSIONS OF IMPROVISATIONAL PERFORMANCE

Each of the 11 dimensions in Fig. 6.1 partially constitutes the phenomenal dimension from *ritualized* to *improvisational*. Unlike the product creativity discussed in chapter 5—which results in musical scores, written prose novels, paintings, or room interiors—group creativity involves a creative process that generates an ephemeral product that will no longer exist after it is over.[17] Composed creative products have been more amenable to structural analysis, while group creativity has been neglected because traditional structural analysis is inadequate to understand this sort of semiotic practice. When analytic methods developed for compositions are applied to improvisations, one is fundamentally distracted from the indexical nature of performance that I emphasized in chapter 3.

Ossification Versus Revivalism

This contrast has been explored within anthropology as a way of explaining the permanence and change of cultural forms, particularly rit-

---

[17]Performers and audience members may retain memories of the performance, but these are not the same as the social fact of the performance itself, because they are psychological perceptions of that social fact; see chapter 7 for additional discussion of this important point.

ual performance. Tambiah (1985) analyzed historical shifts in ritual structure from the extreme of ossification to the opposite extreme of revivalism, and referred to *pragmatic* and *semantic* dimensions of ritual practice. Tambiah's "pragmatic dimension" refers to the way the poetic structure of a ritual text constrains the moment of interaction itself, in a form of indexicality referred to in chapter 3 as reflexive calibration. Reflexive calibration is a form of indexical entailment; rather than projecting a future flow for the interaction, a reflexive performance segment metapragmatically defines that segment itself. Reflexive calibration is present to some extent in all sign usage; for example, speaking in a socially recognized voice reflexively indexes the speaker as a member of a particular social group, and reflexively entails a relation to the addressee.

For Tambiah, ossification of ritual occurs when the reflexive metapragmatics of the ritual begin to constrain the possible interpretations and meanings of the ritual. Tambiah suggested that the natural tendency of all ritual forms was to progressively lose semantic content, which is replaced by reflexive indexical constraints on interpretation, ultimately becoming a "meaningless" formal structure. In contrast, in a period of revival, a new semantic content of the ritual form becomes salient (through forms of ideology such as fundamentalism), and the ossified structures of reflexive indexicality are deconstructed.

Bauman and Briggs (1997) referred to similar processes using the terms *decontextualization* and *entextualization*: "the process of rendering discourse extractable, of making a stretch of linguistic production into a unit—a *text*—that can be lifted out of its interactional setting" (p. 243). They summarized many formal characteristics of language which serve to entextualize speech, including framing, tropes, and indexical grounding. They argued that the performative frame is particularly effective at serving the function of entextualization (see also Kuipers, 1992, pp. 102–103). In my terms, entextualization turns an improvised performance into a ritualized one. Note that this use of the term *entextualization* diverges from that of Silverstein cited in chapter 3: Although he usually used the term to refer to *denotational* entextualization, a "construal of discursive interaction as a structure of expressions each of which is evaluable in terms of reference and modalized predication" (1993, p. 43), he used the term more generally to refer to real-time interactional processes which result in the creation of any text, whether "extractable" or not. To avoid overly script-like connotations, I prefer the term *ritualization* to entextualization, and I prefer the term *emergent* to text as used by the poststructuralists, to refer to an interactional social fact.

This dimension is a property of performative genres; written notational forms are not necessarily involved. Ossification is a property of performed ritual texts *qua* social facts, and is not comparable to the processes which generate composed products that purport to prescribe or represent a performance. Nonetheless, through processes of decontextualization, ritual performance texts take on some of the characteristics of composed products. Cultural rituals typically include both musical and verbal interaction, and the degree of improvisation in each mode tends to develop in parallel. If Tambiah were correct in suggesting that there is a universal tendency toward ossification, performance genres that have retained improvisational elements would be of particular interest.

Degree of Creative Involvement of Performer

Musical and verbal ensemble performance forms can be characterized as either defining and constraining the role an individual can play, or allowing for individual personality and creativity to determine the nature of the role. For example, elaborately specified systems of linguistic interaction, such as the nine Javanese "politeness" registers (Errington, 1985; Geertz, 1972) maximize the role performance aspect, constraining the ability of the individual to make an individual creative statement. Improvisational genres allow a more personality dominant type of performance, since performers may create hybrid social roles for themselves through dialogism or multiple voicing (Bakhtin, 1981). This is an "etic" rather than an "emic" category; as Brenneis (1990) and Nettl (1974) noted, even in improvisational genres performers may not have an awareness of themselves as creative forces. In some genres, such as Sufi devotional songs (Qureshi, 1986, 1987), musicians claim that their performance is a response to the audience, and that the performers are simply vessels performing an evocative, rather than expressive, role. The researcher cannot assume that the local culture will maintain a Western concept of individual agency.

Several researchers have posited a relationship between the formalization of ritual speech and the limitation of individual agency (Bloch, 1975; DuBois, 1992; McDowell, 1983). Bloch (1975) argued that ritualization, or *formalization*, served the function of constraining speaker creativity: "The formalization of speech ... dramatically restricts what can be said . . . if this mode of communication is adopted, there is hardly any *choice* of what can be said" (p. 17). In his formulation, this depersonalization of speech contributes to the political power of oratorical genres. DuBois (1992) referred to the formalized speech of divinations as "meaning without intention," arguing that in ritual speech, the role of performer becomes more distributed and social, more embedded in the performance context.

In unmarked improvisational genres such as everyday conversation, participants often have very little awareness of the degree of creativity they exercise through their indexical entailments. Rather, the tendency is to believe that individual action is determined by the constraints of indexical presupposition (see chap. 3).

Indexically Entailing Poetics Versus Indexically Reflexive Poetics

Ritualized performance forms, by virtue of their relative rigidity, do not provide as many opportunities for individual performers to act in creative ways. These constraints derive from social convention and formalized structure, and thus are of a different order from the constraints deriving from the creative entailments and emergents introduced anew in a given performance. Ritualized genres do not allow individual performers to perform actions which have indexically entailing force on other participants.[18] As a result, the vector of indexical entailment discussed earlier fades asymptotically in importance (the indeterminacy of all performance causes there to be always some potentially entailing effect). Rather than indexical entailment, we find in compositional forms a high degree of reflexively calibrating poetic indexicality, what Tambiah called the "pragmatic dimension" of ritual. This type of indexical poetics constrains the possible audience interpretations of the performance as well.

The more improvisational genres provide individual performers with a range of possible indexical entailments at each moment (see Fig.

---

[18]McDowell (1983) proposed that the formal/informal dichotomy be expanded to include three roughly parallel dimensions: accessibility, formalization, and efficacy. Like the dimensions proposed here, these dimensions tend to covary. Although ritualized genres ("formalized" in McDowell's formulation) reduce the range of indexical entailments available to a speaker, McDowell noted (along with Bloch, 1975) that formalized speech tends to be more effective and powerful for specific ritual functions, usually those effecting rites of passage.

3.2). In improvisational genres, much of the interest for the audience rests in the complex interplay of competing indexical entailments and presuppositions emanating from and impinging on individual performers. Improvisational genres tend to de-emphasize constraining hierarchical structures of poetically reflexive calibration in favor of individual performers' indexical entailments.

Breadth of Genre Definition

Nettl (1974) asserted that one cannot make a sharp distinction between composition and improvisation. Instead, he argued that the ethnographic evidence suggests that all cultures have concepts of "pieces," musical units with their own integrity. Those genres that I call more improvised could be characterized as having basic musical entities, but with a more flexible entity definition. In fact, Nettl (1974) suggested that our terminology may be wrong: Rather than call the Persian *dastgah* a "genre," for example, the performers think of it as a "piece" they are performing.

In a more improvised genre, a greater variety of performances will be considered to be tokens of the same performative event type (culturally defined). In a relatively ritualized genre, a more narrow range of possible performances is considered to be an instance of the performative event type. Sutton (1987) pointed out that in Javanese gamelan music—a relatively ritualized genre—performances that a Westerner might consider to be the same piece (because they contain the same ready-made motifs) are in fact considered to be distinct compositions. A variation on a ritualized performance often will not be conceived of as a variation, but simply as an incorrect performance (often then losing its ritual effectiveness; see Kaeppler, 1987, p. 14).

Size of Ready-Mades and Density of Decision Points

Powers (1980) noted that the ethnographic literature has used the term *improvisation* indiscriminately to refer to two very different types of performance genre: In one type, the performer chooses from among a finite set of "ready-mades" at each point, which form a genre-specific paradigmatic set, and in the other type, the performer selects individual notes to form novel patterns, guided by a "modal model."

The former type, involving selection from paradigmatic sets of ready-mades, has linguistic parallels in the parallel couplets of the island of Roti (Fox, 1974) and in the canonical Slavic epic poetry improvisation (Lord, 1960; Parry, 1971). The former type also seems to be the norm in most traditions of dance that involve improvisation, because the nature of dance performance essentially requires dancers to combine "culturally acceptable pieces of dance" such that it is "essentially a new combination and reordering of culturally (or idiomatically) acceptable movement motifs in real time" (Kaeppler, 1987, p. 21). Powers compared the latter "modal" type to "oratorical discourse," which follows the genre rules specified by rhetoric.

Some improvisational forms (e.g., Javanese *gamelan*, Rotinese parallel oratory, Slavic epic poetry) are constructed by the performer out of pre-existing units, which will be recognized by any member of the culture as being part of the performance genre. The creativity of the performer rests in innovative combinations of these ready-made units. In such genres, the ready-mades cannot be changed, and new ones cannot be created by the performer.[19] These types of genre represent a lower density of decision points than a genre without ready-mades, in which the performer can make an innovative decision at virtually every note. Jazz and *ragas* are of this latter type, although in practice, many jazz performers develop personal sets of ready-mades which are repeatedly used (Berliner, 1994; Owens, 1995; Sawyer, 1992; Tirro, 1974); most performers have a repertoire of two or three dozen licks (Perlman & Greenblatt, 1981, p. 176).

The degree of improvisationality increases as the size of the ready-mades decreases, and the density of decision points increases. In a completely ritualized genre, the only decision point is which performance is appropriate to the event; the entire performance becomes a single ready-made.

Involvement of the Audience

Brenneis (1990) suggested that the relatively passive role of European audiences may have caused Western researchers to neglect the per-

---

[19]Although in practice, new ready-mades are created without the innovation being acknowledged, a process documented by Fox (1974) in Rotinese couplets. These changes can result in indexical entailments which extend outside the performance event, causing historical change.

vasive importance of the audience in musical genres of other cultures. The improvisationality of a genre is generally proportional to the degree of audience involvement; in more improvised genres, the performers are more aware of themselves as responding to the audience. In some genres, performers believe they are not creating as agentive individuals, but are acting as vehicles for the spiritual state of the audience (as in Sufi devotionals). The cultural function of all performances, both ritualized and improvised, includes a desired effect on the audience members; as such, we would expect to find indexical entailments projecting from the performers to the audience members, similar to the indexical entailments acting between the polyphonic voices of the performers. In addition, more improvised genres demonstrate more direct interactional participation by the audience; the audience projects entailments onto the performers, and participates actively in the creation of the emergent. To the degree that a genre is ritualized, this sort of creative indexical entailment will be less salient.

Ensemble Orientation

The more improvisational genres of performance are more likely to involve an ensemble of performers, with interaction among the performers playing an important role in the performance. The more ritualized genres of performance, in contrast, are more likely to include solitary, solo performances.

This dimension partially explains why I have chosen to focus on improvisation in this book. Although my goal is to explain group creativity more generally—even in those genres that are more ritualized and scripted (see chap. 7)—in the more improvisational genres, group creativity and interaction play a more significant role. Thus by studying improvisation, one can better focus on the ensemble elements of performance.

There are some ritualized genres that involve ensembles; perhaps counterintuitively, these tend to be the most ritualized of all genres. The theory of group creativity suggests why this might be the case: Ritual genres are often performed in contexts where an accurate reproduction is essential to the efficacy of the ritual, and the contingent processual dynamics of group creativity mitigate against an accurate reproduction of an identical performance from event to event. Thus extreme ritualization is necessary to constrain performers from the typical contingency of group interaction.

Resistance of Genre to Novelty Versus Receptivity to Novelty

Ritualized performance genres are rigidly defined and are difficult to change; individuals often perceive novelty as a departure from a reified form, and thus inherently bad. This is equally the case with ritualized genres and with formal performances of composed scores, such as the Western orchestral repertoire. In contrast, improvisational performance genres are more receptive to novelty, and may even encourage or require novelty. In American music, the genre of jazz improvisation is perhaps the most receptive to novelty.

Permanence of Genre Change Versus Evanescence of Genre Change

Because ritualized genres are resistant to novelty, once an innovation is accepted it is likely to remain in the genre for a long period of time. In contrast, an innovation in an improvisational genre is not likely to last long before later changes push it out of the genre. Saussure's (1959) view of historical linguistics implied that ordinary language use tends toward the improvisation end of our continuum, since genre changes tend to be incremental and short-lived. Although perhaps inadequate to describe reified linguistic registers associated with high social status (see later), Saussure's view is nonetheless effective in describing low registers, in which genre changes are relatively short-lived.[20]

Notation

Cultures with only highly improvisational genres tend not to have a notational system. If a culture does have a notational system, the more ritualized genres are more likely to be written down using it, and are more likely to be tape-recorded when recorders are first introduced to the culture. If attempts to transcribe a more improvisational genre are made, there is often difficulty because of differences

---

[20]Some poststructuralists incorrectly accuse Saussure of equating standard register with *langue*, and nonstandard with *parole*. Although the issue of "register" is not addressed by Saussure, his concepts of both *langue* and *parole* are more appropriately applied to nonstandard usage, since his focus on the arbitrariness of the sign neglected the ritualizing influence of linguistic ideology and standard register.

in performance practice in ritualized and improvisational genres; notational systems are typically developed primarily to record the more ritualized genres of performance and may be unable to represent important aspects of the performance practice of the more improvisational genres.

Cultural Valuation

In most cultures, ritualized performance genres—which have the first characteristic along each of the above dimensions—are culturally valued, perhaps considered "high art," relative to improvisational genres—those which have the latter characteristics—which are either not considered art at all, or may be grudgingly termed (in the West) "folk art." Improvisational musical genres are rarely accorded the same status as the more ritualized forms. The distinction between high art and low art parallels the sociolinguistic distinction between high and low speech registers. The classic example in American culture is the ideologically tinged debate over accepting jazz into the high art arena. In all cultures having both forms of group creativity, the more ritualized forms are culturally privileged. For example, Caton (1990) analyzed three performance genres among the Yemeni, one completely ritualized, one highly improvised, and one intermediate form. As expected, the cultural value associated with the ritualized form is far higher than either of the other genres. When tape recorders were introduced to Yemen, the ritualized performances were recorded and circulated; whereas this never happened with the more improvised genres of performance. In general, individuals are more likely to record ritualized genres, not only for security but also to ensure that future performances "get it right" so that the performance will be effective (note the relation to the dimension "degree of creative involvement of the performer").

The same trend has been documented among dance genres in Polynesian cultures (Kaeppler, 1987). Both Hawaii and Tonga have a broad range of dance genres, and Kaeppler placed these genres on a single dimension from dances that were strictly choreographed and could not be changed, to dances that could be improvised spontaneously, with some genres midway on the continuum. Kaeppler documented a correlation, in both cultures, between the formality of the context and the degree of improvisation allowed; the more formal the context, the less improvisation is allowed, and the more informal and everyday the context, the more improvisation is allowed. Ritual dances were "performed for the gods" and could not be changed (p. 14), whereas improvised dances were found at drinking parties and moonlight picnics (p. 20).

Many linguistic anthropologists and sociolinguists have documented how high registers take on characteristics of ossification, even to the degree of becoming dead languages to the broader culture (although perhaps remaining the language of religion and education for a privileged class, as in the classic *diglossia* of Ferguson, 1959). Well-known examples include Latin in early modern Europe and high-register "classical" Arabic in the Middle East.

ETHNOGRAPHIC EXAMPLES OF LINGUISTIC PERFORMANCE

A wide range of recent ethnographic studies has supported Jakobson's observation that the poetic function is at work in many linguistic genres. These studies have identified poetic structuring principles in a broad range of ethnographic material (Bauman & Sherzer, 1974; Hymes, 1962). To demonstrate the aforementioned improvisationality dimensions, I present three examples each of musical and verbal performance from the ethnographic literature; the following examples, drawn from the large body of material available, include one highly ritualized genre, one highly improvised, and one that represents partially ritualized improvisation, a midpoint on my continuum.

This section describes three genres of verbal art: a Zinacantecos prayer, representing an extremely ritualized genre; Antiguan contrapuntal conversation, representing an extreme of improvisation; and several genres of Yemeni oratorical poetry, representing intermediate forms. The following section then describes three genres of musical performance.

Ritualized Performance: A Zinacantecos Prayer

Most textually fixed poetic ritual forms tend to be highly ossified. Analysis of these ritualized performance texts shows they are maximally saturated with indexical poetic structures, certainly more so than improvisational forms of performance. Tambiah's theory of the ossification processes of ritual predicts that as a performance form becomes less improvisational, it will be progressively more saturated with this type of reflexively calibrated indexicality. Choosing from a wealth of such examples in the ethnographic literature, I analyze an example from the Tzotzil-speaking Zinacantecos of Chiapas, Mexico (Bricker, 1974; Silverstein, 1981). Figure 6.2 displays a six-verse prayer in parallel couplet form, which is overlain with several other poetic forms of indexicality (A, B, C, and D, following Silverstein, 1981). The structure consists of six couplets, in each one of which are two parts of parallel Tzotzil syntactic form. Note that 1 and 2 play on the substitution of synonymous terms ("grandfather," "Lord"; "earth," "mud"), and 3 can be joined with these two. In contrast, 4 plays on the substitution of antonyms ("poverty," "wealth"), as do 5 and 6 ("laborer," "tribute-payer"; "father," "mother"). Figure 6.2 notes the splitting of the prayer into two equivalent halves, 1-2-3 and 4-5-6 (C). But, as Bricker (1974) noted, the set of substituted items in 1 and 2, and again in 5 and 6, each "evokes a third idea: 'grandfather' and 'Lord' together connote elder; 'earth' and 'mud' together connote arrival (because the traveler's feet are stained with earth and mud); 'laborer' and 'tribute-payer' together connote vassal; 'father' and 'mother' together connote parents" (p. 371). This sets off 1-2 from 3, and 4 from 5-6 (B). We might also note that the contrasts in 1 and in 6 are from the semantic domain of kinship and related status, while those in 2 through 5 play upon the shift of pronominal reference from second person to first person to third person. Thus we have a fourth structure (D), 1 and 6 framing 2 through 5.

All of the patterns just described represent aspects of the poetic function organizing the denotational language of this text, exemplify-

(A) (B) (C) (D)

1. Well grandfather, Lord:
2. How long have you been waiting here for my earth?
   How long have you been waiting here for my mud?
3. I am gathering together here;
   I am meeting here.
4. I see the house of poverty;
   I see the house of wealth
5. Of His laborer,
   Of His tribute-payer.
6. Holy Esquipulas, thou art my father;
   Thou art my mother.

FIG. 6.2. Zinacantecos prayer.

ing reflexively calibrated poetic indexicality. Note in particular the su-
perposition of the asymmetric movement from past through present
to future in couplets 2 through 5 (D) with the forms of symmetricality
identified earlier. The asymmetric movement can be viewed as an
iconic representation of the desired outcome of the prayer: a future
increase in wealth for the supplicant. The net effect of this highly elaborate layering of poetic structures is to produce a highly ossified
form, which is not amenable to individual performance variation.[21]

Improvised Performance: Antiguan "Contrapuntal Conversation"

Reisman (1974) described an interactional verbal genre from Antigua
that represents a highly improvised, nonritualized performance. The
Antiguan "contrapuntal conversation" or "argument" is a form of verbal interaction in which a group of participants stands together, all
speaking simultaneously. As Reisman noted, it is contrapuntal in that
"each voice has a 'tune' and maintains it and that the voices often sing
independently at the same time" (p. 111). It is not immediately apparent that they are listening to each other, but upon closer examination,
one realizes "There is a kind of scanning process at work which lis-
tens with multiple attention and which ultimately determines which
voices will prevail" (p. 121). Reisman explicitly drew a musical analogy: "The repetition of theme characteristic of argument, the lack of
strong norm against interruption, the acceptance of two or more
voices talking at the same time . . . and the personal expressive associations of speaking sometimes add up to give to certain conversations
a *truly contrapuntal air*" (p. 124). Reisman indicated that this type of
verbal interaction occurs in a few ritual contexts, giving the example
of the christening party ritual; but it is more commonly found in everyday settings.

Reisman suggested there is a social preference for indexical entailments to be denotationally implicit, which in practice results in the
use of indexical poetic techniques: "There is a process of condensa-
tion and allusion at work all the time. One is expected in many con-

---

[21]Sebeok (1964) was one of the first to apply this perspective to folkloristic analysis.
His structural analysis of Cheremis charms also revealed multiple layers of mutually reinforcing poetic structure: "This text—at first glance so deceptively simple—is imbued
with a multilevel network of balanced symmetries" (p. 364). He associated this dense
tropic layering with the efficacy of the charm.

texts to 'catch' the meaning. And conversely there is a feeling that undue explicitness implies a dull person" (p. 122). This contrasts with a European emphasis on explicitness, as exemplified in Grice's conversational maxims (Grice, 1975).

Partially Improvised Performance: The Yemeni *Balah*

Most verbal performance genres described in the ethnographic literature fall at a midpoint on the continuum from ritualized to improvised. As Reisman (1974) noted, "between the formulas of prayers and greetings and such totally innovative use of language as may exist there is the large range of speech patterned to communicate meanings" (p. 113). The acceptance of improvisational elements, and provisions for individual creativity within a culturally specified genre, are quite common. Caton (1990) analyzed several poetic performance genres of Yemeni Bedouins. *Balah*, the most highly improvised of the three, is performed competitively by a group of men; it is an ensemble improvisation. "The whole point of the *balah* . . . is to be a game in which poets compete by spontaneously composing lines of verse to see who can outwit whom" (p. 63). Caton contrasted *balah* with two less improvised forms. The second form is *zamil*, which shares some characteristics with *balah*; for example, both are performed at weddings. Yet *balah* is performed only at weddings, whereas in addition to weddings, the *zamil* is used for dispute mediation. At weddings, it is an interactive call and response; in disputes, it is an oratorical performance by a single person, and is not interactive. *Qasidah* is the highest form, and is usually composed in advance rather than improvised. Caton noted that the ritualized nature of the *qasidah* results in reduced indexical entailments, since it is not embedded in a social event (p. 46); as a result, its semantic content becomes more noticeable, and reflexive indexicality plays a primary role. *Qasidah* is considered the pinnacle of the art and only the best poets can compose it, whereas many can perform *balah* or *zamil*.

The *balah* is the most improvised verse: "It is poetry created spontaneously before an audience, not prepared in advance and then delivered by a reciter. The audience witnesses an *act of creation*" (Caton, 1990, p. 79). It is also the most ensemble-oriented: there is always more than one poet, and always in a competition. "Poets are carefully monitored by the chorus, the audience, and each other to make certain they follow the rules of the game" (p. 79).

Caton described a variety of poetic indexical techniques used by skilled performers of *balah*. One of these is the use of culturally recognized formulaic expressions, or ready-mades: "there are hundreds of these formulaic expressions, and they ornament every conversation. It is extremely important to know how to link formulas together and use them in the appropriate social contexts" (p. 60). The formulas may be modified in rule-driven ways to fit into the larger verse; "The general pattern of such performances is for one or two poets to dominate, and the poet who establishes the rhyme has a 'lead' over his competitors" (p. 93). There are many poets who participate; Caton provided an extended analysis of a *balah* with four participants.

Despite the tendency to use ready-mades, the ready-mades may be modified in formulaic ways or completely original "non-formulaic lines" may be used (p. 96). Some originality is expected by the audience. Elements from the specific performance context may be used: for example, the presence or origin of individuals may be noted. Even Caton, the ethnographer, was referenced during one *balah*. The *balah* can include metapragmatic comments on the other's performance, a sophisticated combination of the vectors of indexical presupposition and entailment. As the *balah* progresses, it becomes more improvised, as two poets pair off for challenges and comebacks.

ETHNOGRAPHIC EXAMPLES OF MUSICAL PERFORMANCE

Genres of musical performance display a similar distribution along the above contrast dimensions, paralleling the associations and patterns noted above in my analysis of verbal art. This section describes three musical genres: the *srepegan* genre of Javanese gamelan music, representing an extremely ritualized genre; African-American free jazz, representing an extreme of improvisation; and the *gisaro* of the Kaluli people of Papua New Guinea, representing an intermediate form. It would be difficult to demonstrate specific poetic mechanisms without a detailed musicological analysis; therefore, this section will rely on other analytic sources to demonstrate the presence of these mechanisms.

Ritualized Performance: The Javanese Gamelan

Gamelan music is an appropriate starting point, because so much of the generative grammar approach to music analysis has focused on this form of Javanese court music (Becker & Becker, 1979; Hughes, 1988). As pointed out earlier and in chapter 3, these syntax-based models for music tend to be more appropriate to more ritualized performance; thus, it's not surprising that a genre like gamelan music would be of interest within a structuralist paradigm. The gamelan also demonstrates that even ritualized performance is contingent, with elements of indeterminacy, to an extent that performances of scores are not. Ritualized performance can only asymptotically approach the rigidity of an ostensible product.

One of the most cited ethnographic attempts to apply syntactic models to musical performance is Becker and Becker (1979). The *srepegan* genre has between 30 and 60 distinct "pieces." These pieces are played during traditional theater performances, where they accompany certain movements of shadow-puppets and dancers. Although the genre is quite old, modern compositions are still created (p. 3). Becker and Becker's goal was to identify principles of coherence in the *srepegan* genre. By "coherence," they referred by analogy to the narrative structures of plays. Musical systems of coherence are based on a "hierarchy of constraints," including the paradigmatic and syntagmatic relationships of a musical performance. In Western music, the system of coherence is based on the constraints of tonality and thematic development at the highest level, with lower level constraints including the type of piece being composed. For example, tonality is a basic constraint, because it determines the paradigmatic set for each note choice. Yet, tonality is not the paradigmatic set in Javanese music, since the pitch relations are fixed by the tuning of the set of instruments. Rather, the paradigms of opposition are created from two-note intervals and contours: above, below, the same. Paradigmatic sets are sets of possible four-note contours, or *gatra*.

A gamelan performance is highly structured through a saturation of hierarchic levels of poetic structures. At the lowest level are the four-note contours, *gatra*. There are seven contours which occur frequently in *srepegans*. In each *srepegan*, one contour is dominant, being played 50% of the time; there is also a 2nd and 3rd contour. The 2nd and 3rd contours mark structural boundaries to the piece. Each piece contains from 8 to 18 contours in a sequence, with 9 being canonical.

Becker and Becker suggested that the "deep structure" of the *srepegan* has five additional constraining rules: (1) there are three sets of three contours; (2) in each set, the middle contour is the dominant one; (3) in the middle triplet, the first contour is also the dominant; (4) in the middle triplet, the final contour is 2; (5) the first and last triplets are identical. They then identified several transformational rules whereby *srepegans* of noncanonical length are generated from this base structure.

These multilayered constraints show many isomorphisms with the regimenting tropic figurements of the Zinacantancos prayer of Fig. 6.2. Becker and Becker used this constraint hierarchy to explain the balance of redundancy and innovation observed in *srepegan* performances; this discussion has parallels with my discussion of indexical presupposition and entailment in chapter 3. At certain moments in the performance, the constraints of the piece weaken, and the performer's creativity may emerge. However, three higher level constraints still regiment the performer: the constraint of mode (*pathet*), the constraints of gamelan music, and the constraints of the genre *srepegan*. Real innovation emerges at points when these levels of constraint are in conflict; at these points, the performance is maximally indeterminate: "At these points of conflict, it is never possible completely to anticipate the shape of a particular *srepegan*. The resolutions will vary from region to region, from gamelan group to gamelan group" (p. 32). Thus there is indeterminacy even in a highly ritualized performance genre.[22]

Improvised Performance:
African-American Free Jazz

The relatively recent development of free jazz (the name "free jazz" comes from an Ornette Coleman record in 1960) provides an example of extremely nonritualized musical performance. Jost (1974) noted that free jazz represented an African-American rebellion against the compositional ethic of the dominant European society; it resulted from a form of *cultural inversion* (Hansen, 1989; Hobsbawm & Ranger, 1983;

---

[22]Hughes (1988) also used a generative grammar methodology to analyze another genre of gamelan, the *gendhing lampah*. Each of three subgenres (one of which is the *srepegan*) was characterized by a single four-note contour, combined with a "series of fairly regular transformations" (p. 24). His analysis was more explicitly transformational, with a specification of "deep structure," "surface variation," and "base generative rules."

Jolly, 1992) frequently identified in oppressed cultures.[23] Free jazz is a subgenre of jazz performance in which the participants explicitly attempt to avoid structure. Unlike mainstream jazz, no songs, keys, or chord progressions are selected in advance. A completely improvised emergent group performance is the goal. Like the Antiguan argument, to the uninitiated free jazz sounds like noise; it's difficult to tell if the musicians are listening to each other. Yet also like the Antiguan argument, in fact the musicians are listening closely, and the performance evolves and changes due to a complex musical interaction among the performers. As Jost (1974) noted: "[there are] strong interactions between the improvising soloist and the rhythm section.... In free jazz, this is even more the case, since ... the accompanying function of the rhythm group has been increasingly eliminated in favor of interaction between *all* the musicians in a group" (p. 16). Free jazz is structurally similar to Bakhtin's novel (Bakhtin, 1981), in that it is a "meta-genre" within which musicians can inhabit multiple voices simultaneously or sequentially. These "voices" can be as specific as quoting a known musician's style, or they may be more general stylistic periods or genres. Some critics believe that free jazz's negation of traditional jazz norms has resulted in a wider range of personal styles than had been the case in prior jazz genres (Jost, 1974, p. 10).

Partially Improvised Performance: The Kaluli *Gisaro*

As with verbal art, the majority of musical examples tend to fall in between the extremes of ritualization and improvisation. In fact, the extremely compositional nature of the dominant Western cultural forms may have resulted in the rather extreme nature of free jazz; there is no similar report of such unstructured group improvisation in the ethnographic literature. (In a parallel opposition, the Antiguan argument form is associated with the "lower classes" among those acculturated to colonial values.) Steven Feld's (1982) analysis of the Kaluli *gisaro* outlined the structural constraints of the performance genre, and the balance between cultural form and individual creativity that determines the performance. The *gisaro* genre defines an overall flow or structure of the dancer's performance; it defines the goal (to make men in the audience sorrowful); and it defines a collection of linguistic and musical techniques which are to be used toward this end. The

---

[23]Many researchers have noted parallels with African-American speech genres (Abrahams, 1974; Labov, 1972; Monson, 1996).

dancer is expected to create a musical "map" of the listener's locale through the text, in such a manner that the exact location is not immediately apparent, but only unfolds toward the end of the dance. The word for this technique, *tok*, means "path, road, or gate" (p. 150). Feld pointed out that "the song is successful when listeners are totally suspended into a journeying mood, experiencing the passage of song and poetic time as the passage of a journey" (pp. 150–151). This "map" results in an asymmetric poetic structure: a geographic journey through the locale known to the audience. Each location passed during the narrative is somehow associated with a recently deceased member of the audience's family. Likewise, the presentation of this map darts about like a bird through the familiar territory—a metaphor of the Kaluli belief that the person becomes a bird after death.

A wide range of reflexively calibrating song devices are available to the performer to increase the effectiveness of this underlying asymmetric poetic trope. For example, the performer may use a related language, Sonia, which is only used in these contexts; this is a reflexively indexical use of language. Other techniques project creative entailments through multi-utterance patterns of poetic indexicality. These include pair–part structures such as question and answer pair lines, if/then hypothetical sequences, and metaphors. Finally, the grand trope of bird flight is paralleled by a linear shift in style: Toward the end of the performance, the words used become less denotational in content. In the final portion of the song, there is "the most abbreviation, ellipsis, and syntactic deviation" (p. 137).

Although the overall structure has a reflexively calibrating, relatively fixed structure, the individual performer has local performative opportunities for creative entailment. Audience participation is expected, and in fact is the legendary climax of the event: the burning of the dancers. The words of the song sung by the dancer are canonically written for a man whose young son has recently died. This man is expected to become so overwhelmed with grief that he takes a burning log from the fire and burns the arms of the dancers, sometimes repeatedly throughout the performance.

DISCUSSION

In this chapter, I extended the model of chapter 3 and showed that group creativity is found in both improvised and ritualized performance. The findings of this chapter reinforce my claim that the analysis of group creativity requires a fundamentally interactional semiotics, one that emphasizes indexicality in interactional process, rather than a structural analysis focused on sign systems, paradigmatic equivalence sets, or static notational systems. Both music and verbal art demonstrate the emergence of a performance through complex interactional dynamics, in a process which is unpredictable and is contingent from moment to moment.

I used the model to identify several parallels between musical and verbal performance. One implication of these parallels is that analytic methods developed for the study of verbal group performance within linguistic anthropology (Bauman & Sherzer, 1974) could potentially be applied to music as well (as argued by Monson, 1996). A focus on group creativity allows us to integrate analyses of both musical and verbal performance. Future work in this area could combine studies of verbal and musical performance, since in most cultures, the two are combined in ritual (see Feld, 1982); this could lead to additional elaboration of an integrated, interdisciplinary approach to group creativity in musical and verbal performance.

I described six genres of performance, one verbal and one musical, of each of three types: highly ritualized, highly improvisational, and partially improvised. The purpose of this presentation was to demonstrate that similar indexical mechanisms are in operation in both music and language, and to emphasize how the poetic techniques of indexicality vary in usage in a similar fashion along the proposed dimensions in both musical and verbal performance.

The purpose was also to elaborate on the observation that different genres of group creativity manifest different degrees of improvisationality; not all group performances are equally improvised, and some of them are relatively structured, or "ritualized." I used the semiotic model of chapter 3 to reveal a range of interesting comparisons between group creativity in musical and verbal art.

Figure 6.3 presents a subjective ranking of each of the six genres on most of the contrast dimensions. The leftmost columns represent the most ritualized genres, the rightmost columns are the most improvisational genres, and the middle two are those that are partially improvised. The numbers, on a scale of 1 to 10, are not meant to denote objective measurement, but are only heuristic suggestions for purposes of discussion; based on the above summaries, the reader can confirm the plausibility of these numbers. On each dimension, a value of 1 indicates *high improvisationality*, and a value of 10 indicates *high ritual-*

Contrast Dimension	Zinacantecos prayer	Javanese srepegan	Yemeni balah	Kaluli gisaro	Antiguan conversation	Free jazz
Ossification Revivalism	10 (ossified)	9	5	6	2	1
Reflexive vs. Entailing	10 (reflexive)	9	7	5	2	2
Breadth of Definition	10 (narrow)	8	6	7	1	1
Size of Ready Mades	10 (entire piece)	7	6	4	1	1
Performer's Creativity	10 (low)	10	3	3	2	2
Audience Involvement	10 (low)	10	8	4	1	8
Ensemble orientation	10 (low)	9	4	8	1	1
Receptivity to Novelty	10 (low)	8	4	6	1	1
Cultural Valuation	10 (high)	9	4	8	1	2

FIG. 6.3. The placement of the six genres on nine contrast dimensions (ranked from 1 to 10).

ization. As expected, the nine dimensions are roughly parallel, yet the variations conform to the suggestion that a single linear dimension from improvised to ritualized may be overly simplistic.

One of the dimensions, "Permanence of genre change," is omitted due to lack of historical evidence. I have also omitted the "Notation" dimension because it is essentially a binary rather than a continuous dimension, and of the six only the Javanese gamelan is notated. The gamelan is at the ritualized extreme, so this partially supports the hypothesized dimension. My discussion of Yemeni oral poetry also supports the notation dimension; Caton reported that the most ritualized of the genres, the *qasidah*, was the first to be recorded when tape recorders became available, and tapes of performances are copied and circulated; this has not happened with the *balah*, the most improvised of the genres.

The most important observation is that music and verbal art show almost identical patterns. Ritualized musical performance genres demonstrate almost all of the characteristics found in ritualized verbal performance genres; improvised musical genres demonstrate almost all of the characteristics found in improvised verbal genres. An exception is the low audience involvement of free jazz; as suggested earlier, this could be because free jazz is a recent innovation, created in opposition to European musical genres, yet retaining some of the performance structure of those genres. The partially improvised genres, in both music and language, demonstrate the greatest range of values on each dimension. Although these intermediate genres also reinforce the claim for a similar approach to music and verbal art, the parallels between the musical and verbal genres (Yemeni Bedouin *balah* and Kaluli *gisaro*) are not as exact as those between the genres at the two extremes. For example, the *gisaro* has a high cultural valuation whereas the *balah* has a lower valuation. This is perhaps due to the absence of a more ritualized genre in Kaluli culture, whereas the Yemenis devalue the *balah* relative to the *qasidah* performance.

Although for purposes of argument, I have presented examples of verbal performance and musical performance in distinct analytical groups, one must keep in mind Caton's (1990) observation that "most tribal verse genres include compositions created in a dancelike performance which comprise an aesthetic-semiotic ensemble along with words and music" (p. 19). Although the highly notated compositional genres commonly valued in the West tend to be isolated to a single sense modality (with the exception of opera, as noted by Lidov, 1975, and Noske, 1977), most performance forms described in the ethnographic literature combine at least two semiotic modalities, words and music; generally, other semiotic modalities are also at play, including dance, costume, space, and object placements. This suggests that the parallel indexical poetic structures of these several modalities provides a synergistic indexical power. The Kaluli *gisaro* is an example of this semiotic parallelism; my discussion of *gisaro* suggests that these structures are found in both the musical and verbal modalities, and are synergistically reinforcing.

A comparison of linguistic anthropologists' reports with those of ethnomusicologists leads to an interesting observation: It is less common for music to be as highly ritualized as verbal genres. Musical forms are almost never completely ritualized even when the accompanying verbal text is composed, and marked verbal performance genres are much more commonly ritualized. This observation is confirmed by the contrast in Fig. 6.3 between the most ritualized genres: the verbal genre, Zinacantecos prayer, is slightly more ritualized than the *srepegan*. It is unclear whether this observation is an artifact of the research interests of these two bodies of ethnographers, or whether it reflects a cross-cultural reality; for example, while folklorists have focused on identifying fixed text forms, ethnomusicologists may have been more attuned to the presence of variance within performance genres by the established European tradition of "theme and variations."[24]

---

[24]Note Lévi-Strauss' *The raw and the cooked* (1969), with its constant musical metaphors, from the dedication, "To music," to the title of Part 1, "Theme and variations," to the table of contents, structured like a European musical composition.

7

Collective Ideation: Creativity, Teamwork, and Collaboration

A special branch of sociology, which does not yet exist, should be devoted to research into the laws of collective ideation.
—Emile Durkheim, 1953, p. 32n1

In this book, I have explored group creativity in music and verbal art. My discussions have focused on the creative group interactions of musicians and actors that are performed for the benefit of an audience. Throughout the book, three recurrent themes have been *improvisation*, *emergence*, and *interaction*.

I have emphasized *improvisation* because many of the most creative group genres are particularly improvisational. Although genres vary in their degree of improvisationality (chapter 6), some amount of improvisational creativity is found in all performance traditions that are not scripted or scored in advance. A musical group involves improvisation if the musicians do not each have sheet music specifying their parts; a dramatic or ritual performance involves improvisation if the speaking parts are not written down word for word. This is a broad conception of improvisation, because it includes some relatively ritualized genres. Yet all of these performance genres, whether relatively ritualized or relatively improvised, to some degree involve the improvisational processes of group creativity.

I have emphasized *emergence* because many of the most interesting characteristics of group creativity result from emergence. In emergent groups, the whole is greater than the sum of the parts; the performance is greater than the individual performers. A performing group is a complex dynamical system (Johnson, 2001; Kauffman, 1995), with many properties typically associated with such systems: sensitivity to initial conditions, rapidly expanding combinatorics as time progresses, and global behavior of the system that cannot be predicted even if the analyst has unlimited advance knowledge about the individual components. Because group creativity is emergent, the direction the group will go in is difficult to predict in advance, even if you know quite a bit about the mental states and personalities of the individual performers. Even with this knowledge, there is simply too much potential variability in the moment-to-moment interactional process of the performance itself, and the multiplying moment-by-moment combinatorics make advance prediction practically impossible. This is why creative groups have emergent properties that are at a higher level of analysis than the individual participants.

I have emphasized *interaction* in group creativity because interaction is the processual essence of collaborative emergence; the performance emerges from the symbolic interaction among the performers. Many other scholars have commented on the improvisationality of groups—not only in music and verbal art but also in a wide range of collaborative activities, including teaching, managing, and problem solving—and many scholars have noted that the results of group creativity are unpredictable, and emerge from the collective actions of the participants. But what has been missing from these discussions has been a focus on the interactional processes that occur in creative groups. My goal in this book is to contribute to our understanding of the interactional processes found in group creativity, and the majority of the book is devoted to the presentation and elaboration of a theory of symbolic interaction in groups. This theory builds on prior studies of group creativity in many disciplines, and analyzes the processes whereby group creativity results in emergence from improvisation.

In chapter 1, I introduced the themes of the book. In chapter 2, I drew on a wide range of interviews with both improvisational actors and musicians to identify some of the key characteristics of group creativity. Chapter 3 presented a model of group creativity, drawing on several disciplinary influences, but primarily studies of linguistic interaction—semiotics, conversation analysis, and linguistic anthropology. I briefly summarized the long tradition of applying theories of language to music, and I argued that my approach is different, in that I focus on parallels in the interactional processes—the "pragmatics"—of music and language. Prior attempts have focused on phonology, syntax, or semantics; this is a first attempt to apply notions from the study of language use in context to musical interaction, and my model is designed to theorize the social group processes of interaction in creative groups. I explained why a focus on this level is more likely to be successful in pursuing the analogy between language and music: Whereas the interactional processes of music and verbal art are quite similar, the syntax and semantics of the two have many differences.

In chapter 4, I reached back into the early 20th century to explore the writings of two influential philosophers of aesthetics: John Dewey and R. G. Collingwood. Both of these theorists developed influential theories of art and creativity, and both of their theories were designed to apply to all creative forms. These two are rarely thought to have that much in common, and in fact are often thought to disagree on central theoretical questions. But using the theoretical model of chapter 3, I was able to identify a range of commonalities in their theories. I showed that both theorists made a similar move: They developed their theories by starting from a theory of language as symbolic interaction. By connecting my semiotic model to these influential theories of art, I showed how all creativity may have fundamental similarities with group creativity.

In chapter 5, I elaborated these similarities further by turning to contemporary creativity theory. I summarized a range of influential theories of creativity in social contexts, associated with creativity researchers such as Mihaly Csikszentmihalyi (1988, 1990a), Howard Gardner (1993), and Vera John-Steiner (2000). I then showed a range of interesting parallels between group creativity and these theories of socioculturally situated creativity. These parallels are historical continuations of the parallels I identified in the 1930s-era writings of Dewey and Collingwood. Although Dewey is acknowledged to be an influence by socioculturalists, they have not noted these specific parallels.

In chapter 6, I returned to the central theme of the book: the parallels between music and verbal art that I first explored in chapters 2 and 3. I used chapter 3's theoretical model to develop a range of contrast dimensions of group performance genres—dimensions that are roughly parallel to the ritual-to-improvisation continuum. I used these contrast dimensions to locate six different performance genres—3 musical and 3 verbal—within the theoretical model. This exercise shows how the model can be helpful to all scholars who study group performance, because it identifies a range of properties that apply in similar ways to both musical and verbal performance.

In this closing chapter, I begin by discussing some implications of this approach to group creativity for studies of individual creativity. In the second section, I argue that group creativity plays a role even in performances that are scored or scripted, and I review studies of interactional synchrony in orchestras and in scripted plays. In the third section, I apply my perspective on group creativity to collaborating groups in two everyday settings, organizational teams and classroom collaborations, and I review studies of the improvisational dynamics of these groups.

IMPLICATIONS FOR STUDIES OF INDIVIDUAL CREATIVITY

Creativity research has focused on product creativity, in which the creative process results in objective, ostensible products which remain after the creative act is complete. Creativity studies have tended to neglect group creativity, and particularly, to neglect improvisation. Although not prevalent in Western cultures, cross-cultural study indicates that creative forms employing elements of improvisation are quite common worldwide. Unlike product creativity, which involves a long period of creative work leading up to the creative product, in group creativity, the creative process and the resulting product are co-occurring. The focus in creativity research on product creativity is not surprising, given that our purposes are often to understand the histories of our own creative genres, and to identify and encourage creativity (particularly scientific creativity) in our own societies. However, theories claiming to be directed at underlying universals in the psychological and social processes of creativity must be cognizant of all manifestations of creativity, including both product and group creativity.

When studying product creativity, psychologists often limit their focus to the individual creator. A painting is fully created in an artist's studio, and its entire creation may occur without the presence of any other person. A poem can be composed while on a solitary hike through the woods. Yet to study group creativity, the researcher is forced to focus on groups; it cannot be fully understood by analyzing the creativity of the individual members of the group. The behavior of a group emerges from the interactions among the individual performers, and the study of group creativity requires a focus on the collective, because creative groups are complex dynamical systems and manifest emergent properties. Like many complex systems in nature, creative groups manifest emergent properties at the system level that are not held by any of the individual components.

The emergent performance, although created collaboratively by the performers, takes on a life of its own and begins to constrain the performers, as I proposed in chapter 3. Due to this *downward causation* (Sawyer, 1999, 2001b, 2003), a complete understanding of group creativity requires a methodology that acknowledges the analytic independence of the group as a distinct level of analysis. Group creativity cannot be understood through explanations in terms of individuals and their interactions, an approach known as *methodological individualism* (Sawyer, 2001b, 2002b). Psychology cannot provide a complete explanation of group creativity; we need a group level of analysis, and we need to incorporate methods and concepts from sociology, communication, and organizational behavior.

This claim about group creativity parallels a claim made by the sociocultural psychologists: that a group sometimes learns as a collective, and that it can acquire "group knowledge" without that knowledge necessarily being locatable in the heads of any of the individual members of the group (Hutchins, 1995; Rogoff, 1998). Similarly, I argue that in groups, creativity is a property of the group and not necessarily a property of the individual members of the group. Of course, for a group to learn, the individual members of the group have to change as well, and this change can probably also be characterized as learning in the traditional individualistic sense. And for a group to be creative as a whole, the individual members of the group probably engage in something that a psychologist would recognize as individual creativity. But due to emergence, the group properties may not necessarily be the same as the individual properties; what the group learns does not necessarily correspond to anything learned by any single group member, and what a group creates does not necessarily correspond to anything created by any single group member.

What about the memories of the performance held by the individual performers and the audience members—isn't that internal mental representation essentially the same as the emergent performance? No, because the emergent performance has properties that are collective group properties and do not correspond to any properties of the individual members of the group. Yes, the musicians in a jazz ensemble will remember some properties of the performance: what key they performed in, how many times through the chorus the saxophone player soloed, some particularly exciting moments of musical communication. But many properties of the performance exist only in the moment and are not represented in any musician's head—the measure-to-measure interactional dynamics that held the group together in interactional synchrony, the overall structure and flow of the performance.[25] In the following three sections, I describe three emergent group properties—group flow, group ideation, and group evaluation—and I explore some of their implications for psychological theories of individual creativity.

Group Flow

In chapter 2 I described group flow, a collective state that occurs when a group is performing at the peak of its abilities. The concept of group flow is related to Csikszentmihalyi's (1990b) psychological concept of flow, but with a critical difference; Csikszentmihalyi intended flow to represent a state of consciousness within the individual performer, whereas group flow is an emergent property of the entire group as a collective unit.

Both jazz and improv theater are relatively unstructured, and the group has no explicit goal or task. Yet many groups are formed with a specific goal in mind—task forces, project groups, or committees. How can we extend the concepts of group flow and group creativity to task-oriented groups? Using Csikszentmihalyi's model in Fig. 2.1 as an outline, I propose that group flow is more likely to occur when the degree to which the group must attain an *extrinsic collective goal* is matched by the number of *pre-existing structures* shared and used by the performers (see Fig. 7.1).

By an "extrinsic collective goal," I mean, for example, the task facing a business team when they know that by the end of the meeting they have to come up with a resolution of a budget shortfall, or the task facing an engineering design team when they know that the pur-

---

[25]Halbwachs (1939) made a similar claim regarding individual and collective memory in musical ensembles, basing his argument on Durkheim's theory of collective representations. Although I agree with this aspect of Halbwachs' argument, I also accept Schutz's (1964) critique of Halbwachs as overly focused on musical notation (pp. 162–167).

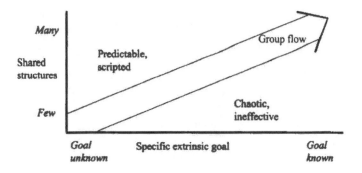

FIG. 7.1. Group flow.

pose of the meeting is to fix a software bug that threatens to spiral out of control. In improvisational groups, in contrast, there is no such extrinsic collective goal; the only goals are intrinsic to the performance itself—to perform well and to entertain the audience.

By "pre-existing structures," I mean the performance elements that are associated with a ritualized performance, as defined in chapter 6. These include at least four types of structure:

1. An overall flow or outline of the performance that all participants know in advance (although the exact length of each segment, and the timing of transitions, must still be improvised).

2. A shared repertory of ready-mades, with a knowledge of how they typically sequence in order (as in the call-and-response regularly improvised by Geri Allen and Art Blakey described in chapter 2).

3. Clearly defined roles for each of the performers. In product-oriented groups, roles tend to be more clearly defined and distinct, and efficiency is a major concern. In improvisational groups, the emphasis is on process and open communication, and there is a more flexible division of roles (John-Steiner & Mahn, 1996).

4. Common agreement on the conventions—the set of tacit practices governing interaction in the group.

If there are many shared structures when there is no specific goal, then the performance will be too predictable and scripted. Shared structures interfere with the generation of new insights. For example, a corporate brainstorming session in which everyone in the group comes from the same corporate culture and has very similar ideas about what counts as a good idea will be so predictable that it will not serve its function of generating new insights.

At the other extreme, if there is a specific goal and the participants do not share enough common structures, then it will be very difficult for the group to accomplish its goal. The interaction will be chaotic and ineffective—both ineffective at attaining its goal, and ineffective in its own right as a performance. When a jazz ensemble is hired to perform what is known as a "society gig"—a wedding reception or a corporate party—they will tend to play relatively straight. In a society gig, there is more of a specific goal than in a late-night jam session performance—the goal of enhancing the experience of the guests and conforming to their perhaps simplistic notions of what jazz is. Society gigs only work if all of the musicians are well-trained in the standard jazz repertoire; a young player who has spent his short musical career at the Berklee School of Music in Boston, playing technically demanding open-ended free jazz, will not share the necessary structures, and the resulting performance will not effectively attain its goal.

The "extrinsic goal" dimension parallels the distinction made in creativity research between *problem-finding creativity* and *problem-solving creativity* (Csikszentmihalyi & Sawyer, 1995; Getzels, 1964). When the group has a specific goal in mind, they are *problem solving*—the purpose of the group is to come up with a solution to the problem. When the group has no goal in mind, they are, in a sense, seeking out a goal or looking for a goal—they are trying to *find the problem*. Improvisational groups are engaged in problem finding—they are not faced with a specific problem to solve, but instead, part of the enjoyment of the performance is in the unexpected moment-to-moment goals that the performers create for themselves. For example, during an extended improvisation of a jazz group, the music may stray quite far from the 32-bar song form that initially inspired the improvisation. By straying from the form, the musicians have collectively created a problem for themselves—how will they return back to the "head," the unison performance of the straight melody?

In a 60-minute performance of a fully improvised play, the group spends the first half of the performance finding problems they will solve in the second half. At the beginning, actors are encouraged to offer new material, and toward the end, to resolve and connect items that have already been introduced. By the second half of the scene, a variety of dramatic material has been introduced, including some conflict and contradictions. After the early work of introducing dramatic material, the performance then requires collaborative work to construct a feasible dramatic frame within which all of this material makes sense. The actors must collectively solve a problem that they have created for themselves, solving a puzzle of which they have created the pieces. The actors don't know how everything will be resolved and connected; the resolution of these problems is an emergent group process, and no one actor can know what will emerge from the subsequent dialogue.

The most improvisational groups fall in the upper-right quadrant of Fig. 7.1, having intrinsic goals and less shared structures. Later, I examine some everyday groups that attain group flow in the center and the lower-left quadrant of Fig. 7.1—work teams, which have the goal of developing a new product or solving a specific problem, and classroom collaborations, which have the educational goal of teaching the participants.

What Is Created?

In product creativity, it is relatively easy to identify what is created—it is the ostensible product that results at the end of the creative process. In group creativity, in contrast, it is harder to identify exactly what is created. The group as a collective creates the emergent performance; but what do the individual members of the group create? What do they offer to the emergent performance? Can one identify a single, quantifiable, creative idea that can be attributed to an individual?

Creativity researchers have different theories about what the "unit of ideation," the basic element of creativity, is. For example, Simonton (1988) proposed that scientific creativity is based on a hierarchical organization of these units, called *configurations of mental elements*. It is difficult to identify a single unit of ideation in a jazz performance, since creativity occurs on many structural levels. Pressing's (1988) model of jazz improvisation proposed that the unit of ideation is the single note. Johnson-Laird (1988) suggested that this unit should be the melodic phrase. Other candidates for a unit of ideation occur at several nonmelodic levels, including timbre or tone of notes, specific note selection, selection of certain scales or "modes," individual

breaths or phrases, and broad concepts such as using a certain performer's style. Any one of these levels, alone or in combination, may
act as an independent level of ideation.

Musicians are particularly aware of rhythmic ideas from the other
band members (as in Monson's interview with Peterson, chapter 2,
pp. 31–32). This seems to indicate a *rhythmic pattern* level of ideation.
"I play something I like and then I'll play it again, and use that little
rhythmic pattern for a little while" (Sawyer interview, Nov. 26, 1990). A
second level of ideation is the melodic phrase itself; selection of the
solo phrase, frequently with elaboration and repetition, is a standard
solo technique. A third level of ideation is *musical style*. Musicians explicitly distinguish "style" from the melodic pattern level: "I might try
and get a feeling like [Miles Davis], but like I say, I don't really deal
with patterns like that. . . . Within the past few months I was listening
to Miles, and I remember noticing that I started playing things that
sounded like his patterns. But it wasn't something I was trying to do.
But it would be on a song that would sound like something he would
play" (Sawyer interview, Nov. 26, 1990).

Not only is it difficult to identify a single level of ideation, it is difficult to identify appropriate segmentable units within a single level of
analysis. At the melodic level, is it the note, the phrase, or the form it-
eration? At the rhythmic level, is it one measure, one phrase, one four-
bar grouping, or one form? An additional complicating factor is the
presence of "ideation units" which seem almost impossible to segment, such as a reference to a musical period or to a specific performer. Personal creativity is a continuous process of combining all of
these levels and units, so that each level intersects with the others
while remaining independently cohesive.

In improvisational theater, the unit of ideation is the individual actor's offer in a turn of dialogue; actors are taught to introduce a new
development in the drama in every turn to keep the drama unfolding
and developing. Offers are often made using shorthand references to
popular culture. These shorthand references are important, because
you have to "make your point in five minutes, to make your character
in five minutes" (Sahlins, in Sweet, 1978, p. 186). Often the audience
suggestions come from the morning newspaper, so that the shared
narratives of recent news events could also serve as units of ideation:
"we all had to be on top of the news because, when we took suggestions from the audience, the great majority of them would invariably

be right on top of what was happening that day" (Troobnick, in Sweet, 1978, pp. 191–192).

However, because a turn can offer a lot of dramatic information or a small amount of information, it's difficult to identify with clarity a single "unit of ideation." Assume that two men are on stage to begin a scene, and one actor speaks toward the audience, looking around frantically:

(1) Where's a cop when you need one?

The offer in (1) proposes that the other actor is the cop; its primary implication is projected toward the other actor, but it is broadcast and is not targeted at him. (1) is a big offer, because it offers many details about the frame.

In contrast, (2), an early turn from a 60-minute long-form performance (from a transcript in chap. 1), is a small offer:

(2) Here are those papers.   Handing a "stack of papers" to
                                   addressee.

Big offers propose fundamental frame properties, such as a character, activity, or location; small offers are rather subtle modifications or qualifications of a frame property: a character's personality quirk, a detail of an unfolding event, or specifics about the location.

As I have emphasized throughout this book, these individual offers do not become complete ideas until retrospectively, during the ensuing flow of the performance. Particularly with small offers like "Here are those papers," the meaning is not determined by the speaker, because the utterance is consistent with several potential future dialogues. The line could be the command of a superior, assigning additional work; it could be that of an assistant, who had earlier been ordered to bring the papers. The creative import of acts of individual performers cannot be fully attributed to them, because the meaning of each act emerges from an ensuing interactional process.

Thus it is problematic to identify individual creative contributions, or to attribute even specific elements of the emergent performance to individual performers. As I show in the next section, group creativity truly is a property of the collective, not of the individual.

Ideation and Evaluation

A tradition in creativity research (Campbell, 1960; Hadamard, 1945; Rothenberg, 1979; Simonton, 1988) holds that creativity occurs in (at least) two stages. Beginning with Guilford's (1963, 1968) seminal studies of creativity in the 1950s, creativity researchers have usually placed the source of novelty in *divergent thinking*, an "ideation stage" that often occurs below the level of consciousness. In this formulation, the conscious mind then filters or *evaluates* these many ideas, using *convergent* or *critical* thought processes. Novelty originates deep in the brain in an undirected, nonconscious fashion, and the conscious mind decides which of those novel ideas are coherent with the creative domain. The two-stage model of ideation followed by evaluation has a strong intuitive validity, and has repeatedly appeared in the history of thought about creativity. Many creative people think their own creativity works this way. In a study of creative individuals (Csikszentmihalyi & Sawyer, 1995), we quoted a chemist who made creativity sound deceptively simple: "You have a lot of ideas, and throw away the bad ones" (p. 346). The intuitive appeal of the two-stage model is reinforced by its parallels with the Freudian model of the mind—with an untamable, difficult-to-understand subconscious, and a rational, structured conscious mind.

The output of the ideation stage has been studied at length by psychologists, in part because they have often equated ideation or divergent thought with something like a "creativity quotient." Precisely how divergent processes generate novelty has been a source of much speculation among creativity researchers, but unfortunately the experimental method has not been successful at revealing these processes. In contrast, psychologists have had more success with the empirical study of evaluative processes, in part because those processes are often accessible to consciousness. Researchers take it for granted that divergent thought somehow drives the system by creating novelty; the research agenda then becomes an exploration of how evaluative thought processes select among these options.

Group creativity raises a fundamental issue for these staged psychological models: is it appropriate to represent creativity as occurring in sequential stages? In group creativity, it is unclear whether there are distinct creative stages corresponding to ideation and evaluation. Evaluation must occur in part at the ideation stage; otherwise, too many ideas would be generated for the limited processing capacity available during live performance. The evaluation stage would be overwhelmed, unable to properly filter the large number of musical ideas (Runco, 1993). Several studies have shown that the ideas generated in the ideation stage are not unrelated, but instead reflect associative patterns (Mednick, 1962; Runco & Okuda, 1991). Thus, even if it is analytically useful to distinguish ideation from evaluation, both types of thought may be constant, ongoing components of the creative mind, moments of a unitary mental process. During improvisational performance new ideas can come from either the nonconscious or the conscious mind, and new ideas are also evaluated partially by the nonconscious mind and also by the conscious mind. Thus, creativity theory may need to be extended to accommodate parallel processes of ideation and evaluation.

Creativity theories also may need to be extended because in group creativity, ideation and evaluation are collective and are accomplished by the group. When one performer introduces a new idea—an indexical entailment—the other performers evaluate it immediately, determining whether or not the performance will shift to incorporate the proposed new idea (chap. 3). The eventual meaning of the new idea is thus determined retrospectively and collectively.

The evaluative filtering of new musical ideas is a collective group process; one could think of it by analogy as the individual's evaluation stage, but externalized into the social world and made into a group process. Jazz musicians evaluate performances by listening to the entire group, not to the soloist or to individual members: "you can only appreciate jazz if you listen to the whole group. The soloist's part by itself is just one line in a whole painting" (Bobby Rogovin, in Berliner, 1994, p. 387). Referring to a musical conversation between a trumpet and bass, bassist Richard Davis commented,

> Sometimes you might put a idea in that you think is good and nobody takes to it. . . . And then sometimes you might put an idea in that your incentive or motivation is not to influence but it does influence. (Monson, 1996, p. 88)

This social process of spontaneous evaluation has interesting parallels with Csikszentmihalyi's analysis of how an evaluation is performed by a field when an individual proposes a new creative product (see chap. 5). For Csikszentmihalyi, after the individual has created a product, a social process of evaluation then takes effect as the members of the field select among new products to evaluate which are appropriate to enter the domain. Thus changes to a product domain depend on both group-level evaluative processes and psychological processes. In this view, social groups play an essential role in evaluating creative products; after all, an individual's evaluative filter may be faulty, and he or she may propose creative products that the field determines are uninteresting, repetitive, or wrong.

Yet unlike in product creativity, in group creativity there is no opportunity for the iterative evaluation and revision common in other forms of creativity. The social filtering occurs in parallel with the creative process of each performer, in the same way that each performer's evaluative processes must be operating in parallel with his or her internal psychological processes of ideation. Thus, not only must intrapsychic evaluation occur in parallel with ideation; interpsychic evaluation also occurs in parallel with creative performance. How can the analyst separate the ideation and evaluation stages, when the time constraints of a performance do not allow conscious reflection and evaluation? If the ideation and evaluation stages are temporally indistinguishable during improvisation, then they may be indistinguishable in other forms of creativity as well.

Evaluation processes result from an internalization of the social processes of person-domain-field (Csikszentmihalyi & Sawyer, 1995). An evaluation is, in part, a judgment about whether or not the new insight will be acceptable to the field, and how it can be integrated with the domain (through an appropriately skillful elaboration). Thus, when an individual evaluates the new idea, whether during the ideation stage or during conscious evaluation, knowledge of the domain and field plays an important role. Because of the long period of professional socialization required by most performance domains, there is ample time for this social process to be internalized by creative individuals. This social process knowledge can be internalized to such an extent that it can take effect at the preconscious level of ideation.

By proposing that ideation and evaluation result from an internalization of social processes, I have been inspired by American pragmatism. The pragmatists, including James (1890), Dewey (1934), and Mead (1934), suggested that mental processes were a reflection of social processes. An individual's ideation and evaluation may be isomorphic to those same group processes in ensembles. If it is not simply a coincidence that social processes of group creativity display a similar processual pattern to individual creativity, then it would be interesting to explore why and how these parallels exist. Perhaps the psychology of creativity is, in fact, the social process of creativity, absorbed and internalized by those individuals we call creative.

GROUP CREATIVITY IN NOTATED GENRES

There is in principle no difference between the performance of a modern orchestra or chorus and people sitting around a campfire and singing to the strumming of a guitar or a congregation singing hymns under the leadership of the organ. And there is no difference in principle between the performance of a string quartet and the improvisations at a jam session of accomplished jazz players.

—Schutz, 1964, p. 177

Scored and conducted ensembles fall in the lower-left quadrant of Fig. 7.1; they have an extreme degree of shared structures (the score of the piece, shared understandings about performance practice), and they have a well-specified problem (to perform the piece accurately and with an appropriate interpretation). In this sense, they represent the opposite extreme from the improvisational genres I have focused on in this book. Yet even in these most structured of genres, group creativity is necessary to an effective performance, because a score underdetermines performance. Otherwise, "performing works would be akin to minting coins" (Godlovitch, 1998, p. 85); as orchestral musicians sometimes put it, "you're either making music or just playing notes" (Faulkner, 1983, p. 74).

Several studies of orchestral interaction have been inspired by Schutz's classic 1964 paper "Making music together," which emphasized the interactional processes in ensemble music. Schutz noted that many musical groups achieve synchrony and intersubjectivity without a conductor. Several studies of interaction in musical groups have been influenced by Shutz and his focus on intersubjectivity; for example, Malhotra (1981) studied the gestural communication that serves to coordinate an orchestral performance. She discovered that although the conductor plays an important role in organizing the performance, musicians do not always attend visually to the conductor, and 15% of them report *never* looking at the conductor. When not attending to the conductor, musicians hear and see those sitting near them, and much of the ensemble coordination occurs through gestures, facial expressions, and bodily movements. For example, "the first violinist's raised eyebrow may indicate to a second violin that he or she is playing slightly flat and must raise his or her pitch. The nodding of the first bassoonist's head or raising of the right eyebrow can cue in the second bassoon" (pp. 105–106).

As Weeks (1996a) noted, much of the group interaction among musicians is hidden from the audience during a performance, and the intention of all involved is to give the audience the somewhat misleading impression that the musicians are reading "the musical text as the composer intended it, under the direction of the conductor *then-and-there*" (p. 248). Weeks focused his research on rehearsals, analyzing the interactions of talk and gesture that serve to coordinate the performance and to help the musicians reach a common understanding of the piece. This coordinating talk is completely absent from public performance, and many of the nonverbal gestures are omitted as well. In Weeks' (1996b) analyses, ensembles require the most interactional work to coordinate temporal features of the performance: the initial tempo of the piece; the rate to slow down the tempo in a ritardando—a passage in which the composer has indicated that the tempo should slow down; and the relative durations of the fermata, a mark on the score that indicates that a note should be held for an indeterminate length of time.

Improvisational coordination becomes salient when one of the performers makes a mistake, playing a wrong note or losing the tempo of the piece. Musicians refer to this as "covering up" a mistake. Weeks (1990) analyzed the interactional processes that occurred during the rehearsal of a chamber group of seven musicians that had no conductor. He documented how a cellist and pianist executed a series of "collaborative maneuvers" (p. 211) to recover from several mistakes made by the cellist, so that the performance could continue in such a way that the average listener would not notice the variation. The covering-up action involved a retrospective contextualization of the mistake, redefining it by modifying the scored performance that immediately followed so that it retroactively seemed to have been the correct note or tempo to have played (p. 216). The ensemble's modification resulted in dropping almost 2 beats from the scored performance. Weeks (1990) concluded that "although the score has served as a guide, the determination of the specific place the group is at a given moment is thereby a complex *collaborative accomplishment*" (p. 219).

Several conversation analysts have examined dramatic dialogue, applying techniques and concepts from conversational study to the scripted creations of playwrights (Burton, 1980; Herman, 1995; Issacharoff, 1985/1989). Yet surprisingly, there are only a few studies (Hafez, 1991; Stucky, 1994) that have transcribed the live performances of scripted theater groups for later conversational analysis. Although the script provides the words for the actors, the actors must perform the words so that they sound like natural human dialogue. For example, they must manage turn transitions between actors so that they sound natural, and doing this requires group interaction and a form of interactional synchrony.

Stucky (1994) focused on pauses between speaker turns; he transcribed live theater performances and compared the detailed transcripts and the scripted directions to pause provided by the playwright. As I noted in chapter 1, conversation analysts have demonstrated that turn transitions are collaboratively improvised, and emerge from the collective actions of the entire group; Stucky's analysis of staged theater dialogues also reveals that actors must collectively improvise the length of these pauses. In some cases, actors improvisationally omit an authorial pause, or insert a pause not indicated in the script. These group improvisations implicitly communicate important meanings to the audience, and can significantly alter the meaning of the text.

Studies like these are rare, but they demonstrate that group creativity is required even in genres in which each performer performs from a score or script, and even in musical genres that employ a conductor to facilitate interactional synchrony. Thus the study of group creativity has relevance for studies of notated ensemble genres as well. If these genres, the most structured and organized of all group interactions, still involve symbolic interaction, interactional synchrony, and emergence, then certainly all groups must involve these processes. In the following section, I examine group creativity in two settings: organizations and classrooms. Although these settings have a more clearly defined problem, and more pre-existing structures, than improvisational performances, they are nonetheless more openended and less structured than scored music or scripted theater.

COLLABORATION AND TEAMWORK

I have focused on creative performance genres in music and verbal art. But as I noted in chapter 1, group creativity is found in a wide range of everyday human social activities. Even the formal and rehearsed performances of a symphony or a scripted play involve group creativity. Group creativity is not only a trivial pastime or an entertainment goal; it is essential in many problem-solving groups, such as a brainstorming session at a small high-technology company, a group of teachers collaborating to develop a new curriculum, or a family working to resolve a financial crisis.

Many genres of group creativity are not culturally recognized as creative performances. Whereas the most performative interactional genres are usually considered to be creative in the folk theory of a culture, the more common genres, including various types of everyday conversation such as gossip and information exchange, are often not recognized as group creativity per se. This taken for granted aspect of many forms of group creativity may contribute to their neglect by creativity theory. Although some scholars have studied creativity in these types of groups, they have not closely studied the symbolic interactional processes that occur within the group. Thus the theory and method that I've outlined in this book have implications for each of those disciplines that study creativity in groups, whether in business teams or classroom collaborations.

Many creative products are generated by groups, not by individuals. In organizations, work teams are designed to develop a new product or to solve a specific preassigned task. They typically have more constraints on the flow of group creativity than improvisational art forms—a work team in a financial services organization would not be able to follow an improvisation that led to an idea for a new consumer electronics device. In classroom collaborations, students are assigned the outlines of a task by the teacher, and the explicit goal of the collaboration is that the students will learn something from the activity.

In my discussion of group flow (Fig. 7.1), I proposed a way to compare the improvisational genres that I focus on in this book and these other forms of group creativity: these other forms are usually oriented toward an endpoint or goal that will result from the activity, whereas in improvisation, "the process is the product" and the group has no intention of generating something that will remain after their performance is done. But in spite of these differences, the interactional processes of group creativity are similar in all groups—from improvisational to ritualized, from scripted to unscripted, from goal-oriented to autotelic. In the following two sections, I briefly review recent studies that emphasize the improvisational, group nature of interaction in organizational creativity and in classroom collaborations.

Organizational Creativity

The newfound urgency in organizational studies to understand improvisa-
tion and learning is symptomatic of growing societal concerns about how to
cope with discontinuity, multiple commitments, interruptions, and transient
purposes that dissolve without warning.

—Karl Weick, 2001, p. 297

In an influential 1988 article, the legendary management guru Peter F. Drucker argued that the "new organization" of the future would be like "the hospital, the university, the symphony orchestra." These organizations have in common a flat management structure rather than a many-leveled hierarchy; and they involve group creativity, as they are "composed largely of specialists who direct and discipline their own performance" (p. 45). Yet Drucker realized that the scored symphonic work was not a perfect metaphor, because his "new organization" would be improvisational: "a business has no 'score' to play by except the score it writes as it plays.... The performance of a business continually creates new and different scores" (p. 49).

In the years since Drucker's article, many influential organizational theorists have elaborated on his ensemble metaphor by emphasizing that organizations are improvisational, like jazz groups (Bastien & Hostager, 1992; Crossan & Sorrenti, 1997; Eisenberg, 1990; Kao, 1996; Miner et al., 2001; Moorman & Miner, 1998; Perry, 1991; Weick, 2001) or like improv theater (Crossan, Lane, White, & Klus, 1996; Crossan & Sorrenti, 1997; Moorman & Miner, 1998; Weick, 2001). An improvisational group is a better metaphor than Drucker's orchestra, because in organizations there is no script, individuals are often surprised by their collaborators, and interaction can result in the emergence of creative insights and solutions. In the writings of these organizational theorists, we find the jazz metaphor used to emphasize the key characteristics of group creativity: improvisation, emergence, and interaction. The team works without a script, and thus its activity is collaboratively improvised; and the outcome is uncertain (in many cases it cannot be known, by definition, because the goal is to generate an innovation) and thus is emergent from the group dynamic. In this new organizational paradigm, the team manages itself through a collective, emergent process. Many of the descriptions of *self-managed teams* are reminiscent of an improvisational jazz group: "multiple leaders emerge and a dynamic pattern of shared team leadership evolves" (Belasen, 2000, p. 259) and "this collaborative action is informal, emergent, and dynamic" (p. 262).

Eisenberg (1990) and Kao (1996) called this collaborative creativity *jamming*, comparing it to the group creativity of a jazz performance. Eisenberg (1990) observed that employees that experience this kind of improvisational creativity at work can easily get addicted to it; they're addicted to the flow state that comes only from group creativity. These conditions are rarely found in large organizations, which tend to focus on structure, script and process, and limit the opportunities for improvisation. Individuals sometimes seek out this flow experience by avoiding large corporations and joining small, entrepreneurial firms, or by working on their own.

Because of my interest in group creativity, I am particularly interested in the finding that more improvisational teams are a common source of technical innovation (Belasen, 2000, pp. 252–258; Eisenhardt & Tabrizi, 1995; Lanzara, 1983; Moorman & Miner, 1998; Weick, 2001). My model of group flow predicts that a more unstructured group is required for problem-finding creativity; and organizational researchers have found that improvisational groups are self-organizing systems that are more effective at problem finding, because they are "fluid and loosely coupled, permitting the emergence of internal networking as the landscape for innovation and creativity" (Belasen, 2000, p. 253). Eisenhardt and Tabrizi (1995) found that improvisational processes shortened the product development cycle, and that advance planning actually retarded product development. Moorman and Miner (1998) asserted that organizations faced with a rapidly changing market environment were more likely to improvise. Many improvisational groups form quickly and spontaneously in response to a crisis; these *ephemeral organizations* are emergent and collaborative, and better at developing innovative solutions quickly than large, formally structured organizations (Lanzara, 1983).

These theorists have found that the superior creativity of the self-managed team results from the interactional processes of information flows: Collaborative emergence is more likely to occur when information flows are faster, with a richer and deeper network of links among the team members. This finding supports my emphasis on communication dynamics and interactional process. For example, Moorman and Miner (1998) found that product design teams frequently improvise in response to a changing environment, and that interaction among team members is critical, because the level of "organizational real-time information flows" among individuals increases the effectiveness of improvisation (p. 12).

Several researchers have identified the same tension between structure and improvisation that I identified in chapter 2—the emergence of group riffs or scripted skits from repeated improvisations has been referred to as a form of emergent organizational learning (Miner et al., 2001). If the group performs together for too long then so many group riffs may emerge that this high degree of "organizational memory" may inhibit the originality of the performance (Moorman & Miner, 1998). Moorman and Miner (1998) found that the degree of organizational memory reduced the degree of improvisation in a group; this supports the hypothesized relationship in Fig. 7.1 between shared structures and amount of improvisation.

Weick (2001), discussing improvisation in organizations, noted that for many organizational tasks improvisation may not be desired; rather, consistency and repetition may be more appropriate. Improvisation might be an effective technique in some organizational situations, but "a liability under other conditions" (p. 301). In stable business environments where the problems are well understood, problem-solving creativity is sufficient, and groups may in fact need more shared structures. Weick (2001, pp. 287–288) emphasized the importance of "degrees of improvisation," using the phrase in much the same sense as I did in chapter 6. The variable that he emphasized is time pressure; he argued that full-scale improvisation should be rare in time pressure settings (p. 288; also see Kuiper, 1996).

It is intriguing that contemporary organization theorists are focusing on the group creativity of work teams, and that they have identified the same key features of these groups that I have identified in this study of group creativity in music and verbal art: the importance of collective improvisation; the ephemeral nature of the interaction as contrasted with the permanent product nature of designs or plans; the emergent aspects of the group; the importance of interactional dynamics and communication among group members in this process; and the role played by the pre-existing structures of organizational memory. These features of work groups, noted by prominent organization theorists, suggest that the theory of group creativity might fruitfully be extended to creativity in organized teams.

Educational Collaboration

In chapter 5, I noted that my study of group creativity falls within the sociocultural tradition in psychology. The socioculturalists have focused primarily on the social and cultural contexts of learning in educational settings, and of child development in family settings. These studies have demonstrated the importance of social interaction in groups, and have shown that a microgenetic focus on interactional process can reveal many insights into how learning takes place.

A central theme in the sociocultural tradition is the focus on the group rather than the individual. Socioculturalists hold that groups can be said to "learn" as collectives, and that knowledge can be a possession or property of a group, not only of the individual participants in the group (Rogoff, 1998). For example, Hutchins (1995) documented actions taken by the crew of a ship to make their way into a harbor, but with a broken navigational system that forced the crew to collectively improvise. A transcript of their interactions indicated that no one crew member understood the complete system they had improvised or exactly why it was succeeding; thus, the crew's solution to the problem they collectively faced emerged from group improvisation, and this emergent solution can be thought of as a form of collective learning.

Studies of group creativity have some suggestive implications for sociocultural studies of educational contexts. I have described how improvising groups collectively create emergent group products, including the group riffs of a jazz group and the increasingly routinized performances of an improv theater group. Here, I'll focus my comments on how teaching can be reconceived of as an improvisational activity, and how peer collaboration can be analyzed as a group creation.

Improvisational Teaching. Even when teachers are following a rather strict lesson plan—a script—there is always some residual requirement to improvise responses to students in the class. Mehan (1979) found that even when teachers are following conventionalized classroom routines they subconsciously and effortlessly improvise variations on the routine in response to the unique demands of each classroom. For example, one of the most common classroom routines is the Initiation-Response-Evaluation (IRE) discourse sequence: the teacher asks a question of a student, the student answers, and the teacher provides feedback on whether or not the student's answer was correct. Mehan discovered that even this simple routine requires an ability to improvise; for example, a student who was not called on may shout out the answer, and the teacher must decide whether to acknowledge that student or to ignore the unapproved speech. Or a student may respond with a question, perhaps not understanding the original question or even being reminded of some earlier misunderstanding that has little to do with the current lesson. The teacher has to improvise a way to respond to the question and then return to his or her own script for the class.

In many ways creative teaching is an improvisational performance, and the best teachers are good improvisational performers. But it usually takes years of practice to be an effective classroom improviser. In the first few years, young teachers tend to stick with the rigid curriculum and lesson plans they were taught to use; they get nervous if a child does something unexpected that takes them off schedule. As teachers gain more and more experience, their teaching becomes increasingly improvisational. In a study of improvisational teaching, Borko and Livingston (1989) compared experienced mathematics teachers and student teachers. They found that the experienced teachers improvised in every class, in that their lesson plans were flexible and they were responsive to students, using an interactional teaching style. They made decisions on the spot to respond to the unique demands of that class. Rather than preparing a detailed lesson plan, they prepared a flexible outline that allowed them to be responsive to the students. One expert teacher said "I play off the kids" (p. 483), comparing his teaching method to a tennis match.

In contrast, inexperienced teachers developed specific and detailed lesson plans. They planned ahead every few pages of the textbook, they developed word-for-word scripted lectures rather than loose outlines, and they rehearsed a script for each class, which the experienced teachers almost never did. One new teacher said "I can't ad-lib it too well" (p. 487). When the students did something that took the class in a different direction, the inexperienced teachers had trouble, because their ability to improvise a response was not fully developed.

Experienced teachers use a more improvisational style, and are more comfortable with the give-and-take of group interaction. This is consistent with studies of jazz and improv theater that show it typically takes years before performers become fully socialized into the community as expert improvisers. This perhaps accounts for the popularity of team teaching, in which one member of the team is an experienced senior teacher and the other member is a junior apprentice; this format provides the younger teacher with a period of several years to become socialized into the unique demands of improvisational performance.

Peer Collaboration. In addition to lectures, IRE recitations, and solitary work on problems, many teachers use the technique of collaborating groups. In this technique, a group of approximately four students is placed in a circle and given an assignment to solve collectively. In many cases, the members of the group are graded on the performance of the entire group as well as on their own performance, providing them with an incentive to contribute to the group's overall learning. For the reasons described in the previous section on organizational teams, employers are increasingly interested in educational strategies that train students in collaborative group skills (Webb, 1995). Effective teams require participants who can coordinate, communicate, resolve conflicts, solve problems, make decisions, and negotiate, and these teamwork skills are now widely recognized to be an important set of skills that high school students must acquire (O'Neil, Allred, & Baker, 1992).

Group creativity requires a give-and-take in which each of the members is contributing equally. In the most collaborative groups, constructive appropriation is a collaborative and creative process (Sawyer et al., in press); children work together to create their own knowledge, and learning is akin to a creative insight. These effective collaborating groups manifest emergence—the outcome cannot be predicted, and the whole is greater than the sum of the parts.

More than two decades of research have shown that this form of collaborative practice is uniquely beneficial to learning in a wide range of content areas, including mathematics, biology, and writing (Sawyer & Berson, 2002). Different forms of collaboration may be differentially effective for different types of learning. The model of group flow (Fig. 7.1) predicts that a collaboration with a more specific goal will need more scaffolding and structuring from the teacher, and in fact, there is some evidence for this correlation in the classroom. Cohen (1994) proposed that for learning tasks with well-defined goals, procedures, and clear answers, children tend to help each other in an asymmetric, instructional style of interaction. In contrast, for unstructured tasks with no clear-cut procedures or answers, the most effective interactions depend on "a mutual exchange process in which ideas, hypotheses, strategies, and speculations are shared" (Cohen, 1994, p. 4). The joint negotiation of Cohen's "mutual exchange process" corresponds to the give-and-take of the more improvisational groups, and is more likely to result in the unexpected novelty that arises through collaborative emergence.

In the most collaborative learning settings, students interact in a joint constructive process, and the free-flowing interaction of collaborative conversation scaffolds each participant in their appropriation of the material. John-Steiner and Mahn (1996) identified several levels of collaboration, from *complementary*—the clear division of roles associated with business teams and classroom groups, to *family* and *integrative*—more collective group styles in which roles were fluid or "braided" and the group began to speak with a unified voice. As in creative groups, the development toward the more integrative group style required a high degree of trust among participants.

When teachers organize collaborating groups of students, they face a tension familiar to improvising groups: between the need for pre-existing structures and the need to leave flexibility for emergent interaction to occur. Research has shown that the most effective collaborating groups are those that are partially structured, in careful ways, by the teacher (Azmitia, 1996; Cohen, 1994). For example, the teacher may constrain the collaboration by instructing students in specific conversational strategies or requiring them to follow a certain sequence of actions; or the teacher may assign specific functional roles, such as "facilitator," to individual students (Cohen, 1994, pp. 17–22). Empirical studies of a range of different techniques have shown that the most effective collaborations involve some structure, but not too much, and of a type appropriate to the learning task (Webb & Palincsar, 1996). If teachers do nothing to structure a collaborating group of students, the students can easily fall from a flow state into anxiety (Fig. 2.1) as they become overwhelmed by the challenges of the task (Azmitia, 1996, p. 139); consequently, they tend to stick to a more concrete mode of interaction. On the other hand, if the collaboration is overly structured, then the students are prevented from thinking for themselves and co-constructing their own knowledge, thus preventing the benefits that collaboration was intended to accomplish (Cohen, 1994, p. 22). The balance that results in group flow varies with age, as children become increasingly capable of renegotiating roles during a collaboration, and increasingly capable of engaging in John-Steiner and Mahn's "integrative" style of collaboration in which the group functions as a unit, speaking with one voice and working toward a joint goal (Azmitia, 1996, p. 141).

As with studies of organizational teams, educational research on collaborating groups has begun to emphasize the features that they have in common with creative performance: their interactional dynamics, their give-and-take, and the fact that properties of the group emerge from individual actions and interactions, requiring a shift in focus from the psychological analysis of individual participants to a collective, group level of analysis. These education researchers have discovered that the benefits of collaboration accrue from the complex processes of interaction in the group (Sawyer & Berson, 2002). The lessons of group creativity could be fruitfully applied to classroom peer collaborations, and more generally to any social constructivist environment in which the interaction is unstructured and improvisational.

SUMMARY

In the epigraph to this chapter, I quoted from Durkheim's (1953) important article "Individual and Collective Representations." This article is perhaps Durkheim's most concise and influential argument that the discipline of sociology is of necessity distinct from psychology, and that collective phenomena cannot be understood by attempting to reduce them to explanations in terms of the individual members of the group. Durkheim's rhetorical strategy in this essay was to draw an analogy with the biologist's attempt to reduce psychology to the study of neurons:

> Each mental condition is, as regards the neural cells, in the same condition of relative independence as social phenomena are in relation to individual people. . . . Those, then, who accuse us of leaving social life in the air because we refuse to reduce it to the individual mind have not, perhaps, recognized all the consequences of their objection. If it were justified it would apply just as well to the relations between mind and brain. (p. 28)

This essay is an elaboration of Durkheim's earlier claim that "there is between psychology and sociology the same break in continuity as between biology and the physiochemical sciences" (1964, p. 104), and such claims lead many sociologists to consider Durkheim to be the first emergence theorist (Sawyer, 2002a).

Durkheim's arguments are still relevant today, because most scholarly studies of group creativity have attempted to explain the phenomenon in psychological terms: in terms of the creative mental processes and the personalities and skills of the individual performers. Psychologists of music study jazz performance by studying the cognitive processes of individual performers (Pressing, 1988; Sloboda, 1988); psychologists study verbal speech and discourse by focusing on mental representations and cognitive processing (Gernsbacher & Givón, 1995). These psychologists focus on the individual performer, and as a result, they have not developed a methodology nor a theory appropriate for analyzing how groups collectively improvise an emergent performance as their members create simultaneously and in parallel. There has been almost no sustained scholarly study of group creativity (cf. Sawyer, 1997a), although it has been more than a century since Durkheim called for a "special branch" of scholarship that would focus on group creativity, "the laws of collective ideation" (Durkheim, 1953, p. 32n1). In this book I have attempted to contribute to the development of this branch. Given the disciplinary structure of contemporary social science, I am not as certain as Durkheim that this branch belongs within sociology proper, although I agree with Durkheim that it cannot be solely the province of psychology. Taking a lesson from the socioculturalists, who combine psychological and anthropological approaches, I believe that the study of group creativity must draw on a range of disciplines.

I have presented evidence of a theoretical convergence across many distinct spheres of scientific activity (cf. Sawyer, 1998). In chapter 1, for example, I discussed how several disciplines have shifted to a focus on the interactional practices of groups. The ethnography of speaking within anthropology has shifted from a folklorist focus on texts to a focus on performance process. The ethnography of musical performance has argued for a similar shift with regard to music. Conversation analysis in sociology has argued for a fundamentally social approach to language use, in contrast to the individualistic approach of Chomskian linguistics. Both sociocultural psychology and creativity research have demonstrated the importance of considering the social and cultural context of individual psychological activity. All of these new approaches emphasize emergence, contingency, unpredictability, and social interaction. These parallel paradigm shifts, at the same time yet in disciplines so far apart that they rarely reference each other, are exciting because they show us how the social sciences might become unified around a focus on group creativity. Many scholars have recently called for a re-thinking of the disciplinary structure of the social sciences (Abbott, 2001; Abu-Lughod, 1999; Wallerstein, 1998; Wertsch, 1998) and these parallel shifts suggest a potential path toward a new unification somewhat distinct from these proposals.

Communication scholars focusing on interactional synchrony were some of the first to identify the importance of group interaction in everyday social activities (Davis, 1982; also see chap. 2). Although this approach was much more microlevel and biological than my approach here, there are two interesting parallels between the emphases of these scholars and the approach to groups that I propose here: the need for interdisciplinarity, and the need for a systems-oriented methodology. The study of interactional synchrony was always interdisciplinary, combining the research of developmental biologists on mother–child interaction patterns with anthropologists studying cross-cultural variations in dance rhythms. As Scheflen (1982) noted, the paradigm had its roots in the systems-focus of 1950s era cybernetics, "control and communication in the animal and the machine," the subtitle of Wiener's classic text *Cybernetics* (1948). Complex dynamical systems theory is the contemporary manifestation of this mid-20th century systems thinking, and it is an interdisciplinary paradigm shift that is similar to my approach here. In spite of the shift to a social system level of analysis, none of those disciplines that have studied groups have drawn substantively on complex systems concepts. My focus on improvisation, emergence, and interaction could be thought of as a type of complex dynamical systems theory. I have avoided elaborating these connections because I have not drawn explicitly on complex systems theory; that will have to wait for another book.

References

Abbott, A. (2001). *Chaos of disciplines*. Chicago: University of Chicago Press.

Abrahams, R. D. (1974). Black talking on the streets. In R. Bauman & J. Sherzer (Eds.), *Explorations in the ethnography of speaking* (pp. 240–262). New York: Cambridge University Press.

Abu-Lughod, J. L. (Ed.). (1999). *Sociology for the twenty-first century: Continuities and cutting edges*. Chicago: University of Chicago Press.

Alexander, T. M. (1987). *John Dewey's theory of art, experience, and nature: The horizons of feeling*. Albany, NY: State University of New York Press.

Alperson, P. (1984). On musical improvisation. *Journal of Aesthetics and Art Criticism, 43*, 17–29.

Austin, J. L. (1962). *How to do things with words*. Oxford: Clarendon Press.

Azmitia, M. (1996). Peer interactive minds: Developmental, theoretical, and methodological issues. In P. B. Baltes & U. M. Staudinger (Eds.), *Interactive minds: Life-span perspectives on the social foundation of cognition* (pp. 133–162). New York: Cambridge University Press.

Baker-Sennett, J., Matusov, E., & Rogoff, B. (1992). Sociocultural processes of creative planning in children's playcrafting. In P. Light & G. Butterworth (Eds.), *Context and cognition: Ways of learning and knowing* (pp. 93–114). Hillsdale, NJ: Lawrence Erlbaum Associates.

Bakhtin, M. M. (1981). Discourse in the novel. *The dialogic imagination* (pp. 259–422). Austin, TX: University of Texas Press.

Barthes, R. (1979). From work to text. In J. V. Harari (Ed.), *Textual strategies: Perspectives in post structuralist criticism* (pp. 73–81). Ithaca, NY: Cornell University Press.

Bastien, D. T., & Hostager, T. J. (1992). Cooperation as communicative accomplishment: A symbolic interaction analysis of an improvised jazz concert. *Communication Studies, 43*, 92–104.

Bauman, R., & Briggs, C. L. (1997). Poetics and performance as critical perspectives on language and social life. In R. K. Sawyer (Ed.), *Creativity in performance* (pp. 227–264). Norwood, NJ: Ablex.

Bauman, R., & Sherzer, J. (Eds.). (1974). *Explorations in the ethnography of speaking.* New York: Cambridge University Press.

Beardsley, M. C. (1965). On the creation of art. *The Journal of Aesthetics and Art Criticism, 23*(3), 291–304.

Beardsley, M. C. (1966). *Aesthetics from classical Greece to the present: A short history.* New York: Macmillan.

Becker, H. (1982). *Art worlds.* Berkeley: University of California Press.

Becker, H. S. (1986). *Writing for social scientists.* Chicago: University of Chicago Press.

Becker, H. (2000). The etiquette of improvisation. *Mind, Culture, and Activity, 7*(3), 171–176.

Becker, J., & Becker, A. (1979). A grammar of the musical genre *Srepegan. Journal of Music Theory, 23*(1), 1–43.

Belasen, A. T. (2000). *Leading the learning organization: Communication and competencies for managing change.* Albany, NY: SUNY Press.

Belgrad, D. (1998). *The culture of spontaneity: Improvisation and the arts in postwar America.* Chicago: University of Chicago Press.

Berliner, P. (1994). *Thinking in jazz: The infinite art of improvisation.* Chicago: University of Chicago Press.

Blacking, J. (1977). *The ethnography of musical performance.* Unpublished background paper for "The ethnography of musical performance," a panel at the twelfth IMS conference, University of California, Berkeley.

Blacking, J. (1981). Ethnography of musical performance. In D. Heartz & B. Wade (Eds.), *IMS Report of the twelfth congress, Berkeley 1977* (pp. 383–401). New York: Bärenreiter.

Bloch, M. (1975). Introduction. In M. Bloch (Ed.), *Political language and oratory in traditional society* (pp. 1–28). New York: Academic Press.

Blumer, H. (1969). *Symbolic interactionism: Perspective and method.* Englewood Cliffs, NJ: Prentice-Hall.

Borko, H., & Livingston, C. (1989). Cognition and improvisation: Differences in mathematics instruction by expert and novice teachers. *American Educational Research Journal, 26*(4), 473–498.

Bourdieu, P. (1977). *Outline of a theory of practice.* New York: Press Syndicate of the University of Cambridge.

van Boxtel, C., van der Linden, J., & Kanselaar, G. (2000). Deep processing in a collaborative learning environment. In H. Cowie & G. van der Aalsvoort (Eds.), *Social interaction in learning and instruction: The meaning of discourse for the construction of knowledge* (pp. 161–178). New York: Elsevier Science.

Brenneis, D. (1984). Grog and gossip in Bhatgaon: Style and substance in Fiji Indian conversation. *American Ethnologist, 11*, 487–506.

Brenneis, D. (1990). Musical imaginations: Comparative perspectives on musical creativity. In M. A. Runco & R. S. Albert (Eds.), *Theories of creativity* (pp. 170–189). Newbury Park, CA: Sage.

Bricker, V. R. (1974). The ethnographic context of some traditional Mayan speech genres. In R. Bauman & J. Sherzer (Eds.), *Explorations in the ethnography of speaking* (pp. 368–388). New York: Cambridge University Press.

Bright, W. (1963). Language and music: Areas for cooperation. *Ethnomusicology, 7*(1), 26–32.

Brown, R. (1981). How improvised is jazz improvisation? *Jazz Research Papers, 1*, 22–32.

Brustein, R. (1963, May 11). Tonight we try to improvise. *The New Republic,* 28–29.

Burgoon, J. K., Stern, L. A., & Dillman, L. (1995). *Interpersonal adaptation: Dyadic interaction patterns*. New York: Cambridge University Press.

Burton, D. (1980). *Dialogue and discourse: A sociolinguistic approach to modern drama dialogue and naturally occurring conversation*. London: Routledge & Kegan Paul.

Cambor, C. G., Lisow, G. M., & Miller, M. D. (1962). Creative jazz musicians: A clinical study. *Psychiatry, 25*, 1–15.

Campbell, D. T. (1960). Blind variation and selective retention in scientific discovery. *Psychological Review, 67*, 380–400.

Cappella, J. N. (1991). The biological origins of automated patterns of human interaction. *Communication Theory, 1*, 4–35.

Caton, S. C. (1987). Contributions of Roman Jakobson. *Annual Review of Anthropology, 16*, 223–260.

Caton, S. C. (1990). *Peaks of Yemen I summon: Poetry as cultural practice in a North Yemeni tribe*. Berkeley: University of California Press.

Chafe, W. (1997). Polyphonic topic development. In T. Givon (Ed.), *Conversation: Cognitive, communicative and social perspectives* (pp. 41–53). Amsterdam: John Benjamins.

Cicourel, A. V. (1974). *Cognitive sociology: Language and meaning in social interaction*. New York: The Free Press.

Clarke, E. F. (1988). Generative principles in music performance. In J. A. Sloboda (Ed.), *Generative processes in music: The psychology of performance, improvisation, and composition* (pp. 1–26). New York: Oxford University Press.

Coates, J. (1997). The construction of a collaborative floor in women's friendly talk. In T. Givon (Ed.), *Conversation: Cognitive, communicative and social perspectives* (pp. 55–89). Amsterdam: John Benjamins.

Cohen, E. G. (1994). Restructuring the classroom: Conditions for productive small groups. *Review of Educational Research, 64*(1), 1–35.

Collingwood, R. G. (1938). *The principles of art*. New York: Oxford University Press.

Comte, A. (1842/1854). *The positive philosophy of Auguste Comte* (Harriet Martineau, Trans.). New York: D. Appleton. (Originally published in French in six volumes, from 1830 to 1842).

Condon, W. S. (1980). The relation of interactional synchrony to cognitive and emotional processes. In M. E. Key (Ed.), *The relationship of verbal and nonverbal communication* (pp. 49–65). New York: Mouton.

Condon, W. S., & Ogston, W. D. (1966). Sound film analysis of normal and pathological behavior patterns. *Journal of Nervous and Mental Diseases, 143*, 338–347.

Condon, W. S., & Ogston, W. D. (1967). A segmentation of behavior. *Journal of Psychiatric Research, 5*, 221–235.

Condon, W. S., & Ogston, W. D. (1971). Speech and body motion synchrony of the speaker-hearer. In D. L. Horton & J. J. Jenkins (Eds.), *Perception of language* (pp. 150–173). Columbus, OH: Charles E. Merrill.

Corbett, J. (1995). Ephemera underscored: Writing around free improvisation. In K. Gabbard (Ed.), *Jazz among the discourses* (pp. 217–240). Durham, NC: Duke University Press.

Crease, R. P. (1993). *The play of nature: Experimentation as performance*. Bloomington, IN: Indiana University Press.

Croce, B. (1948). On the aesthetics of Dewey. *Journal of Aesthetics and Art Criticism, 6*, 203–207.

Crossan, M. M., Lane, H. W., White, R. E., & Klus, L. (1996). The improvising organization: Where planning meets opportunity. *Organizational Dynamics, 24*(4), 20–35.

Crossan, M., & Sorrenti, M. (1997). Making sense of improvisation. In J. P. Walsh & A. Huff (Eds.), *Advances in strategic management, Vol. 14* (pp. 155–180). Greenwich, CT: JAI Press.

Csikszentmihalyi, M. (1988). Society, culture, and person: A systems view of creativity. In R. J. Sternberg (Ed.), *The nature of creativity* (pp. 325–339). New York: Cambridge University Press.

Csikszentmihalyi, M. (1990a). The domain of creativity. In M. A. Runco & R. S. Albert (Eds.), *Theories of creativity* (pp. 190–212). Newbury Park, CA: Sage.

Csikszentmihalyi, M. (1990b). *Flow: The psychology of optimal experience.* New York: HarperCollins.

Csikszentmihalyi, M. (1996). *Creativity: Flow and the psychology of discovery and invention.* New York: HarperCollins.

Csikszentmihalyi, M., & Sawyer, R. K. (1995). Creative insight: The social dimension of a solitary moment. In R. J. Sternberg & J. E. Davidson (Eds.), *The nature of insight* (pp. 329–363). Cambridge, MA: MIT Press.

Dalhaus, C. (1982). *Esthetics of music* (William W. Austin, Trans.). New York: Cambridge (Original work published in German as *Musikästhetik* by Musikverlag Hans Gerig, Cologne, 1967).

Davis, M. (Ed.). (1982). *Interaction rhythms: Periodicity in communicative behavior.* New York: Human Sciences Press.

Davis, M. (1986). *Miles ahead: The music of Miles Davis* [video]. Mark Obenhaus and Yvonne Smith. WNET/Thirteen and Obenhaus Films, Inc. in association with Channel 4 Television, London. "Great Performances" public television program #1303, 60 minutes, October 17, 1986.

de Certeau, M. (1984). *The practice of everyday life.* Berkeley: University of California Press.

Derrida, J. (1978). Structure, sign, and play in the discourse of the human sciences, *Writing and difference* (pp. 278–294). Chicago: University of Chicago Press.

Dewey, J. (1934). *Art as experience.* New York: Perigree Books.

Dewey, J. (1948). A comment on the foregoing criticisms. *Journal of Aesthetics and Art Criticism, 6,* 207–209.

Donagan, A. (1962). *The later philosophy of R. G. Collingwood.* Oxford, England: Oxford University Press.

Douglas, G. H. (1970). A reconsideration of the Dewey-Croce exchange. *Journal of Aesthetics and Art Criticism, 28,* 497–504.

Drucker, P. F. (1988). The coming of the new organization. *Harvard Business Review, 66*(1), 45–53.

DuBois, J. W. (1992). Meaning without intention: Lessons from divination. In J. T. Hill & J. T. Irvine (Eds.), *Responsibility and evidence in oral discourse* (pp. 48–71). New York: Cambridge University Press.

Dunbar, K. (1995). How scientists really reason: Scientific reasoning in real-world laboratories. In R. J. Sternberg & J. E. Davidson (Eds.), *The nature of insight* (pp. 365–395). Cambridge, MA: MIT Press.

Duranti, A. (1988). Intentions, language, and social action in a Samoan context. *Journal of Pragmatics, 12,* 13–33.

Duranti, A. (1992). Language in context and language as context: The Samoan respect vocabulary. In A. Duranti & C. Goodwin (Eds.), *Rethinking context: Language as an interactive phenomenon* (pp. 77–99). New York: Cambridge University Press.

Duranti, A., & Brenneis, D. (Eds.). (1986). *The audience as co-author*. Special issue of *Text*,
6(3). Amsterdam: Mouton de Gruyter.

Durkheim, E. (1951). *Suicide*. Glencoe, IL: Free Press. (Originally published as *Le Suicide:
Etude de sociologie*, Paris: Alcan, 1897).

Durkheim, E. (1953). Individual and collective representations, *Sociology and philosophy*
(pp. 1–34). Glencoe, IL: Free Press (Originally published in *Revue de Metaphysique et
de Morale*, *6*, 1898).

Durkheim, E. (1964). *The rules of sociological method*. New York: The Free Press (Originally
published as *Les régles de la mèthode sociologique*, Paris: Alcan, 1895).

Eisenberg, E. M. (1990). Jamming: Transcendence through organizing. *Communication Research*, *17*(2), 139–164.

Eisenhardt, K. M., & Tabrizi, B. N. (1995). Accelerating adaptive processes: Product innovation in the global computer industry. *Administrative Science Quarterly*, *40*, 84–110.

Engeström, Y. (1994). Teachers as collaborative thinkers: Activity-theoretical study of an
innovative teacher team. In I. Carlgren, G. Handal, & S. Vaage (Eds.), *Teachers' minds
and actions: Research on teachers' thinking and practice* (pp. 43–61). London: The
Falmer Press.

Engeström, Y., & Middleton, D. (Eds.). (1996). *Cognition and communication at work*. New
York: Cambridge University Press.

Errington, J. J. (1985). On the nature of the sociolinguistic sign: Describing the Javanese
speech levels. In E. Mertz & R. J. Parmentier (Eds.), *Semiotic Mediation: Sociocultural
and Psychological Perspectives* (pp. 287–310). Orlando, FL: Academic Press.

Evans, K. B., & Sims, Jr., H. P. (1997). Mining for innovation: The conceptual underpinnings, history and diffusion of self-directed work teams. In C. L. Cooper & S. E. Jackson
(Eds.), *Creating tomorrow's organizations: A handbook for future research in organizational behavior* (pp. 269–291). New York: Wiley.

Falk, J. (1980). The conversational duet. *Proceedings of the Sixth Annual Meeting of the
Berkeley Linguistics Society*, 507–514.

Faulkner, R. (1983). Orchestra interaction: Communication and authority in an artistic organization. In J. B. Kamerman & R. Martorella (Eds.), *Performers and performances:
The social organization of artistic work* (pp. 71–83). New York: Praeger.

Feld, S. (1974). Linguistics and ethnomusicology. *Ethnomusicology*, *18*(2), 197–217.

Feld, S. (1982). *Sound and sentiment: Birds, weeping, poetics, and song in Kaluli expression*.
Philadelphia: University of Pennsylvania Press.

Ferguson, C. A. (1959). Diglossia. *Word*, *15*, 325–340.

Fish, S. (1980). *Is there a text in this class? The authority of interpretive communities*. Cambridge, MA: Harvard University Press.

Foreman, K., & Martini, C. (1995). *Something like a drug: An unauthorized oral history of
Theatresports*. Alberta, Canada: Red Deer College Press.

Foucault, M. (1972). *The archeology of knowledge and the discourse on language*. New York:
Pantheon Books. Originally published as *L'Archéologie du Savoir* (Paris: Editions Galli-
mard, 1969).

Fox, J. J. (1974). "Our ancestors spoke in pairs": Rotinese views of language, dialect, and
code. In R. Bauman & J. Sherzer (Eds.), *Explorations in the ethnography of speaking* (pp.
65–85). New York: Cambridge University Press.

Friedrich, P. (1971). Structural implications of Russian pronominal usage. In W. Bright (Ed.), *Proceedings of the UCLA sociolinguistics conference, 1964* (pp. 214–259). Los Angeles: Center for Research in Languages and Linguistics.

Frost, A., & Yarrow, R. (1990). *Improvisation in drama.* London: The MacMillan Press Ltd.

Gardner, H. (1993). *Creating minds.* New York: Basic Books.

Gardner, W., & Rogoff, B. (1990). Children's deliberateness of planning according to task circumstances. *Developmental Psychology, 26*(3), 480–487.

Garfinkel, H. (1967). *Studies in ethnomethodology.* Englewood Cliffs, NJ: Prentice-Hall.

Geertz, C. (1972). Linguistic etiquette. In J. B. Pride & J. Holmes (Eds.), *Sociolinguistics: Selected readings* (pp. 167–179). New York: Penguin Books. (Excerpt from C. Geertz, *The religion of Java,* 1960, Free Press).

Gernsbacher, M. A., & Givón, T. (Eds.). (1995). *Coherence in spontaneous text.* Amsterdam: John Benjamins.

Getzels, J. W. (1964). Creative thinking, problem-solving, and instruction. In E. R. Hilgard (Ed.), *Theories of learning and instruction* (pp. 240–267). Chicago: University of Chicago Press.

Getzels, J. W., & Csikszentmihalyi, M. (1976). *The creative vision.* New York: Wiley.

Gioia, T. (1988). *The imperfect art: Reflections on jazz and modern culture.* New York: Oxford University Press.

Godlovitch, S. (1998). *Musical performance: A philosophical study.* New York: Routledge.

Goffman, E. (1971). *Relations in public.* New York: Basic Books.

Goodwin, C. (1981). *Conversational organization: Interaction between speakers and hearers.* New York: Academic Press.

Greenberg, C. (1986a). Avant-garde and kitsch. In J. O'Brian (Ed.), *The collected essays and criticism, Volume 1: Perceptions and judgments, 1939–1944* (pp. 5–22). Chicago: University of Chicago Press. (Originally published in *Partisan Review,* Fall 1939).

Greenberg, C. (1986b). Towards a newer laocoon. In J. O'Brian (Ed.), *Clement Greenberg: The collected essays and criticism, Volume 1: Perceptions and judgments, 1939–1944* (pp. 23–38). Chicago: University of Chicago Press. (Originally published in *Partisan Review,* July–August 1940).

Grice, H. P. (1975). Logic and conversation. In P. Cole & J. L. Morgan (Eds.), *Syntax and semantics 3: Speech acts* (pp. 41–58). New York: Academic Press.

Griffin, P., & Mehan, H. (1981). Sense and ritual in classroom discourse. In F. Coulmas (Ed.), *Conversational routine: Explorations in standardized communication situations and pre-patterned speech* (pp. 187–213). The Hague: Mouton.

Grout, D. J. (1980). *A history of Western music.* New York: Norton.

Gruber, H. E., & Davis, S. N. (1988). Inching our way up Mount Olympus: The evolving-systems approach to creative thinking. In R. J. Sternberg (Ed.), *The nature of creativity* (pp. 243–270). New York: Cambridge University Press.

Guilford, J. P. (1963). Intellectual resources and their values as seen by scientists. In C. W. Taylor & F. Barron (Eds.), *Scientific creativity* (pp. 101–118). New York: Wiley.

Guilford, J. P. (1968). *Creativity, intelligence, and their educational implications.* San Diego, CA: EDITS/Knapp.

Gumperz, J. J. (1982). *Discourse strategies.* New York: Cambridge University Press.

Gumperz, J. J., & Hymes, D. (Eds.). (1972/1986). *Directions in sociolinguistics: The ethnography of communication.* New York: Basil Blackwell.

Habermas, J. (1987). *Theory of communicative action* (Vols. 1–2). Boston: Beacon Press.

Hadamard, J. (1945). *The psychology of invention in the mathematical field.* Princeton, NJ: Princeton University Press.

Hafez, O. M. (1991). Turn-taking in Egyptian Arabic: Spontaneous speech vs. drama dialogue. *Journal of Pragmatics, 15,* 59–81.

Hagberg, G. L. (1995). *Art as language: Wittgenstein, meaning, and aesthetic theory.* Ithaca, NY: Cornell University Press.

Halbwachs, M. (1939). La mémoire collective chez les musiciens. *Revue Philosophique, 127,* 136–165.

Halpern, C., Close, D., & Johnson, K. (1994). *Truth in comedy: The manual of improvisation.* Colorado Springs, CO: Meriwether Publishing.

Hanks, W. F. (1996). *Language and communicative practices.* Boulder, CO: Westview Press.

Hansen, A. (1989). The making of the Maori: Cultural invention and its logic. *American Anthropologist, 91,* 890–902.

Harrington, D. M. (1990). The ecology of human creativity: A psychological perspective. In M. A. Runco & R. S. Albert (Eds.), *Theories of creativity* (pp. 143–169). Newbury Park, CA: Sage.

Hatten, R. (1980). Nattiez's semiology of music: Flaws in the new science. *Semiotica, 31*(1/2), 139–155.

Hatten, R. (1990). The splintered paradigm: A semiotic critique of recent approaches to music cognition. *Semiotica, 81*(1/2), 145–178.

Herman, V. (1995). *Dramatic discourse: Dialogue as interaction in plays.* New York: Routledge.

Hermelin, B., O'Connor, N., Lee, S., & Treffert, D. (1989). Intelligence and musical improvisation. *Psychological Medicine, 19,* 447–457.

Hobsbawm, E., & Ranger, T. (1983). *The invention of tradition.* New York: Cambridge University Press.

Hollenberg, D. (1978). Performance review: Ran Blake/Ray Bryant trio. *Downbeat, 45*(10), 40–42.

Hopper, R. (1992). *Telephone conversation.* Bloomington: Indiana University Press.

Hopper, R. (1993). Conversational dramatism and everyday life performance. *Text and Performance Quarterly, 13,* 181–183.

Hughes, D. W. (1988). Deep structure and surface structure in Javanese music: A grammar of *Gendhing Lampah. Ethnomusicology, 32*(1), 23–74.

Hutchins, E. (1995). *Cognition in the wild.* Cambridge, MA: MIT Press.

Hymes, D. H. (1962). The ethnography of speaking. In T. Gladwin & W. C. Sturtevant (Eds.), *Anthropology and human behavior* (pp. 13–53). Washington, DC: Anthropological Society of Washington.

Hymes, D. (1972). Models of the interaction of language and social life. In J. J. Gumperz & D. Hymes (Eds.), *Directions in sociolinguistics: The ethnography of communication* (pp. 35–71). New York: Basil Blackwell.

Ingram, P. (1978). Art, language, and community in Collingwood's *Principles of Art. Journal of Aesthetics and Art Criticism, 27,* 53–64.

Irvine, J. T. (1974). Strategies of status manipulation in the Wolof greeting. In R. Bauman & J. Sherzer (Eds.), *Explorations in the ethnography of speaking* (pp. 167–191). New York: Cambridge University Press.

Issacharoff, M. (1989). *Discourse as performance.* Palo Alto, CA: Stanford University Press.

Jackson, P. W. (1998). *John Dewey and the lessons of art.* New Haven, CT: Yale University Press.

Jakobson, R. (1960). Closing statement: Linguistics and poetics. In T. A. Sebeok (Ed.), *Style in language* (pp. 350–377). Cambridge, MA: MIT Press.

Jakobson, R. (1971). Shifters, verbal categories, and the Russian verb, *Selected writings of Roman Jakobson. Volume 2: Word and language* (pp. 130–147). The Hague: Mouton.

James, W. (1890). *The principles of psychology*. New York: H. Holt.

Jimerson, J. B. (1999). *Interpersonal flow in pickup basketball*. Unpublished manuscript, Indiana University.

John-Steiner, V. (1985). *Notebooks of the mind: Explorations of thinking*. Albuquerque, NM: University of New Mexico Press.

John-Steiner, V. (1993). Creative lives, creative tensions. *Creativity Research Journal, 5*(1), 99–108.

John-Steiner, V. (2000). *Creative collaboration*. New York: Oxford University Press.

John-Steiner, V., & Mahn, H. (1996). Sociocultural approaches to learning and development: A Vygotskian framework. *Educational Psychologist, 31*(3/4), 191–206.

Johnson, S. (2001). *Emergence: The connected lives of ants, brains, cities, and software*. New York: Scribner.

Johnson-Laird, P. N. (1988). Freedom and constraint in creativity. In R. J. Sternberg (Ed.), *The nature of creativity* (pp. 202–219). New York: Cambridge University Press.

Jolly, M. (1992). Spectres of inauthenticity. *The Contemporary Pacific, 4*, 49–72.

Jost, E. (1974). *Free jazz*. Vienna: Universal Edition A. G.

Kaeppler, A. L. (1987). Spontaneous choreography: Improvisation in Polynesian dance. *Yearbook for Traditional Music, 19*, 13–22.

Kao, J. (1996). *Jamming: The art and discipline of business creativity*. New York: Harper-Collins.

Kauffman, S. (1995). *At home in the universe: The search for laws of self-organization and complexity*. New York: Oxford University Press.

Keenan, E. (1971). Two kinds of presupposition in natural language. In C. J. Fillmore & D. T. Langendoen (Eds.), *Studies in linguistic semantics* (pp. 45–54). New York: Holt.

Keenan, E. (1973). A sliding sense of obligatoriness: The poly-structure of Malagasy oratory. *Language in Society, 2*, 225–243.

Keil, C., & Feld, S. (1994). *Music Grooves*. Chicago: University of Chicago Press.

Kendon, A. (1990). *Conducting interaction: Patterns of behavior in focused encounters*. New York: Cambridge University Press.

Kimmelman, M. (1998, Sunday, August 9). Installation art moves in, moves on. *New York Times*, Section 2, pp. 1, 32.

Krampen, M. (1981). A bouquet for Roman Jakobson. *Semiotica, 33*(3/4), 261–299.

Kuhn, T. S. (1960). *The structure of scientific revolutions*. Cambridge, MA: MIT Press.

Kuiper, K. (1996). *Smooth talkers: The linguistic performance of auctioneers and sportscasters*. Mahwah, NJ: Lawrence Erlbaum Associates.

Kuipers, J. C. (1992). Obligations to the word: Ritual speech, performance, and responsibility among the Weyewa. In J. T. Hill & J. T. Irvine (Eds.), *Responsibility and evidence in oral discourse* (pp. 88–104). New York: Cambridge University Press.

Labov, W. (1972). Rules for ritual insults. In T. Kochman (Ed.), *Rappin' and stylin' out: Communication in black urban America* (pp. 265–314). Urbana: University of Illinois Press.

Langer, S. (1953). *Feeling and form*. New York: Scribner's.

Lanzara, G. F. (1983). Ephemeral organizations in extreme environments: Emergence, strategy, extinction. *Journal of Management Studies, 20*(1), 71–95.

Latour, B., & Woolgar, S. (1979). *Laboratory Life: The social construction of scientific facts*. London: Sage.

Lévi-Strauss, C. (1955). The structural study of myth. *Journal of American Folklore, 68*(270), 428–444.

Lévi-Strauss, C. (1969). *The raw and the cooked: Introduction to a science of mythology: 1* (J. Weightman & D. Weightman, Trans.). New York: Harper and Row. (Originally published in 1964 as *Le Cru et le Cuit* by Librairie Plon.).

Levinson, S. C. (1983). *Pragmatics*. New York: Cambridge University Press.

Lewes, G. H. (1875). *Problems of life and mind. Series 1, Volume II*. London: Trubner & Company.

Lidov, D. (1975). *On musical phrase*. (Monographies de sémiologie et d'analyses musicales, I). Montréal: Groupe de Recherches en Sémiologie Musicale, Faculté de Musique, Université de Montréal.

Lidov, D. (1980). Musical and verbal semantics. *Semiotica, 31*(3/4), 369–391.

Lomax, A. (1982). The cross-cultural variation of rhythmic style. In M. Davis (Ed.), *Interaction rhythms: Periodicity in communicative behavior* (pp. 149–174). New York: Human Sciences Press.

Longman, J. (2002, June 18). Makeover is doing wonders for U.S. soccer team. *New York Times*, pp. A1, D3.

Lord, A. B. (1960). *The singer of tales*. New York: Cambridge University Press.

Malhotra, V. A. (1981). The social accomplishment of music in a symphony orchestra: A phenomenological analysis. *Qualitative Sociology, 4*(2), 102–125.

Margolis, J. (1980). *Art and philosophy*. Atlantic Highlands, NJ: Humanities Press.

Martindale, C. (1990). *The clockwork muse: The predictability of artistic change*. New York: Basic Books.

Matusov, E. (1996). Intersubjectivity without agreement. *Mind, Culture, and Activity, 3*(1), 25–45.

McDowell, J. H. (1983). The semiotic constitution of Kamsa ritual language. *Language in Society, 12*, 23–46.

McLeod, N., & Herndon, M. (Eds.). (1980). *The ethnography of musical performance*. Norwood, PA: Norwood Editions.

McNeill, D. (1992). *Hand and mind: What gestures reveal about thought*. Chicago: University of Chicago Press.

Mead, G. H. (1932). *The philosophy of the present*. Chicago: University of Chicago Press.

Mead, G. H. (1934). *Mind, self, and society*. Chicago: University of Chicago Press.

Mednick, S. A. (1962). The associative basis of the creative process. *Psychological Review, 69*(3), 220–232.

Mehan, H. (1979). *Learning lessons*. Cambridge: Harvard University Press.

Mertz, E., & Parmentier, R. J. (Eds.). (1985). *Semiotic mediation: Sociocultural and psychological perspectives*. Orlando, FL: Academic Press.

Meyer, L. (1956). *Emotion and meaning in music*. Chicago: University of Chicago Press.

Meyer, L. (1973). *Explaining music: Essays and explorations*. Chicago: University of Chicago Press.

Miner, A. S., Bassoff, P., & Moorman, C. (2001). Organizational improvisation and learning: A field study. *Administrative Science Quarterly, 46*, 304–337.

Monson, I. T. (1991). *Musical interaction in modern jazz: An ethnomusicological perspective*. Unpublished doctoral dissertation, New York University.

Monson, I. (1995). Commentary on Keil. *Ethnomusicology, 39*(1), 87–89.

Monson, I. (1996). *Saying something: Jazz improvisation and interaction*. Chicago: University of Chicago Press.

Moorman, C., & Miner, A. S. (1998). The convergence of planning and execution: Improvisation in new product development. *Journal of Marketing, 62*, 1–20.

Moran, S., & John-Steiner, V. (in press). Creativity in the making: Vygotsky's contemporary contribution to the dialectic of development and creativity. In R. K. Sawyer et al., *Creativity and development*. New York: Oxford University Press.

Moreno, J. L. (1973). *The theatre of spontaneity*. Beacon, NY: Beacon House (2nd ed., original work published in German in 1923, First English edition published in 1947).

Mukarovsky, J. (1964). Standard language and poetic language. In P. L. Garvin (Ed.), *A Prague school reader on esthetics, literary structure, and style* (pp. 17–30). Washington, DC: Georgetown University Press.

Nardi, B. A. (Ed.). (1996). *Context and consciousness: Activity theory and human-computer interaction*. Cambridge, MA: MIT Press.

Nattiez, J. J. (1975). *Fondemonts d'une sémiologie de la musique*. Paris: Union Générale d'Éditions.

Nattiez, J. J. (1977). The contribution of musical semiotics to the semiotic discussion in general. In T. A. Sebeok (Ed.), *A perfusion of signs* (pp. 121–142). Bloomington: Indiana University Press.

Nattiez, J. J. (1990). *Music and discourse: Toward a semiology of music* (Carolyn Abbate, Trans.). Princeton, NJ: Princeton University Press.

Nettl, B. (1958). Some linguistic approaches to musical analysis. *Journal of the International Folk Music Council, 10*, 37–41.

Nettl, B. (1974). Thoughts on improvisation: A comparative approach. *The Musical Quarterly, 60*(1), 1–19.

Nicolopoulou, A., & Cole, M. (1993). Generation and transmission of shared knowledge in the culture of collaborative learning: The Fifth Dimension, its play-world, and its institutional contexts. In E. A. Forman, N. Minick, & C. A. Stone (Eds.), *Contexts for learning: Sociocultural dynamics in children's development* (pp. 283–314). New York: Oxford University Press.

Noske, F. (1977). *The signifier and the signified: Studies in the operas of Mozart and Verdi*. The Hague: Nijhoff.

O'Neil, Jr., H. F., Allred, K., & Baker, E. L. (1992). *Measurement of workforce readiness: Review of theoretical frameworks* (CSE Technical Report 343). Los Angeles, CA: National Center for Research on Evaluation, Standards, and Student Testing (CRESST), University of California, Los Angeles.

Owens, T. (1995). *Bebop: The music and its players*. New York: Oxford.

Papaeliou, C., & Trevarthen, C. (1994). The infancy of music. *Musical praxis, 1*(2), 19–33.

Parry, M. (1971). *The making of Homeric verse: The collected papers of Milman Parry*. Oxford: The Clarendon Press.

Peirce, C. S. (1931). *Collected papers of Charles Sanders Peirce, Vol. 2*. Cambridge, MA: Harvard University Press.

Pepper, S. C. (1939). Some questions on Dewey's esthetics. In P. A. Schilpp (Ed.), *The philosophy of John Dewey*. Chicago: Northwestern University Press.

Perlman, A. M., & Greenblatt, D. (1981). Miles Davis meets Noam Chomsky: Some observations on jazz improvisation and language structure. In W. Steiner (Ed.), *The sign in music and literature* (pp. 169–183). Austin: University of Texas Press.

Perry, L. T. (1991). Strategic improvising: How to formulate and implement competitive strategies in concert. *Organizational Dynamics, 19*(4), 51–64.

Philips, S. U. (1992). The routinization of repair in courtroom discourse. In A. Duranti & C. Goodwin (Eds.), *Rethinking context: Language as an interactive phenomenon* (pp. 311–334). New York: Cambridge University Press.

Picasso, P. (1982). *The mystery of Picasso* [Film]: MK2 Diffusion and Ines Clouzot.

Pikovsky, A., Rosenblum, M., & Kurths, J. (2001). *Synchronization: A universal concept in nonlinear sciences*. New York: Cambridge University Press.

Powers, H. S. (1980). Language models and musical analysis. *Ethnomusicology, 24*(1), 1–60.

Pratt, M. L. (1977). *Toward a speech act theory of literary discourse*. Bloomington: Indiana University Press.

Pressing, J. (1988). Improvisation: Methods and models. In J. A. Sloboda (Ed.), *Generative processes in music: The psychology of performance, improvisation, and composition* (pp. 129–178). New York: Oxford University Press.

Qureshi, R. (1986). *Sufi music of India and Pakistan*. New York: Cambridge University Press.

Qureshi, R. (1987). Music sound and contextual input: A performance model for music analysis. *Ethnomusicology, 31*, 56–86.

Reddy, M. J. (1979). The conduit metaphor: A case of frame conflict in our language about language. In A. Ortony (Ed.), *Metaphor and thought* (pp. 284–324). New York: Cambridge University Press.

Reisman, K. (1974). Contrapuntal conversations in an Antiguan village. In R. Bauman & J. Sherzer (Eds.), *Explorations in the ethnography of speaking* (pp. 110–124). New York: Cambridge University Press.

Ridley, A. (1997). Not ideal: Collingwood's expression theory. *Journal of Aesthetics and Art Criticism, 55*(3), 263–272.

Rinzler, P. (1988). Preliminary thoughts on analyzing musical interaction among jazz performers. In D. Morgenstern, C. Nanry, & D. A. Cayer (Eds.), *Annual Review of Jazz Studies 4* (pp. 153–160). New Brunswick, NJ: Transaction Books.

Rogoff, B. (1990). *Apprenticeship in thinking: Cognitive development in social context*. New York: Oxford University Press.

Rogoff, B. (1995). Observing sociocultural activity on three planes: Participatory appropriation, guided participation, and apprenticeship. In J. V. Wertsch, P. del Rio, & A. Alvarez (Eds.), *Sociocultural studies of mind* (pp. 139–164). New York: Cambridge University Press.

Rogoff, B. (1998). Cognition as a collaborative process. In D. Kuhn & R. S. Siegler (Eds.), *Handbook of child psychology, 5th edition, Volume 2: Cognition, perception, and language* (pp. 679–744). New York: Wiley.

Rogoff, B., Baker-Sennett, J., Lacasa, P., & Goldsmith, D. (1995). Development through participation in sociocultural activity. In J. Goodnow, P. Miller, & F. Kessel (Eds.), *Cultural practices as contexts for development* (pp. 45–65). San Francisco: Jossey-Bass.

Rosaldo, M. Z. (1982). The things we do with words: Ilongot speech acts and speech act theory in philosophy. *Language in Society, 11*, 203–237.

Rothenberg, A. (1979). *The emerging goddess: The creative process in art, science, and other fields*. Chicago: University of Chicago Press.

Runco, M. A. (1993, May). *Critical creative thought*. Paper presented at the Wallace Symposium, University of Kansas.

Runco, M. A., & Albert, R. S. (Eds.). (1990). *Theories of creativity*. Newbury Park, CA: Sage.

Runco, M. A., & Okuda, S. M. (1991). The instructional enhancement of the ideational originality and flexibility scores of divergent thinking tests. *Applied Cognitive Psychology*,
5, 435–441.

Ruwet, N. (1967). Linguistics and musicology. *International Social Science Journal*, *19*,
79–87.

Ruwet, N. (1972). *Langage, musique, poésie*. Paris: Éditions du Seuil.

Saussure, F. d. (1959). *Course in general linguistics* (Wade Baskin, Trans.). New York:
McGraw Hill.

Sawyer, R. K. (1992). Improvisational creativity: An analysis of jazz performance. *Creativity Research Journal*, *5*(3), 253–263.

Sawyer, R. K. (Ed.). (1997a). *Creativity in performance*. Greenwich, CT: Ablex.

Sawyer, R. K. (1997b). *Pretend play as improvisation: Conversation in the preschool classroom*. Mahwah, NJ: Lawrence Erlbaum Associates.

Sawyer, R. K. (1998). The interdisciplinary study of creativity in performance. *Creativity
Research Journal*, *11*(1), 11–19.

Sawyer, R. K. (1999). The emergence of creativity. *Philosophical Psychology*, *12*(4), 447–469.

Sawyer, R. K. (2001a). *Creating conversations: Improvisation in everyday discourse*. Cresskill,
NJ: Hampton Press.

Sawyer, R. K. (2001b). Emergence in sociology: Contemporary philosophy of mind and
some implications for sociological theory. *American Journal of Sociology*, *107*(3), 551–
585.

Sawyer, R. K. (2002a). Durkheim's dilemma: Toward a sociology of emergence. *Sociological Theory*, *20*(2), 227–247.

Sawyer, R. K. (2002b). Emergence in psychology: Lessons from the history of non-reduc-
tionist science. *Human Development*, *45*, 2–28.

Sawyer, R. K. (2003). *Improvised dialogues: Emergence and creativity in conversation*.
Westport, CT: Greenwood.

Sawyer, R. K. (in press). Emergence in creativity and development. In R. K. Sawyer et al.,
Creativity and development. New York: Oxford University Press.

Sawyer, R. K., & Berson, S. (2002). *The study group: How external representations affect collaborative discourse* (Unpublished manuscript). St. Louis, MO: Washington University.

Sawyer, R. K., John-Steiner, V., Moran, S., Sternberg, R., Feldman, D. H., Csikszentmihalyi,
M., & Nakamura, J. (in press). *Creativity and development*. New York: Oxford University Press.

Scheflen, A. E. (1982). Comments on the significance of interaction rhythms. In M. Davis
(Ed.), *Interaction rhythms: Periodicity in communicative behavior* (pp. 13–22). New York:
Human Sciences Press.

Schegloff, E. A. (1986). The routine as achievement. *Human Studies*, *9*, 111–151.

Schegloff, E. A. (1990). On the organization of sequences as a source of "coherence" in
talk-in-interaction. In B. Dorval (Ed.), *Conversational organization and its development*
(pp. 51–77). Norwood, NJ: Ablex.

Schegloff, E. A. (1992). Repair after next turn: The last structurally provided defense of
intersubjectivity in conversation. *American Journal of Sociology*, *97*(5), 1295–1345.

Schegloff, E. A., & Sacks, H. (1973). Opening up closings. *Semiotica*, *8*, 289–327.

Schögler, B. (1998). Music as a tool in communications research. *Nordic Journal of Music
Therapy*, *7*(1), 40–49.

Schögler, B. (1999–2000). Studying temporal co-ordination in jazz duets. *Musicae
Scientiae*, *3* (suppl.), 75–92.

Schutz, A. (1964). Making music together: A study in social relationships. In A. Brodessen (Ed.), *Collected papers, Volume 2: Studies in social theory* (pp. 159–178). The Hague: Martinus Nijhoff.

Searle, J. R. (1969). *Speech acts.* New York: Cambridge University Press.

Sebeok, T. A. (1964). The structure and content of Cheremis charms. In D. Hymes (Ed.), *Language in culture and society* (pp. 356–371). New York: Harper & Row. (Reprinted from *Anthropos*, 1953, *48*, 369–388).

Seham, A. E. (2001). *Whose improv is it anyway? Beyond Second City.* Jackson: University Press of Mississippi.

Senderovich, S. (1982). Rhythm, trope, myth: The early poetics of Roman Jakobson. *Semiotica, 40*(3/4), 347–370.

Silverstein, M. (1976). Shifters, linguistic categories, and cultural description. In K. Basso & H. Selby (Eds.), *Meaning in anthropology* (pp. 11–55). Albuquerque: University of New Mexico Press.

Silverstein, M. (1979). Language structure and linguistic ideology. In P. R. Clyne (Ed.), *The elements: A parasession on linguistic units and levels* (pp. 193–247). Chicago: Chicago Linguistic Society.

Silverstein, M. (1981). *Metaforces of power in traditional oratory.* New Haven, CT: Text of a lecture read to the Department of Anthropology, Yale University.

Silverstein, M. (1984). On the pragmatic "poetry" of prose: Parallelism, repetition, and cohesive structure in the time course of dyadic conversation. In D. Schiffrin (Ed.), *Meaning, form, and use in context: Linguistic applications* (pp. 181–198). Washington: Georgetown University Press.

Silverstein, M. (1993). Metapragmatic discourse and metapragmatic function. In J. A. Lucy (Ed.), *Reflexive language* (pp. 33–58). New York: Cambridge University Press.

Silverstein, M. (1997). The improvisational performance of culture in realtime discursive practice. In R. K. Sawyer (Ed.), *Creativity in performance* (pp. 265–312). Norwood, NJ: Ablex.

Simonton, D. K. (1988). *Scientific genius: A psychology of science.* New York: Cambridge University Press.

Sloboda, J. A. (1985). *The musical mind: The cognitive psychology of music.* New York: Oxford University Press.

Sloboda, J. (Ed.). (1988). *Generative processes in music.* New York: Oxford University Press.

Smith, S. (1995, April 9). Funny business: Improvisational comedy seeks its own inspired level, in new forms, new cities, new media. *Chicago Tribune*, Section 13, pp. 1, 24.

Solomon, A. (1997, February 9). The jazz martyr. *New York Times Magazine*, pp. 32–35.

Spolin, V. (1963). *Improvisation for the theater.* Evanston: Northwestern University Press.

Springer, G. P. (1956). Language and music: Parallels and divergences. In M. Halle (Ed.), *For Roman Jakobson* (pp. 504–513). The Hague.

Stankiewicz, E. (1983). Commemorative essay: Roman Jakobson. *Semiotica, 44*(1/2), 1–20.

Steedman, M. J. (1984). A generative grammar for jazz chord sequences. *Music Perception, 2*(1), 52–77.

Steinberg, L. (1972). *Other criteria: Confrontations with twentieth-century art.* New York: Oxford University Press.

Sternberg, R. J. (Ed.). (1988). *The nature of creativity.* New York: Cambridge University Press.

Sternberg, R. J., & Davidson, J. E. (Eds.). (1995). *The nature of insight*. Cambridge, MA: MIT Press.

Stewart, M. L. (1986). Player interaction in the 1955–1957 Miles Davis quintet. *Jazz Research Papers, 6*, 187–210.

Stucky, N. (1988). Unnatural acts: Performing natural conversation. *Literature in Performance, 8*(2), 28–39.

Stucky, N. (1993). Toward an aesthetics of natural performance. *Text and Performance Quarterly, 13*, 168–180.

Stucky, N. (1994). Interactional silence: Pauses in dramatic performance. *Journal of Pragmatics, 21*, 171–190.

Suchman, L. A. (1987). *Plans and situated actions: The problem of human-machine communication*. New York: Cambridge University Press.

Suhor, C. (1986). Jazz improvisation and language performance: Parallel competencies. *Etc.: A Review of General Semantics, 43*(2), 133–140.

Sutton, R. A. (1987). Variation and composition in Java. *Yearbook for Traditional Music, 19*, 65–95.

Sweet, J. (1978). *Something wonderful right away: An oral history of the Second City & the Compass Players*. New York: Avon Books.

Tagg, P. (1987). Musicology and the semiotics of popular music. *Semiotica, 66*(1/3), 279–298.

Tambiah, S. J. (1985). *Culture, thought, and social action: An anthropological perspective*. Cambridge, MA: Harvard University Press.

Tarasti, E. (1993). From *Mastersingers* to Bororo Indians: On the semiosis of improvisation. In T. Bram (Ed.), *Proceedings from the Congress on Improvisation* (pp. 62–81). Luzern, Switzerland.

Tirro, F. (1974). Constructive elements in jazz improvisation. *Journal of the American Musicological Society, 27*, 285–305.

Tunstall, P. (1979). Structuralism and musicology: An overview. *Current Musicology, 27*, 51–64.

Vygotsky, L. S. (1978). *Mind in society* (Alex Kozulin, Trans.). Cambridge, MA: Harvard University Press.

Vygotsky, L. S. (1986). *Thought and language* (E. Hanfmann & G. Vakar, Trans.). Cambridge, MA: MIT Press. (Original work published 1934).

Wallerstein, I. (Ed.). (1998). *The heritage of sociology and the future of the social sciences in the 21st century*. Thousand Oaks, CA: Sage.

Webb, N. M. (1995). Group collaboration in assessment: Multiple objectives, processes, and outcomes. *Educational Evaluation and Policy Analysis, 17*(2), 239–261.

Webb, N. M., & Palincsar, A. S. (1996). Group processes in the classroom. In D. C. Berliner & R. C. Calfee (Eds.), *Handbook of educational psychology* (pp. 841–873). New York: Simon & Schuster Macmillan.

Weeks, P. (1990). Musical time as a practical accomplishment: A change in tempo. *Human Studies, 13*, 323–359.

Weeks, P. (1996a). A rehearsal of a Beethoven passage: An analysis of correction talk. *Research on Language and Social Interaction, 29*(3), 247–290.

Weeks, P. (1996b). Synchrony lost, synchrony regained: The achievement of musical coordination. *Human Studies, 19*, 199–228.

Weick, K. E. (2001). *Making sense of the organization*. London: Blackwell.

Weinraub, B. (2002, January 14). You loved Elaine, now meet Ellie. *New York Times*, pp. B1, B3.

Wertsch, J. V. (1992). Keys to cultural psychology. *Culture, Medicine, and Psychiatry, 16*, 273–280.

Wertsch, J. V. (1998). *Mind as action*. New York: Oxford University Press.

Wiener, N. (1948). *Cybernetics: or, control and communication in the animal and the machine*. New York: Wiley.

Wilkes-Gibbs, D. (1995). Coherence in collaboration: Some examples from conversation. In M. A. Gernsbacher & T. Givón (Eds.), *Coherence in spontaneous text* (pp. 239–267). Amsterdam: John Benjamins.

Wollheim, R. (1980). *Art and its objects*. New York: Cambridge University Press.

Woodman, R. W., & Schoenfeldt, L. F. (1989). Individual differences in creativity: An interactionist perspective. In J. A. Glover, R. R. Ronning, & C. R. Reynolds (Eds.), *Handbook of creativity* (pp. 77–91). New York: Plenum Press.

Author Index

Subject Index

A

Actor's Studio, 68
Alda, Alan, 47
Allen, Geri, 32, 61, 168
Alton, Bill, 10
Anthropology, 14-16, 68, 138, 188
Arena, Bruce, 7
Arkin, Alan, 48, 50, 64, 69, 70
Armstrong, Louis, 62
Audience, 17-18, 68-72, 110, 131, 132, 145, 146, 177

B

Belushi, Jim, 47
Bepha musical expedition, see Venda
Berman, Shelly, 48, 60
Blakey, Art, 32, 61, 168
Brubeck, Dave, 62
Bryant, Ray, 59, 60
Byrne, David, 11

C

Cheers (TV show), 11
Chemistry, interpersonal, 4, 37, 48, 49
Child development, 6, 22
Children's play, 85
Chomsky, N., 76, 77n4
Chudnow, Dick, 57
Classrooms, 22, 23, 27, 120, 122
Close, Del, 7, 42, 47, 52, 64, 70
Coherence, 33, 50, 83, 86, 88, 90, 95, 154
Coleman, Ornette, 155

Collaboration, 97-98, 134, 177
    in education, 185-187
    in organizations, 180-182,
        see also Teamwork
    in product creativity, 109-111,
        116, 125, 132
    and socioculturalism, 120-123
Collaborative emergence, 12, 19, 78, 116, 181, 186
Coltrane, John, 54
Combinatorics, 7, 12, 91, 163
ComedySportz (theater group), 57, 58, 72
Commedia dell'Arte, 59
Communication, 10, 37
Compass Players (theater group), 8, 41, 42, 48, 59, 64
Composition, 79-81, 92, 136, 143, 144
Complexity, 7, 12, 38-39, 163, 166, 189
Conduit metaphor, 38
Contextualization, 15, 90, 136, 141, 142
Conventions, 50-53, 56-58, 113, 168, see also Ready-mades
Conversation, everyday, 18-21, 33, 87, 131, 143
    comparison to improv theater dialogues, 3, 29
    comparison to product creativity, 107-108
    creativity of, 26
    diachronic change in, 128
Conversation analysis, 18-21, 74, 77, 82, 107, 177, 178, 188
Copeau, Jacques, 5
Creole Jazz Band, 62

An environmentally friendly book printed and bound in England by www.printondemand-worldwide.com

PEFC Certified

This product is
from sustainably
managed forests
and controlled
sources

www.pefc.org

PEFC/16-33-415

MIX

Paper from
responsible sources

FSC® C004959

This book is made entirely of sustainable materials; FSC paper for the cover and PEFC paper for the text pages.

#0159 - 170513 - C0 - 234/156/12 - PB